A SHOW TRIAL UNDER LENIN

STUDIES IN SOCIAL HISTORY

issued by the

INTERNATIONAL INSTITUTE OF SOCIAL HISTORY
AMSTERDAM

1. W.H. Roobol. *Tsereteli — A Democrat in the Russian Revolution. A Political Biography*. 1976. ISBN 90-247-1915-1

2. Zvi Rosen. *Bruno Bauer and Karl Marx. The Influence of Bruno Bauer on Marx's Thought.* 1977. ISBN 90-247-1948-8

3. Marian Sawer. *Marxism and the Question of the Asiatic Mode of Production*. 1977. ISBN 90-247-2027-3

4. Klaus Fröhlich. *The Emergence of Russian Constitutionalism. The Relationship Between Social Mobilization and Political Group Formation in Pre-Revolutionary Russia.* 1981. ISBN 90-247-2378-7

5. Fritjof Tichelman. *The Social Evolution of Indonesia. The Asiatic Mode of Production and Its Legacy.* 1980. ISBN 90-247-2389-2

6. Tom Nieuwenhuis. *Politics and Society in Early Modern Iraq. Mamlūk Pashas, Tribal Shayks and Local Rule Between 1802 and 1831.* 1982. ISBN 90-247-2576-3

7. Marc Jansen. *A Show Trial Under Lenin. The Trial of the Socialist Revolutionaries, Moscow 1922.* 1982. ISBN 90-247-2698-0

SERIES ISBN 90-247-2347-7

A SHOW TRIAL UNDER LENIN
The Trial of the Socialist Revolutionaries, Moscow 1922

by

MARC JANSEN

Translated from the Dutch by
Jean Sanders

1982

MARTINUS NIJHOFF PUBLISHERS THE HAGUE/BOSTON/LONDON

Distributors:

for the United States and Canada
Kluwer Boston Inc.
190 Old Derby Street
Hingham, MA 02043
USA

for all other countries
Kluwer Academic Publishers Group
Distribution Center
P.O. Box 322
3300 AH Dordrecht
The Netherlands

*Published with financial support from the Netherlands Organization for the Advancement
of Pure Research (ZWO).*

Library of Congress Card Number: 82–14183

ISBN 90 247-2698-0 (this volume)
ISBN 90-247-2347-7 (series)

CONTENTS

LIST OF ILLUSTRATIONS

Front cover. Accused and defenders. Seated (left to right).
  Donskoi, Evgeniia Ratner, Vandervelde, and Gots.
  Standing third from left Zhdanov, fifth from left Wauters,
  third from right Timofeev, and second from right Rosenfeld.(IISH)
Back cover. Piatakov reading the verdict. On the left some of the
  accused, probably of the 'second group'. (IISH)
1. Abram Gots. (IISH)
2. Evgenii Timofeev. (IISH)
3. Mikhail Gendel'man. (IISH)
4. Viktor Chernov. (IISH)
5. Accused and defenders. Middle row (left to right).
  Gershtein, Likhach, Timofeev, Evgeniia Ratner, and Gots. Top
  row second from left Donskoi, fifth from left Zhdanov, sixth
  from left Theodor Liebknecht, second from right Tager, and far
  right Rosenfeld. (IISH)
6. The Tribunal. In the centre the president, Georgii Piatakov.
  (Spaarnestad)
7. Defending counsel Nikolai Murav'ev talking with the accused.
  (IISH)
8. The demonstration of 20 June in Moscow. (IISH)
9. Abram and Sara Gots in exile, Alma Ata, 1930's.
  (B.I. Nicolaevsky Collection, Hoover Institution Archives)

PREFACE

Soviet Russia will conquer all the millions of problems that stand in its way, on one condition: as long as the cause of the political education of the broad masses of the people continually advances. We have nothing to be afraid of, if our people fully learns to distinguish who are its friends and who are its enemies. The trial of the Socialist Revolutionaries must and shall be a great step forward in the cause of the political instruction of the very broadest masses in town and country.

(Grigorii Zinov'ev, *Pravda* and *Krasnaia gazeta*, 20 June 1922)

For my part, I considered this trial to be unnecessary: the Socialist Revolutionaries had been beaten and represented no visible danger at all.

(Charles Rappoport, *Ma vie*, Paris 1926-1927, Vol. 2, p. 80)

The Bolsheviks seized power in Russia in October 1917 by staging a coup d'état, and then established a dictatorship. The new rulers suppressed all armed resistance in a bloody civil war, after which they made every effort to uproot and exterminate even peaceful political opposition of all kinds.

Even now it is impossible in the Soviet Union to subject these developments to critical historical study. The political opponents of the Soviet regime of the time are still regarded by official Soviet historiography as counter-revolutionaries and the measures taken against them are seen as completely justified.

Two prominent representatives of the political opposition in the early years of Soviet rule, the Socialist Revolutionary Abram Gots and the Menshevik Mark Liber, were sentenced to death in 1937 after many years of imprisonment and exile. Before being led away they asked a western fellow prisoner to try to get into touch with those of their comrades who were living outside Russia:

Greet our friends for us and tell them that we have born the name of revolutionary with pride. However difficult it is for us to be accused of being counter-revolutionaries, we know that history will pass a different judgement.... Better times will come for Russia and for the whole world. And then history will judge our actions.[1]

Gots was the best-known of the Socialist Revolutionary Party leaders still in Russia. In a nutshell, the history and nature of this party, the PSR, was as follows. Established in 1901, it had originated in an older Russian tradition, that of Populism. As their name indicates, the 19th century Populists (*Narodniki*) were concerned with 'the people', which in Russia at the time meant the peasantry. In addition to Populism, Socialist Revolutionary ideology was influenced by western Marxism. While Populism was oriented towards the peasantry and Marxism towards the 'proletariat', i.e. the workers, the PSR was concerned with the 'toilers', i.e. the peasants *and* the workers, and was also oriented towards the intelligentsia. Nevertheless, the PSR, other than the Russian Social Democratic Workers' Party which had been founded in the same period and which later was divided between the Bolsheviks and Mensheviks, was regarded as the party of agrarian socialism. In fact, one of the most important items on its agenda was the socialization of the land.

Another important point of departure for the PSR was the sovereignty of the people (*Narodovlastie*), to be embodied in a Constituent Assembly elected on the basis of universal suffrage. The PSR also considered it justifiable to make use of terrorism in its struggle against the Tsarist regime.

It is difficult to give an exact characterization of the PSR because one of its most important elements was the fact that it united a multitude of opinions and trends of thought. In a positive sense, this was a result of the PSR's internal party democracy; negatively, it resulted from the fact that the Socialist Revolutionaries formed an incoherent movement rather than a cohesive party. Socialism and democracy were equally important in the view of the PSR, and the one could not be realized without the other. A left wing of the party stressed the social character of the revolution, while a right wing emphasized democracy. Furthermore, as a party of violent action and one which, after the February Revolution of 1917, became influential through its role in the Provisional Government and in the Soviets, the PSR attracted many elements of unsettled political convictions. After 1917, in fact, internal dissension put the PSR at a disadvantage versus the far more tightly organized Bolshevik Party.[2]

In 1917, in the most liberal elections ever held in Russia, the PSR obtained 16 million votes and, together with her national sister parties, realized more than half the total of 42 million (the Bolsheviks had a total of ten million).[3] According to the PSR's own data, in the summer of 1917, it had more than a million members,[4] and some hundreds of thousands in 1918-1919.[5] The leaders of the PSR were condemned in 1922 in the greatest political trial ever held in communist Russia prior to the Stalinist era, a trial with the means of which the communists settled with their socialist rivals for once and for all time.

'Some of them may find solace in the idea that some future chronicler will commend them or their behaviour during this trial', said Public Prosecutor Nikolai Krylenko in his speech for the prosecution.[6] Abram Gots, one of the accused in the trial, apparently also had to console himself in this way in 1937. For a long time, however, it seemed that the accused would be committed to record as 'counter-revolutionaries' and would be further forgotten. Even now, official Soviet historiography describes the 1922 trial as a measure that was completely justified and correct.[7]

Nevertheless, it seems that 'history's final judgement' still has to be pronounced. In 1966, during the trial of the authors Andrei Siniavskii and Iulii Daniel', the accused in the 1922 trial were given favourable mention in Russia for the first time in many years. The anonymous writer of a letter published in *Samizdat* drew a comparison with earlier political trials in Soviet Russia. He observed that the trial of Siniavskii and Daniel' was the first political trial to be held in public since 1922 at which the accused had carried themselves with dignity and had not 'confessed'. 'Since the time of the trial of the Right Socialist Revolutionaries — those heroes of revolutionary Russia who have already become legendary — this is the first political trial of such a nature,' he wrote. 'Only the Right Socialist Revolutionaries left the courtroom without evoking pity, contempt, abhorrence and embarrassment.'[8] The use of the epithet 'Right' betrays the fact that the author of this opinion was born and brought up in the Soviet Union.

During the last few years the trial has been given fresh publicity. In discussions among Russian dissidents about whether, and if so in how far, Stalinism should be seen as a consequence of the political system established in Russia by Lenin and the Bolsheviks in 1917, the matter of the 1922 trial has also been raised. The best-known participants in these discussions are Aleksandr Solzhenitsyn and Roi Medvedev. Solzhenitsyn sees no essential difference between Leninist and Stalinist terror. In *The Gulag Archipelago* he ranks the 1922 trial together with the infamous show trials of a later period, although he observes that the earlier accused showed themselves to be somewhat less accommodating. In Solzhenitsyn's view, these socialists deserved little more sympathy than their Bolshevik judges.[9] Medvedev does not consider Stalinism to be the same as Leninism but, in *Let History Judge*, he has to acknowledge that the trial of the Socialist Revolutionaries showed serious shortcomings. He exonerates Lenin, however, and considers that even then Stalin was to blame.[10]

Historical works published in the West also show that the 1922 trial has not been forgotten.[11] It was this recent interest that made me decide to undertake further research into the trial and into the circumstances under which it was held, even though such research could only be tentative. A comprehensive treatment of the trial of the Socialist Revolutionaries requires the consultation of archives that are available only in the Soviet Union. Although both during and after the trial it was said that the trial proceedings might be published,[12] these plans have never been realized. The records are preserved in Moscow in the *Tsentral'nyi gosudarstvennyi arkhiv Oktiabr'skoi revoliutsii* (f.1005, op.1a). A few Soviet historians have been able to examine the documents and to use excerpts for their work. These and other Archives in the Soviet Union (in particular the *Tsentral'nyi partiinyi arkhiv Instituta marksizma-leninizma*) also have more materials concerning the subject of this study. Western researchers are not permitted to use them, however, and I have been able only to consult such archive material that is available outside the Soviet Union.

Instead of the trial records I have made use of the trial reports published in the Soviet press, although these are somewhat deceptive. The arguments of the accused, of their defenders, and of the witnesses for the defence, are recounted only briefly and tendentiously, interspersed with biased comment. Further, I have used those parts of the trial proceedings which have been published, namely, the Indictment, the addresses by the prosecuting counsels, the closing addresses to the court by the accused of the 'second group' (Socialist Revolutionary renegades who were thrown in with the accused under orders to 'confess'), the pleas of their defending counsels, and the verdict passed by the Tribunal. I have been able to glean supplementary material from the works of those Soviet historians who have been allowed to examine the official proceedings, and from publications about the trial which appeared in the Soviet Union at the time. Newspapers published by Russian emigrés and by the underground press in Russia also contained information about the trial. Parts of the speeches by the accused of the 'first group' (the Socialist Revolutionaries) in their own defence and of the closing addresses to the court by these accused were smuggled out of the country and published in the PSR's journal *Revoliutsionnaia Rossiia*, or were preserved in handwritten form. There is no reason to doubt the authenticity of these texts. Finally, there is a report of the first days of the trial written by the Belgian socialist, Arthur Wauters, who, together with his fellow national and party member, Emile Vandervelde, has also published a book about the trial. Further references will be found in the Bibliography and the Notes to this work.

This study is concerned with the 1922 trial of the Socialist Revolutionaries and with everything connected with it, with the nature of the trial, the attitudes of the people concerned, and with their motives. It does not represent research into PSR policy after the October Revolution in 1917, although that will be touched upon whenever necessary. I have not attempted to answer the question why the Socialist Revolutionaries did not succeed in realizing their ideals.

The introductory chapter briefly discusses the relationship between the Bolsheviks and the Socialist Revolutionaries after the October Revolution. The subsequent two chapters are devoted to the preparations for the trial and to the part played by the international socialist movement. The actual trial is discussed in four chapters: the first is concerned principally with the course of the trial, with particular emphasis on the attitudes and treatment of the various groups of participants; a following chapter is devoted to the judicial examination; a third is concerned with the political debate that went on during the trial; while the last of these four chapters examines the sentences passed and the manner in which they were reached. Chapter 8 discusses the propaganda campaign with which the trial was surrounded, and Chapter 9 the reactions caused by the trial, particularly outside Russia; Chapter 10 then scrutinizes the outcome of the whole affair, giving special attention to the further fate of the accused. An attempt is made to draw some conclusions in the closing chapter.

The chronology used is that which applied in Russia in the particular period. Dates prior to 1/14 February 1918, when the calendar was adjusted, are thus indicated according to the Old Style, or 13 days behind the calendar used in the West; thereafter, dates are given according to the New Style Gregorian calendar of the West. Transliteration is based on the US Library of Congress system, although diacritics are omitted.

Finally, a remark about the name Socialist Revolutionaries. Similar to the way in which the Russian Constitutional Democrats were named 'Kadets', the Socialist Revolutionaries were frequently referred to as SRs (*esery*). I prefer to use the name in full, however, even in quotations in which the abbreviation was used in the original Russian text.

The material for this study has been compiled at the International Institute of Social History (IISH), the Institute for Eastern European Studies and the Library of the University of Amsterdam; the Documentation Office for East European Law and the Library of the University of Leyden; the Hoover Institution on War, Revolution, and Peace, in Stanford, California; the New York Public Library; the Archive of Russian and Eastern European History and Culture, and other institutions of Columbia University, New York; and the Institute for Jewish Research (YIVO), also in New York. Robert Abs of the Emile Vandervelde Institute in Brussels kindly sent me a copy of a document. Information on a personal basis was provided by Boris Sapir, Amsterdam; Mrs Olga Lang and Mrs Oksana Iatsenko, New York; Boris Souvarine, Paris; and the late Mrs Mina Svirskaia, Herzlia-Pituach, Israel.

I owe thanks to many people who have contributed in some way to the finalization of this work. They include members of all the institutions listed above; those who gave me personal information; Mrs Anna Bourguina who helped me to select material in the Nicolaevsky Collection of the Hoover Institution; and Mrs Vera Kovarsky and Vadim Pavlovsky in New York. Professor Jan Bezemer of the University of Amsterdam has constantly supervised my work; without his encouragement this book would never have attained its present form. Boris Sapir has helped in many ways; he, Willem Roobol, and Bruno Naarden have read and criticized early versions of the original Dutch manuscript. I am indebted to Mrs Jean Sanders for the translation, which was made possible by the financial support of the Netherlands Organization for the Advancement of Pure Research (ZWO).

LIST OF ABBREVIATIONS

Cheka	*Chrezvychainaia Komissiia* (Extraordinary Commission)
GPU	*Gosudarstvennoe Politicheskoe Upravlenie* (State Political Administration)
IISH	International Institute of Social History (Amsterdam)
Inprekorr	*Internationale Presse Korrespondenz*
Komuch	*Komitet chlenov Uchreditel'nogo Sobraniia* (Committee of Members of the Constituent Assembly)
LSI	Labour and Socialist International
MPSR	*Men'shinstvo Partii Sotsialistov-Revoliutsionerov* (Minority of the Party of Socialist Revolutionaries)
NEP	*Novaia Ekonomicheskaia Politika* (New Economic Policy)
NKVD	*Narodnyi Komissariat Vnutrennikh Del* (People's Commissariat of Internal Affairs)
PSR	*Partiia Sotsialistov-Revoliutsionerov* (Party of Socialist Revolutionaries)
RSDRP	*Rossiiskaia Sotsial-Demokraticheskaia Rabochaia Partiia* (Russian Social Democratic Workers' Party)
SAI	*Sozialistische Arbeiter Internationale*
SPD	*Sozial-Demokratische Partei Deutschlands*
TsIK	*Tsentral'nyi Ispolnitel'nyi Komitet* (Central Executive Committee)
USPD	*Unabhängige Sozial-Demokratische Partei Deutschlands*
USSR	Union of Soviet Socialist Republics
VTsIK	*Vserossiiskii Tsentral'nyi Ispolnitel'nyi Komitet* (All-Russian Central Executive Committee)

1. *Abram Gots. (IISH)*

2. *Evgenii Timofeev. (IISH)*

3. *Mikhail Gendel'man. (IISH)*

4: *Viktor Chernov. (IISH)*

5. *Accused and defenders. Middle row (left to right): Gershtein, Likhach, Timofeev, Evgeniia Ratner, and Gots. Top row second from left Donskoi, fifth from left Zhdanov, sixth from left Theodor Liebknecht, second from right Tager, and far right Rosenfeld. (IISH)*

6. *The Tribunal. In the centre the president, Georgii Piatakov. (Spaarnestad)*

7. *Defending counsel Nikolai Murav'ev talking with the accused. (IISH)*

8. *The demonstration of 20 June in Moscow. (IISH)*

9. *Abram and Sara Gots in exile, Alma Ata, 1930's. (B.I. Nicolaevsky Collection, Hoover Institution Archives)*

CHAPTER 1

THE SOCIALIST REVOLUTIONARIES
AND THE SOVIET REGIME

The Bolsheviks seized power in Petrograd on 25 October 1917 and established the Soviet regime. They were not the only socialist party in Russia. The largest socialist party was that of the Socialist Revolutionaries who had supported the Provisional Government during the previous months, although not without hesitation and reservation.

The October Revolution caused a rift in the ranks of the Socialist Revolutionaries. While the majority opposed the new regime, a left wing of the Party concurred with the October Revolution. These Left Socialist Revolutionaries broke away and joined the Council of People's Commissars. In March 1918 they broke again with the government in protest against the Treaty of Brest-Litovsk. In July 1918 they attempted a coup d'état with the intention of re-opening the war against Germany. This effort failed and with it their role in politics came to an end.

In the days that immediately followed the October Revolution, the major Socialist Revolutionary Party, the PSR, took part in efforts to form a counter-government and even supported an attempt at a counter-uprising, all without result. In the following weeks direct encounters between the Bolsheviks and the Socialist Revolutionaries did not occur. The PSR leaders did not dare to undertake any armed conflict with the new regime while the military power at their disposal was inadequate. The Bolsheviks therefore had no need to resort to extreme measures, always assuming that they would have been in a position to do so. Moreover, there were Bolsheviks as well as Socialist Revolutionaries who did not wish to exclude the possibility of future cooperation. For a time, therefore, the Socialist Revolutionaries could continue to operate as before: to publish newspapers, to arrange meetings, and to hold their Fourth Party Congress in late November-early December 1917, all comparatively unhindered. Those few party members who were arrested were mostly released again with little delay.

The hopes of the Socialist Revolutionaries were now fixed on the Constituent Assembly, elections for which were held in the weeks after the October Revolution. These elections resulted in a great victory for the Socialist Revolutionaries. As the party of agrarian socialism they were given wholesale support by the peasantry. Together with its national sister parties, the PSR gained over half the total vote. The Bolsheviks had a quarter of the vote and, even with the support of the Left Socialist Revolutionaries, were unable to form a majority in the Constituent Assembly. When this had become abundantly clear, the Bolsheviks disbanded the Constituent Assembly after a sitting that lasted only one day (5 January 1918). A peaceful demonstration in support of the transfer of power to the Constituent Assembly was dispersed with the use of arms, causing a number of dead and wounded. The Socialist Revolutionaries had refused to take up arms and had contented themselves with taking part in that peaceful demonstration.

After the Bolsheviks had dissolved the Constituent Assembly and had signed a separate peace treaty with Germany in Brest-Litovsk on 3 March 1918, plans for armed resistance began to ripen within the PSR. A party conference (the Eighth Party Council) held in Moscow in May 1918 passed a resolution supporting those plans. The council determined that the PSR should not accept foreign help in its fight against the Bolsheviks but that it would do so in its fight against Germany as long as the foreigners, i.e. the Allies, did not intervene in Russia's internal affairs.

The opportunity for revolt came sooner than had been expected. A legion of Czechoslovakian soldiers, who had fought on the Russian front against the Habsburg monarchy and had started to withdraw from Russia along the Trans-Siberian railway after the signing of the Brest-Litovsk Treaty, clashed with the Bolshevik authorities and took control of the railway. The Bolshevik regime in the whole of Siberia and in the East of European Russia as far as the Volga then collapsed.

On 8 June 1918 the *Komuch* (*Komitet chlenov Uchreditel'nogo Sobraniia*: Committee of Members of the Constituent Assembly) was inaugurated in the town of Samara (now Kuibyshev) on the Volga, with the aim of seizing power in the country on behalf of the Constituent Assembly. The *Komuch* was chiefly made up of Socialist Revolutionaries and, with the aid of the Czechs, gained control over a large part of the Volga region. It declared war on the Soviet regime and on Germany, and established a People's Army.

The following months were difficult ones for the Bolsheviks. In addition to the *Komuch* other local power centres sprang up, as a result of which a large part of the country escaped Bolshevik control. The Allies started to intervene. In that part of the country where they were able to hold their own, the Bolsheviks had to deal with revolts such as those of the Left Socialist Revolutionaries and of the former Socialist Revolutionary, Boris Savinkov. Attempts were made on the lives of leading Bolsheviks, including Lenin.

In reprisal, the Bolsheviks started a rule of terror. On 14 June 1918 the Socialist Revolutionaries, together with the Mensheviks, were expelled from the Soviets.[1] Their newspapers were suppressed. They were more or less outlawed and many lost their lives in the Red Terror.

The Socialist Revolutionaries failed in their efforts to organize a democratic counter-government against the Bolsheviks. In September 1918, in Ufa in the Urals, a conference in which a number of local governments and political groupings took part, managed to form a Directory of five members which was to act as national government until sufficient members of the Constituent Assembly should have assembled early in 1919. This government was overthrown in a coup d'état on 18 November, however, and replaced by a military dictatorship led by admiral Kolchak. In the main, the civil war now became a struggle between 'Reds' and 'Whites'.

Although the PSR was a large party, it was a very divided one and showed little coherence. The day-to-day leadership was in the hands of a Central Committee of 20 members, all of whom were widely scattered by the civil war. Eight members were needed to form a quorum; if it proved impossible to get such a quorum together, however, directives could be given by a smaller number of members, sometimes united in a local bureau of the Central Committee. In practice, all kinds of groupings in the party were inclined to act according to their own understanding of affairs, without giving much attention to the directives of the Central Committee. This was due partly to the fact that communications with the centre were frequently disrupted for long periods by the civil war, but also to considerable disagreement over the policy which should be followed with regard to the Bolsheviks: the PSR included both supporters and opponents of armed resistance against the Bolsheviks; the former in turn included both supporters and opponents of cooperation with non-socialists (i.e. in particular the Kadets) and of the acceptance of foreign aid. The opponents of armed resistance to the Bolsheviks were considered to belong to the left wing; those who advocated such resistance, if they simultaneously supported cooperation with non-socialists, to the right wing.

Serious conflict did not arise within the party in the period immediately preceding the Ufa Conference. The right wing was reasonably satisfied with the events that led up to the conference. The left wing showed opposition from the start, but this was at first fairly moderate.

In the first few months after the October Revolution the most vigorous representative of the left wing was Matvei Kogan-Bernshtein. A member of the Central Committee, Kogan-Bernshtein denounced the Bolshevik coup d'état but at the same time opposed any use of violence among socialists. If it proved impossible to reach agreement with the Bolsheviks then, in his opinion, the Socialist Revolutionaries should restrict themselves to peaceful opposition. He therefore protested when the Eighth Party Council decided in May 1918 to use force against the Bolsheviks. Although he joined the *Komuch* movement, he continued to be critical and to voice his opinions in public. In Kogan-Bernshtein's view, cooperation with non-socialists and the acceptance of foreign aid were quite unthinkable. The policy followed by the party at the Ufa Conference was so contradictory to his opinions that he left the meeting demonstratively with the intention of returning to Bolshevik-controlled territory.[2]

Kogan-Bernshtein was not alone in his opposition to the Ufa decisions. The agreement reached in Ufa was in fact a compromise between the Socialist Revolutionaries and non-socialists. The Directory that was set up on the basis of the agreement consisted, apart from two Socialist Revolutionaries, of representatives of more rightist groupings and, for the time being, was responsible to no-one. In the eyes of the Socialist Revolutionary critics, this signified a breach of the powers of the Constituent Assembly.

Roughly half the Socialist Revolutionaries who took part in the Ufa Conference nursed considerable objections to the decisions taken there,[3] one member of the Central Committee, Vadim Chaikin, going so far as to refuse to sign the agreement.[4] The ultimate acceptance of the agreement by the remaining Socialist Revolutionaries was due largely to the difficult situation of the *Komuch* whose territory was threatened by the approaching Red Army, a fact that urged a compromise.

The majority of a quorum of nine members of the Central Committee who met in Ufa shortly after the conference, rallied behind their most authoritative member, Viktor Chernov, who had reached Ufa too late to be able to attend the conference. Chernov had the greatest possible reservations against the Ufa Agreement. He defended the view that the PSR should form a democratic 'third force' (*tret'ia sila*) and should fight on two fronts, i.e. against the Bolsheviks and against the bourgeois reactionaries. The Central Committee supported this opinion by six votes to two. The ninth member of the Central Committee, the aforementioned Chaikin, abstained from voting because he wanted to go even further and to reject the entire agreement.[5]

The result of these deliberations was that a circular letter was distributed by the Central Committee, which has become known as the 'Chernov Charter' (*Chernovskaia gramota*). This circular, dated 22 October 1918, was very critical of the Ufa Conference although without renouncing the Directory in so many words. What did create contention, however, was an appeal to the party to mobilize all its forces so that, if need be, it could resist the organizers of a counter-revolution behind the anti-Bolshevik front.[6]

The 'Chernov Charter' made a very bad impression on the non-socialists. A month later, when they ousted the Directory, Kolchak and his supporters did not neglect to produce the circular as proof of the unreliability of the Socialist Revolutionaries.

After Kolchak's coup d'état, many Socialist Revolutionaries began to doubt whether the idea of fighting on two fronts was still tenable and whether it would not be better to drop the fight against the Bolsheviks for the time being and to launch all their forces against Kolchak. A number of prominent Socialist Revolutionaries – the former Chairman of the *Komuch*, Vladimir Vol'skii, the members of the Central Committee, Nikolai Rakitnikov and Konstantin Burevoi, together with two of Vol'skii's immediate colleagues, Nikolai Sviatitskii and Nikolai Shmelev – remained in Ufa when the town was occupied by the Red Army and some of them sought contact with the new Bolshevik authorities. Negotiations started on 10 January 1919, with the consent of Moscow.[7] As a result, the group, which was given the name of the 'Ufa Delegation', appealed to the soldiers of the People's Army of the *Komuch* 'to stop the civil war against the Soviet regime which, at the present juncture, is the only revolutionary power of the exploited classes able to suppress the exploiters, and to direct their weapons against the Kolchak dictatorship.'[8] In return, the Bolshevik partner in the negotiations, the Military-Revolutionary Committee of Ufa, guaranteed that soldiers of the People's Army and those Socialist Revolutionaries who chose the side of the Red Army would not be prosecuted. The 'Ufa Delegation' then left for Moscow to continue the negotiations at a higher level.[9]

The 'Ufa Delegation', however, in no way represented general party opinion. Delegates of the party organizations in Bolshevik-controlled territory met in Moscow from 6 to 9 February 1919, the various currents of opinion within the party all being represented. The Vol'skii group demanded that the party should reach an agreement with the Bolsheviks. Another group upheld the former tactic of armed struggle against the Bolsheviks, but both these extreme positions were rejected by the majority.[10]

The negotiations which Vol'skii *et al.* had held with the Bolsheviks were stigmatized by the conference as capitulation. Agreement with the Bolsheviks could only be possible if the latter accepted the principle of the sovereignty of the people, the *Narodovlastie*, embodied in the Constituent Assembly. On the other hand, the conference also rejected all attempts to overthrow the Soviet regime with the use of arms, being of the opinion that this would only play into the hands of the counter-revolutionaries. Where Bolsheviks were in control the Socialist Revolutionaries should organize the working masses for a *political* fight; where the counter-revolutionaries were in control they should be opposed with all available means, including force. The conference further denounced the Allied intervention which was no longer justified by the international war situation since Germany had been defeated, and any form of cooperation with the bourgeois parties.[11]

Notwithstanding the rejection of its policy by an authoritative party conference and against the emphatic advice of that conference, the 'Ufa Delegation' continued to negotiate with the Bolsheviks. The Central Committee nevertheless refrained from taking measures against the negotiators, although some favoured their expulsion from the party.[12] The negotiations were welcomed by the Soviet regime for reasons of foreign policy. In a memorandum to the Allied governments on 4 February 1919, People's Commissar Georgii Chicherin referred to the negotiations as evidence that in Russia the Soviet regime was recognized in broad democratic circles as the legal government.[13]

On 19 February the Central Committee of the Communist Party accepted the notion of 'legalization of the Right Socialist Revolutionaries', and the highest Soviet authority promulgated the relevant decree on 26 February.

The motivations for the decree were that the PSR, at its recent conference, had condemned both the idea of armed struggle against the Soviet regime and also the Allied intervention, that it had rejected cooperation with the bourgeois parties, and that it had called on its organizations to overthrow the reactionary governments. It also took note of the 'Ufa Delegation's' call to the soldiers of the People's Army and of its negotiations with the Soviet authorities. Taking all this into account, the All-Russian Central Executive Committee (VTsIK) decided 'to repeal its decree of 14 June [1918] with respect to all Right Social Revolutionary Party groups who accept as binding the aforementioned decisions and actions of the Social Revolutionary Party and of the Committee of Members of the Constituent Assembly, and to grant them the right to participate, together with other parties, in the work of the Soviets'. And further, 'to propose to the administrative and judicial organs of the Soviet Republic that those members of the Right Social Revolutionary Party who share the position that is laid down in the aforementioned resolutions and declarations should be released from prison.'

'The Central Executive Committee', the decree ended, 'will continue as in the past the merciless fight against all groupings who directly or indirectly support the counter-revolution at home or abroad, irrespective of the flag behind which they may hide. But it considers it its duty to offer the parties of the petit-bourgeois democracy the opportunity to show actively and in public their willingness to support the proletariat and the peasants in their fight against the counter-revolution, both at home and abroad.'[14]

The decree of 26 February 1919 was not based on any agreement between the Soviet government and the Central Committee of the PSR. The Moscow Bureau of the Central Committee dissociated itself from the decree even before it was submitted to the VTsIK for approval, and passed a resolution in which it rejected any responsibility for the activities of the 'Ufa Delegation'. The PSR had not taken steps to achieve its legalization. The fact that the party had suspended the armed struggle against the Bolsheviks, declared the Bureau, did not signify that it had changed its position as regards the

Bolshevik regime. The PSR would continue to try to form a genuine-ly democratic government.[15]

According to the Socialist Revolutionary Nikolai Berezov, the text of this resolution was handed to Kamenev shortly before the sitting of the VTsIK at which he had intended, with some ceremony, to legalize the Socialist Revolutionaries. Kamenev, who is said to have strongly urged legalization, then restricted himself in a short speech to referring to the 'necessity, by way of experiment, to give the Socialist Revolutionaries, just as any other group of citizens, the opportunity to prove actively their genuine willingness to serve the Workers' and Peasants' Government.'[16]

What was the significance of the 26 February 1919 decree? It was far from being a general amnesty for the Socialist Revolutionaries. If a Socialist Revolutionary wanted amnesty, he had to sign a personal declaration that he felt himself to be bound by the decisions in which his party renounced the use of force against the Soviet regime. In this way, 43 Socialist Revolutionaries were indicted for deeds perpetuated in 1918 because they refused to sign such a statement, considering such an act as an humiliation.[17] The end of this 'Saratov affair', about which little further is known,[18] was that charges against 18 of the accused were dismissed when they decided after all to sign the necessary declaration.[19] The amnesty apparently did not apply to those who did not sign such a statement, although this was never put into so many words.

In common with the amnesty, the legalization laid down in the decree was of little significance. According to the decree, it applied to party *groups* who supported not only the decisions taken at the February 1919 party conference but also the activities of the 'Ufa Delegation', although the latter in no way represented the party. It was not at all clear, however, as regards the rights which legalization would give such groups in practice. Whoever 'supported the counter-revolution', even though only 'indirectly', would continue to be persecuted.

In March 1919 the Socialist Revolutionaries were briefly able to appear in public. Their Central Committee was able to meet in Mos-cow without restraint. They were again able to publish their news-paper, *Delo naroda*, of which they printed 100,000 copies. Their speakers won much acclaim at political meetings. According to Cher-nov, who reports this in his memoirs, the leaders of the party were under no illusion. They made use of the opportunity to propagate

their opinions in public and to ventilate their criticisms of the Bolsheviks, but their organization was kept secret. And rightly so because their freedom was of short duration. After only ten days
Delo naroda was again banned. The newspaper campaign against the
party and the arresting of its members were resumed. According
to Chernov, the legalization was nothing other than a political
manoeuvre with a view to the conference which the Allies wanted
to hold on the island of Prinkipo in the Marmara Sea, with the
groups and movements that were fighting each other in Russia.[20]
Perhaps this is too narrow a view and some Bolsheviks really favoured cooperation with the other socialist parties, although within
limits to be laid down by the Bolsheviks. After all, the Mensheviks
had also been legalized. If this were the case then their effort undoubtedly encountered opposition among the other Bolsheviks.
Moreover, it found no support among the PSR leadership who did
not agree with the limits laid down by the Bolsheviks.

What remained was a fierce conflict between the Central Committee
of the PSR and the group surrounding the 'Ufa Delegation'.

The Central Committee clung to the notion that the Socialist
Revolutionaries should form a 'third force'. This excluded cooperation with the Bolsheviks which would only be feasible if the Bolsheviks declared themselves willing to acknowledge a Constituent
Assembly as the legal expression of the people's will; in other words,
if they acknowledged the principle of sovereignty of the people or, as
the Socialist Revolutionaries put it, *Narodovlastie*. If the Bolsheviks
were not prepared to give this recognition voluntarily, then the
people would force them to do so in the not too distant future, and
the place of the PSR would then be at the head of the popular
movement for *Narodovlastie*.[21]

The Vol'skii group, on the other hand, thought that the party
should cooperate with the Bolsheviks. In a pamphlet which, in addition to other literature, the group was allowed to publish in Moscow
in 1919, Sviatitskii made a reasoned plea for such cooperation, for
the sake of which the Socialist Revolutionaries should accept the
Soviet system as being the best approximation available at that juncture to the *Narodovlastie*, which would continue to be their ultimate
goal. For their part, the Bolsheviks would have to give up their party
dictatorship, to grant the peasants the same political rights as the

workers, and to allow the other socialist parties to take part in elections to the Soviets on an equal footing.[22]

The conflict between the Central Committee and the Vol'skii
group came to a head at the Ninth Party Council which the Socialist
Revolutionaries managed to hold in the neighbourhood of Moscow
between 18 and 20 June 1919. The council voted by 31 votes to one
and one abstention in favour of the ideas of the Central Committee,
opting for the position of 'third force'. The council thus confirmed
the decisions taken by the February 1919 Party Conference, but
made it clear that the decision not to carry on the armed struggle
against the Bolsheviks was a tactical one and was not a matter of
principle.[23]

This resolution by the Ninth Party Council was reason for Rakitnikov and Burevoi to resign their membership of the Central Committee. Together with the other opponents in the Vol'skii group they
were of the opinion that the Party Council had been one-sidedly
made up by the Central Committee and was not representative of the
party. For that reason they thought themselves entitled to make a
direct appeal to the members of the party. In August 1919 they
issued an appeal for the formation of a socialist united front, criti-
cizing the inflexibility of both the PSR leadership and of the Bolsheviks.[24]

The members of the opposition began to be known as the 'Narod
group' after the name of the paper Narod (The People) which they
started to publish in August 1919.[25] The Narod group's intention in
the first instance was to convert the party to its opinions, but some
of its adherents immediately went beyond that. The local party organization in Ufa, for instance, made it known in Izvestiia on 17
August that it had decided to work in Soviet institutions, and appealed to all PSR members to follow this example. In reply, the Central Committee declared the Ufa party organization to be dissolved,[26] and sent a cautionary letter to the Narod group, asking its
members to dissociate themselves from the Ufa action.[27]

A rift was inevitable. In the autumn of 1919, when general Denikin's troops approached Moscow from the south and the Bolshevik
regime seemed to be in serious jeopardy, the Narod group sent a
declaration of solidarity to the highest military authority of the
Soviet Republic, the Defence Council, putting its followers at the
Council's disposal.[28] Two days later, on 17 October, the group sent
an ultimatum to the Central Committee of the PSR, demanding that

the Committee should call upon the party and its adherents to support the Red Army and that this should be done before 25 October. If the Committee were to ignore this demand, the group would itself make the appeal.[29] The Central Committee reacted by issuing a statement to the party organizations in which the *Narod* group was declared dissolved.[30] The group then decided to break away from the party and to form its own organization, the 'Minority of the PSR' (MPSR), with its own Central Organization Bureau. In a statement to the party, this Bureau declared its intention of thrashing out its differences with the Central Committee at a party congress that would be elected in regular fashion.[31]

A representative of the *Narod* group was allowed to speak at both the Seventh and the Eighth Soviet Congresses (December 1919 and December 1920),[32] but the Bolsheviks showed not the slightest willingness to regard the group as an ally. In a circular dated 1 June 1920 the *Cheka* (political police) said that the *Narod* group was nothing other than a legal cloak for the illegal core of PSR members who supported Chernov.[33] Although in another circular dated 18 December of the same year the *Cheka* did express some appreciation of the group's efforts to persuade PSR members to show loyalty to the Soviet regime, the group's political aspirations were described in the most disparaging terms. The group was said to want to revitalize the PSR as an organization which could lay claim to power in Russia in opposition to the communists, that it attempted to take advantage of the difficult situation in the country to win over the peasants and the petit-bourgeois strata of the population, and levelled inadmissible criticisms against Soviet government policies. In this way, according to the *Cheka*, the *Narod* group endangered the social revolution.[34]

The *Narod* group, notwithstanding its reconciliatory attitude towards the Bolsheviks, was in fact exposed almost as much to persecution by the *Cheka* as was the party from which it had seceded.[35] Its loyalty to the Soviet regime was poorly rewarded. The resulting disillusionment caused the group to fall apart: some withdrew altogether from politics, others joined the Communist Party, yet others returned to the PSR where they were welcomed with open arms.[36] In July 1921 the PSR leadership appealed to MPSR members to return to the mother party: by then it was only too clear that the Bolsheviks were no more prepared to allow freely-elected Soviets than they would the Constituent Assembly.[37]

In February 1922 Burevoi, one of the founders, together with a number of supporters, appealed to the group to disband itself. The MPSR had not been able to come a step nearer to the goal which it had set itself on its formation, i.e. cooperation with the Soviet government. The dictatorship of the Communist Party was uncurtailed and the MPSR, persecuted and muzzled as it was, had been unable to make its ideas known among the working masses. The signatories declared that they would no longer accept responsibility for the group's actions.[38] For a time, until their arrest prevented it, Vol'skii and others tried to keep alive the organization, which also showed strong internal dissension, but in effect this was the end of the *Narod* group.

In accordance with the decisions taken by the party, various PSR organizations took up arms against the White movement in Siberia, the Ukraine, and the Black Sea region, thus playing an important part in the defeat of the movement. In the course of the struggle they sometimes took positions that were akin to those of the *Narod* group: cooperation with the Bolsheviks and acceptance of the Soviet system. Notwithstanding this, however, the Bolsheviks also turned against them once the Whites had been defeated. In common with the *Narod* group, these Socialist Revolutionaries now experienced that the Bolsheviks did not tolerate any other independent political organization.[39] The Menshevik Iulii Martov rightly said that 'Bolshevism does not admit the idea of an opposition party, even if it is ultraloyal and accepts the Soviet principle.'[40] The Bolsheviks were in no way prepared to share their power or to tolerate other political groupings, even as a loyal opposition.

After the Ninth Party Council, the Central Committee also came into conflict with the party's right wing. This right wing considered that efforts should primarily be directed towards realizing democracy in Russia, and that only then should consideration be given to the realization of socialism. In this way, these Socialist Revolutionaries deviated from general party opinion, namely, that no democracy could exist in Russia without socialism, just as socialism could not exist without democracy.

A leading figure in the party's right wing was Nikolai Avksent'ev who, together with the Central Committee member Vladimir Zenzinov, had joined the Directory that had been formed in Ufa. After the overthrow of the Directory they left Russia and settled in Paris, where they became members of a group of right Socialist Revolutionaries. This group was somewhat irritated by the party leadership's offhand treatment of the Ufa Agreement, and issued a statement in which it refused to accept the resolutions of the Ninth Party Council. Zenzinov found it sufficient reason to resign from the Central Committee. The group did not agree with the Party Council's unconditional rejection of cooperation with non-socialist parties and of foreign intervention in the struggle against the Bolsheviks, and considered it faulty tactics to oppose the entire White movement without discrimination. In the group's opinion, Denikin's entourage included a 'healthy' stream.[41]

The right wing also had its representatives in Russia, particularly in the south where some party groups showed loyalty to Denikin in the opinion that this was the best way to serve democracy. In Kiev, for example, Socialist Revolutionaries were members of the town council appointed by Denikin. In October and November 1919 the Central Committee took steps against these Socialist Revolutionaries: it declared both the Paris group and the Kiev party organization to be disbanded, and expelled two members of the latter who had called for support for Denikin.[42]

We have seen that the Central Committee that was elected during the Fourth Congress of the PSR in November 1917 had 20 members.[43] In the course of the civil war some of these members had resigned, for various reasons: Kogan-Bernshtein, Chaikin,[44] Rakitnikov and Burevoi, for example, because they found the Central Committee's policies to be insufficiently to the left, Zenzinov because he found them too much to the left. Others who had resigned their Central Committee membership included I. Prilezhaev, Mikhail Sumgin, Vladimir Rikhter and Valerian Lunkevich. Nikolai Rusanov and the alternate member of the Central Committee, Vasilii Sukhomlin, had been sent abroad as PSR representatives. Alternate member Ivan Teterkin lost his life in the Red Terror; his colleague Aleksandr El'iashevich had stood down. Those who disappeared from the Central Committee were replaced by others.

Towards the end of 1919 the *Cheka* began in earnest to hunt down the members of the Central Committee of the PSR. The party's intellectual and political leader, Viktor Chernov, managed to escape his pursuers for some time by continually changing his place of concealment. He was even able to give a speech at a meeting of the Printers Union with an English delegation. In the end, however, it was thought advisable that he should leave the country. He left

Russia in 1920 to act as the PSR's official representative abroad. In December 1920 he started publication of *Revoliutsionnaia Rossiia*, which from then on was to be the party's official journal.[45]

Chernov's departure from the country was preceded by a number of arrests of Central Committee members. Dmitrii Donskoi, Sergei Morozov[46] and Evgeniia Ratner[47] had been arrested in 1919. In the first half of 1920 the arrests followed of Abram Gots, Evgenii Timofeev,[48] Mikhail Vedeniapin, Dmitrii Rakov and Mikhail Tseitlin. In the following few months Mikhail Likhach, Florian Fedorovich, Mikhail Gendel'man, Lev Gershtein, Boris Ivanov and Nikolai Ivanov were rounded up. In this way, all active members of the Central Committee were in prison by the middle of 1921 with the exception of those who had left the country. Apart from members of the Central Committee, the *Cheka* arrested all active party members on whom it could lay hands.

This continual persecution made the existence of the party organization more and more difficult. In June 1920, in view of the numerous arrests of Central Committee members, an Organization Bureau was set up in Moscow, to include those members of the Central Committee who were still at liberty and also other prominent party members. In August 1921, when the entire Central Committee had been imprisoned, the Organization Bureau was replaced by a five-member Central Bureau which was intended to provide guidance to those PSR organizations that were still in existence.[49] But the Central Bureau was also harassed by arrests. The history of the PSR now became increasingly the story of its persecution.

The leadership which the Central Committee, plagued as it was by arrests of its members, was able to offer at the end of the civil war was far from inspiring. In September 1920, ten representatives of PSR organizations held a conference in Moscow. They declared in a resolution that there was no hope that the Bolshevik regime would eventually evolve along democratic lines. They ascertained 'the presence of a broad rebellious popular movement', and considered it therefore inevitable that the party would, at some time in the future, renew its armed struggle against the Bolshevik regime, this in view of the fact that, due in particular to that popular movement, the counter-revolution was in retreat. Since the masses were 'atomized', however, it was necessary that the party should first organize the 'active forces of the people.'[50]

Even this resolution went too far for the Central Committee. In a response on 1 October 1920 it ruled out absolutely any armed resistance against the Bolsheviks in the near future. In the opinion of the Central Committee, the PSR could otherwise make itself guilty of 'narrow conspiratorial adventurism'. In its political and social struggle the party should not 'depend on the weak basis of a politically unshapen insurgency' because this would only open the way to 'all sorts of demagoguery and speculation with the embitterment of the people.' This would be all the more dangerous in that the counter-revolution had not yet been fully put down. For the time being, therefore, the party should restrict itself to organizational work.[51]

Central Committee member Vedeniapin reacted even more strongly from his prison, in effect condemning any violence against the Bolshevik regime. In his opinion, it was not difficult to organize uprisings, even over a large territory, but the consequences could only be unfavourable: 'At this time, under the given balance of power, armed struggle could only give a new lease of life to Bolshevism which is now in the process of disintegrating, or would free the way for the Russian reactionaries with the imperialism of the Entente in their wake.'[52]

What it amounted to was that the political leaders of the Socialist Revolutionaries, while continually repeating in their agitational activities that the Bolshevik regime must vanish, made absolutely no attempt to give leadership and direction to the anti-Bolshevik feelings that were manifest among broad layers of the population at the end of the civil war, and which found their most striking though by no means only expression in a peasant uprising in Tambov province and in the famous revolt by the Kronstadt sailors. The Organization Bureau of the PSR even dissociated itself from the Tambov uprising in July 1921, calling it a 'semi-banditry movement.'[53]

This political passivity thus arose from two somewhat contradictory arguments: on the one hand the party leadership considered that the PSR had insufficient forces at its disposal to be able to combat the Bolsheviks effectively and, in addition, not to play into the hands of the counter-revolutionaries; on the other hand they thought that history was on their side. To take action now, the leaders thought, would only further postpone the ultimate victory which they were making for.

In August 1921 the Socialist Revolutionaries managed to convene a last party council, the tenth, in Samara on the Volga. The inevitable resolution declared that the issue of the revolutionary overthrow of the Bolshevik dictatorship was becoming more and more urgent. The Bolsheviks had been able to stay in power only because the masses were not organized or politically educated. The principal task of the PSR, therefore, was to organize the working masses.[54]

This resolution by the Tenth Party Council also encountered objections from the Central Committee. In September 1921, ten members of the Central Committee managed to smuggle a letter out of Butyrki Prison in which they expressed their opinion that the resolution did not make it sufficiently clear that, in its struggle against the Bolshevik dictatorship, the PSR wanted to depend only on the working masses, that it rejected any form of cooperation with bourgeois groupings and foreign powers, and that it considered uprisings and guerrilla activities to be a waste of effort. The party's task was to organize the working masses.[55] The ten members of the Central Committee did not say how this was to be done under the watchful eye of the *Cheka*, any more than did the resolution which they amended.

The impotence to which the PSR had been doomed by the course of events during the civil war, and the lack of inspirational leadership on the part of the Central Committee, caused many members to leave the party. Some elected to give active support to the Soviet regime, some even joined the Communist Party. The motives of a few are known because they explained their move in open letters to the press. It should be remembered, however, that these open letters formed part of the propaganda campaign which the Soviet press increasingly carried on against the PSR.

Many letter writers criticized PSR tactics: its armed struggle in the past against the Soviet regime — sometimes in cooperation with non-socialist elements — and its subsequent refusal to decide *on principle* that the armed struggle should be terminated. In this way, according to the letter writers, the PSR continued to support the counter-revolution.

A rejection of some of the PSR's basic principles can be found, for instance, in the appeal 'To All Socialist Revolutionaries', published in both *Pravda* and *Izvestiia* on 27 January 1921. The appeal was signed by a number of former members of the PSR and of the *Narod* group, including Grigorii Ratner, brother of the Central Committee member, Evgeniia Ratner.[56] According to the signatories, the recent events had shown that the Socialist Revolutionary theory of

unity of peasants and proletariat was illusory under existing circumstances. Moreover, they rejected the democratic principles and voiced
the opinion that in a revolutionary era there was only place for the
dictatorship of an organized minority and for a system of political
terror. They called upon the Socialist Revolutionaries to join the
Communist Party because, in their opinion, this was preferable to the
two other possibilities: joining the counter-revolution, or inactive opposition which excluded any participation in the political life of the
country.

In a letter of similar tenor, published in *Pravda* on 4 February
1922, Arkadii Krakovetskii, who had been elected as PSR member to
the Constituent Assembly late in 1917 and had been Minister of War
in the local Siberian government in 1918, reproached his former
party for having aimed only at establishing a bourgeois parliamentary
system in Russia, thereby ignoring the social character of the revolution.

Iakov Dvorzhets, the former Socialist Revolutionary Head of
Chancellery (*upravdel*) of the *Komuch*, stated in a letter published in
Izvestiia on 26 January 1921 that it was wrong to continue to oppose the Communist Party. The revolution demanded unity, and
criticisms of the Communist Party should only be voiced from within by its own members. That was why he, just as Ratner *et al.* and
Krakovetskii, sought to join the communists.

But by no means all the renegade Socialist Revolutionaries wanted
to join the Communist Party. The majority withdrew from active
politics and tried to earn a place in Lenin's Russia by making themselves useful in their own professions. Their motivations can perhaps
be clarified by a few examples. At the end of 1917 the sociologist
Pitirim Sorokin was elected member of the Constituent Assembly for
the PSR. During the following months, however, he lost all his illusions about revolution and socialism and became convinced that it
would be impossible to replace the Bolshevik dictatorship in Russia
by a democratic government in the near future.[57] On 29 October
1918 Sorokin explained in an open letter how greatly politics had
disappointed him during the past year, so that he had come to the
conviction that only work in the field of science and education was
always of benefit to the people. His letter attracted the attention of
Lenin who saw it as a symptom of a change in the attitude of the
'petit bourgeois intelligentsia'.[58] Sorokin was released from prison
and allowed to resume his work at the University of Petrograd. (In

1922, however, he was exiled abroad as a 'counter-revolutionary intellectual'.)

Like Sorokin, the influential economist Nikolai Kondrat'ev, director of the famous Moscow Institute for Conjunctural Research, dissociated himself from the PSR for which he had also been elected
member of the Constituent Assembly. In a statement made in February 1920 he told the party that he was resigning his membership because he found its ideas too utopian and its tactics oriented too
much towards illegality.[59] This step enabled him to continue his
work, though not completely without hindrance.

General Aleksandr Verkhovskii, Minister of War in the Provisional
Government, dropped his opposition to the Bolshevik regime when
the Brest-Litovsk Treaty was invalidated at the end of 1918 by the
German defeat and when Kolchak's coup d'état had convinced him
of the impotence of the Constituent Assembly. He was then released
from prison and allowed to make himself useful to the Red Army as
military expert.[60]

These three had all belonged to the right wing of the PSR. Left-
oriented Socialist Revolutionaries were thus far from being the only
ones who sought political or personal accommodation with the
Soviet regime.

The Bolsheviks encouraged such defections which they surrounded
with a great deal of publicity, as numerous open letters in the press
gave eloquent witness. The *Cheka* department which was responsible
for combating the PSR played an important part in the management
of these affairs. According to *Revoliutsionnaia Rossiia*, in the second
half of 1920 the *Cheka* even attempted to convene a congress of
Socialist Revolutionaries who, in return for legalization, were prepared to pass a resolution acknowledging the Soviet regime.[61] There
are strong indications that police services were asked from those
Socialist Revolutionaries who came into contact with the *Cheka*, and
that these were obtained in certain cases.[62]

The Bolshevik attitude towards the Socialist Revolutionaries is
described by what one of *Cheka*'s principal officers, Martyn Latsis,
said in 1921 with regard to all socialist parties: they had no right to
exist. 'Even if these parties did not take active part in the armed
struggle against the Soviet regime, we must still eliminate them because every hindrance in our path and every weakening of our forces
in this final and decisive struggle can help the counter-revolution towards victory.' And he added: 'From time to time we give these

parties the opportunity to improve their ways, to direct their work
in other directions, and we release their members from prison. But so
far this has had no effect: these parties cannot belie their nature.'[63]
The Bolsheviks could not tolerate any political groupings with
deviant views. They desired no opposition, nor allies, but only followers.

The Socialist Revolutionaries who remained faithful to their party
were kept on the run by the *Cheka* and were arrested and imprisoned
whenever possible. They were not brought to trial. The idea was
rather to isolate them. In general, and certainly in Butyrki Prison in
Moscow, they were treated as political prisoners — perhaps because
they were comrades of former times. They could associate with each
other and speak freely about politics. They were allowed to have
political literature sent in from outside the prison and were even able
to maintain some degree of contact with their fellow party members
who were still at liberty. This broke the isolation in which the *Cheka*
wanted to keep them, however, sometimes giving rise to drastic
measures with which it might be restored. In April 1921, for instance, all socialist prisoners were transferred from Butyrki Prison to
provincial prisons where the regimen was stricter. After some time,
however, prison life invariably resumed its old course. Whenever their
circumstances became too difficult and protests were of no avail, the
prisoners would have recourse to the familiar weapon of the hunger
strike.

The attempts to convert individual Socialist Revolutionaries were
paralleled by a continuous baiting of the PSR. The apparent intention of this campaign was to make the people think that the Socialist
Revolutionaries were counter-revolutionaries just as all other opponents of the Bolsheviks and that they must equally be held responsible for all past and present misdeeds of the counter-revolution. (To
some extent the Bolsheviks *believed* in their presentation of affairs.
'Subjectively you are a revolutionary such as we would wish to have
more of, but objectively you serve the counter-revolution', said the
head of the *Cheka*, Feliks Dzerzhinskii, in 1921 to an arrested Socialist Revolutionary.)[64]

On 30 November 1920 *Izvestiia* published an announcement by
the Soviet government that those Socialist Revolutionaries who were
then in prison would be considered as hostages. The reason given was
that 'the Chernov group', in cooperation with the anti-Bolshevik or-

ganization led by Boris Savinkov from Poland and with funds provided by the Entente, had prepared attacks on the lives of Soviet
leaders. The next day, Dzerzhinskii appeared in person in Butyrki
Prison to reassure the Socialist Revolutionaries who were detained
there. He said that he also realized that there was a great difference
between Chernov and Savinkov and assured them that they need
have no fear that they would really be treated as hostages. That
threat was nothing other than 'high politics'. He asked them, however, to dissociate themselves publicly from Savinkov. The prisoners
replied that this had been done on many occasions by the Central
Committee since Savinkov had been expelled from the party even
before the October Revolution and that it did not intend to do so
again merely to please the *Cheka*, which wanted them all to dissociate from one another. The accusation that there should be any
conspiracy between the PSR and Savinkov was after all completely
without foundation.[65]

The transfer of the political prisoners from Butyrki Prison in April
1921 had caused some amount of uproar — it was said that force had
been used — and the Moscow Soviet therefore set up a commission of
inquiry. This commission, as could have been expected, concluded
that the *Cheka* had not made use of improper force, but it also stated
that a great many party documents had been found among the imprisoned Socialist Revolutionaries.[66] This was further elucidated by
the *Cheka* in a report published in *Izvestiia* on 24 July 1921.

According to the *Cheka*, the documents that had fallen into its
hands in the April 1921 operations proved that 'the PSR has been
the organizer and inspirator of the kulak uprisings and has worked
energetically on the preparation of a general uprising against the
Soviet regime.' The members of the Central Committee of the PSR,
according to the *Cheka*, had mis-used the privileges granted them in
Butyrki Prison on humane grounds, 'to lead the counter-revolutionary movement in the country.' The PSR was said to have been in
touch with both the rebellious peasants in Tambov province and with
Savinkov's organization and other White Guard groupings.

There is no doubt that the imprisoned Central Committee members had been able to maintain some degree of contact with fellow
party members outside the prison. But it is pure demagoguery to say
that they had used these contacts to 'lead the counter-revolutionary
movement in the country.' We have seen that the Central Committee
did almost nothing but restrain the remnants of the party from force-

ful action and that it had emphatically warned against participation in spontaneous movements such as the Tambov uprising.

In the difficult months that followed the end of the civil war the Socialist Revolutionaries were given the role of scapegoat. In July 1921 a conference of Communist Party agitators was told that all the troubles suffered by the nation, the famine and the international isolation, must be attributed primarily to the PSR.[67] 'If there is still a dearth of bread and other foodstuffs in the towns of Soviet Russia', wrote the propagandist Sergei Zorin in 1921, 'if the frost holds the mightly limbs of our factories and industries in its grasp, then we have to thank the PSR for it.'[68]

CHAPTER 2

THE ANNOUNCEMENT OF THE TRIAL
AND THE INTERNATIONAL SOCIALIST MOVEMENT

THE DECISION TO ORGANIZE A TRIAL OF THE SOCIALIST
REVOLUTIONARIES AND THE ANNOUNCEMENT OF THE TRIAL

We have seen in the previous chapter that at the end of the civil war the Bolsheviks were confronted with considerable dissatisfaction among the population. In 1921, therefore, they decided to introduce a series of drastic measures in the economic sphere, intended particularly to bring some relief to the peasants. This package of measures was given the name of the New Economic Policy (NEP).

The Socialist Revolutionaries and the Mensheviks had much earlier pressed for such reforms. In their opinion, however, an economic liberalization could only have beneficial consequences for the ruined economy if it was coupled with a political liberalization.

It is conceivable that the Bolsheviks gave some thought to the idea of political reform,[1] but if that was so they ultimately rejected it.[2] Under the NEP they actually intensified their suppression of the political opposition with the goal of eliminating it altogether.[3]

The NEP was also accompanied by certain legal reforms that were intended to create greater 'legality' (*zakonnost'*) i.e. legal security. In February 1922, the *Cheka* was abolished and replaced by the 'State Political Administration', the GPU, which had more restricted powers. In future, political crimes were to be handled 'solely through the courts'. Exceptions to this rule could only be made with the permission of the VTsIK.[4]

The decision to abolish the *Cheka* seemingly contradicted the decision to intensify the suppression of the political opposition, but as we shall see, the GPU simply carried on the work of the *Cheka*. The decision to expand the competences of the courts, however, had its own particular significance.

'Properly considered, there is no "affair of the Socialist Revolutionaries",' *Revoliutsionnaia Rossiia* had written in December 1920 with reference to the fact that many people were being detained in connection with such an 'affair', 'and the Soviet government does not appear to be preparing to frame one, because that would prove to be a very difficult task, even for the present judiciary.'[5]

A year later, however, the Bolshevik leaders decided to tackle this 'very difficult task'. On 28 December 1921, after an exposition by the head of the *Cheka*, Dzerzhinskii — we shall come back to the probable content of that exposition later — the Central Committee of the Communist Party decided to organize a trial of the Central Committee of the PSR. A committee consisting of Dzerzhinskii, Kamenev and Stalin was given the task of determining when this decision could best be made publicly known.[6]

The preparations began to bear fruit about two months later. A pamphlet was published in Berlin in February 1922 which had been written by G. Semenov (Vasil'ev) and was entitled: 'The work in the army and the terrorist activities of the Party of Socialist Revolutionaries during 1917-1918'. The text of this pamphlet appeared as early as 24 February in the newspaper *Novyi mir*, published in Berlin in the Russian language and a Bolshevik mouthpiece.

The author, Grigorii Ivanovich Semenov (Vasil'ev was his pseudonym), born in 1891, was himself a former Socialist Revolutionary and had had a fairly adventurous career. He did not join the PSR until 1917, in the post-February Revolution period.[7] After the October Revolution, as a member of the Military Commission of the PSR, he had at first been at loggerheads with the Central Committee because he considered the Committee's attitude towards the Bolsheviks to be ineffectual. On his own initiative he had then organized a group to fight the Bolsheviks with terrorist methods. Later, however, his attitude showed a complete reversal. He was arrested in the autumn of 1918, but was given amnesty in June 1919 after having signed the requisite personal declaration. Thereafter he had first joined the *Narod* group and then, in January 1921, the Communist Party.[8]

Inconstant as Semenov was in his political convictions, he showed great constancy in the methods that he used: he preferred clandestine work. He seems to have rendered services to the *Cheka* even before he crossed from the *Narod* group to the Communist Party. According to his pamphlet he had realized the error of his ways during his imprisonment.[9] In 1919 his close colleague, Konopleva, told Chernov that Semenov had conceived the idea of informing the

Cheka of his conversion while in prison.[10] In 1920, on behalf of the Red Army's intelligence service, he had carried out a special mission in Poland against Savinkov.[11] After his return to Russia he is said to have informed the *Cheka* about a conspiracy between Savinkov and the PSR, thereby providing the motivation for the Soviet government's statement in *Izvestiia* on 30 November 1920, mentioned above, in which the imprisoned Socialist Revolutionaries were declared hostage.[12] Later in the same year, according to a spokesman for the Socialist Revolutionary newspaper *Golos Rossii*, published in Berlin, Semenov worked for the *Cheka* in the Crimea.[13] The *Narod* group apparently expelled him because of his work for the *Cheka*.[14] After joining the Communist Party, Semenov was given a post abroad where, early in December 1921, he finished writing his pamphlet. This was thus completed even before the Central Committee of the Communist Party decided on 28 December 1921, on the basis of a proposal by Dzerzhinskii, to organize a trial of the Central Committee of the PSR. The publication of the pamphlet at that particular moment cannot be accidental. It seems warranted to conclude that the *Cheka* had started preparing for the trial even before the Central Committee had taken its decision. That Semenov wrote his pamphlet on *Cheka* instructions seems beyond doubt. That he published it in Berlin rather than in Soviet Russia was perhaps intended to give the impression that he was working independently of the government.

In 40-odd pages Semenov 'revealed' the activities of his former party which had been directed against the Soviet regime in the year following the October Revolution, clearly with the intention of drawing these as much as possible into the criminal sphere. In doing so, he was remarkably liberal in giving the names of the people with whom he had cooperated at that time. In 1922 some of these people were in Russian prisons; others were now threatened with persecution, thanks to Semenov's 'frankness'.

Semenov recounted a series of attempts to overthrow the Soviet regime which the PSR was said to have undertaken. In doing so, the PSR was said to have cooperated with, and to have received funds from, reactionary organizations and foreign missions. Moreover, the PSR was said to have been guilty of terrorist activities. Semenov alleged that he had organized the terrorist group which he had led on instructions from members of the Central Committee. The hold-ups ('expropriations' in the language of revolutionary circles) and the murderous attacks on Bolshevik leaders which his group had committed were also said by Semenov to have been made on instructions from Central Committee members, in particular Abram Gots and Dmitrii Donskoi. According to Semenov, Elena Ivanova, a sister of the Central Committee member Nikolai Ivanov, was one of those who had maintained contacts between the group and the Central Committee. The attacks on the Bolshevik People's Commissar for Press Affairs, Moisei Volodarskii (who was killed on 20 June 1918) and on Lenin (who was wounded by Fania Kaplan on 30 August 1918) had been perpetrated by members of his group. In addition, the group was said to have prepared attacks on other Bolshevik leaders, i.e. on Trotskii, Zinov'ev and Uritskii.

Semenov's most serious accusation was that the PSR was responsible for the attack on Lenin. After having drawn up the plan in Moscow to organize an attack on Lenin, he wrote, he had got into touch with Gots. Gots had twice given him permission for the attack and on the second occasion had given his word of honour that after the attack the Central Committee would claim responsibility on behalf of the party. Semenov had then admitted Fania Kaplan into his group and had nominated her to carry out the attack. He had also introduced her in that capacity to Donskoi who had then again confirmed what Gots had promised earlier. A short time later Kaplan had made her attack. But notwithstanding the promises by Gots and Donskoi, the Central Committee had denied in the press that it had had anything to do with the attack, just as it had done previously with respect to the attack on Volodarskii.

Semenov's story ended in September 1918 at the time of his arrest. In prison, so he declared, he had realized that the dictatorship of the proletariat was essential and that the position taken by the PSR was wrong. And now, after long hesitation (so he alleged), he had decided in the interests of the revolution — again according to his own words — to expose the past of his former party. Socialists all over the world would then be able to assure themselves that the lamentations of the Socialist Revolutionaries that they had nothing on their conscience and were kept imprisoned without cause, were nothing but lies. In his Foreword Semenov also pointed out that many members of the PSR had long realized 'the complete falsity of their double-faced position' and had long understood that they were 'a pawn in the hands of a few political bunglers'. These people were not sufficiently resolute, however, to openly break with the party, to acknowledge their errors, and to genuinely associate themselves with 'all true fighters for the Revolution'. Semenov said that he was convinced that his action would help these Socialist Revolutionaries 'to cross to the camp of the Revolution.'

According to the date on his pamphlet, Semenov had finished it on 2 December 1921. That he knew quite well with which intention his pamphlet was published is shown by the fact that, in the Foreword that was added between 2 December and the date of publication, he placed himself at the disposal of the court as an offender: 'I do not reject the responsibility that I bear with regard to the Russian Revolution and shall, when demanded by the Supreme Revolutionary Tribunal, feel myself obliged to return to Soviet Russia to undergo the punishment I deserve.'

A few days after their publication, Semenov's 'revelations' — as the Soviet press called his pamphlet which was reprinted in full — were endorsed and amplified by statements by his collaborator Lidiia Konopleva, which were published on 28 February in *Pravda* and *Izvestiia* and subsequently also in other papers. Her statements were of similar content and nature to those of Semenov.

Lidiia Vasil'evna Konopleva, also born in 1891 and a teacher by profession, had been an active member of Semenov's terrorist group in 1918 and had since been his closest collaborator. Like Semenov, after leaving the PSR she had joined the Communist Party early in 1921 after a brief spell with the *Narod* group; like Semenov, she is said to have earlier rendered services to the *Cheka*.[15] When, like Semenov, she went abroad after joining the Communist Party, she had seen — at least, according to what she said a few months later — how the Socialist Revolutionary emigré press fulminated against Soviet Russia. In the summer of 1921, to continue with her own story, she had reached agreement with Semenov that they would take action together to expose the PSR. Semenov had then gone to Russia to investigate whether such an action would be worthwhile (i.e. whether the *Cheka* found it worthwhile — it seems reasonable to assume). On his return he had confirmed this to Konopleva, after which first Semenov and then Konopleva had made their statements.[16]

On 28 February, *Izvestiia* also published a statement by the GPU regarding the 'revelations' of Semenov and Konopleva. The GPU stated that on the basis of their criminal acts proved by this and other material, the Central Committee and a number of active members of the PSR would be 'delivered to the court of the Supreme Revolutionary Tribunal'. People like Semenov were also summonsed to appear at the forthcoming trial.

Why did the Central Committee of the Communist Party decide on 28 December 1921 to bring the Socialist Revolutionaries to trial and why, after taking that decision, did it wait another two months before announcing the trial?

The proposal that a trial should be held of the Socialist Revolutionaries was probably made by Dzerzhinskii. He had commented on the Socialist Revolutionaries and the Mensheviks prior to the decision being taken, and was subsequently appointed to the three-member committee which was entrusted with the preparations for the trial. His intentions are made clear by a memorandum which he had had circulated among the *Cheka* staff, apparently a short time earlier, and in which he complained that the material at the *Cheka*'s disposal regarding the PSR was 'not sufficiently utilized from the political point of view,' and that this 'is our principal shortcoming.' According to Dzerzhinskii, the material in question should be given large-scale propagandist use in the press in order that the people might clearly understand 'the sort of treason to which Chernov and Co. have fallen.'[17]

The Bolsheviks' objective in bringing the Socialist Revolutionaries to trial was made quite clear by the Instructions which Lenin sent to the People's Commissar for Justice, Dmitrii Kurskii, on 20 February 1922, i.e. one week before the announcement of the trial, and in which he insisted that the People's Commissariat of Justice should in future take over more of the *Cheka*'s repressive task:

Intensification of the repression of the political enemies of the Soviet regime and of the agents of the bourgeoisie (*in particular* the Mensheviks and the Socialist Revolutionaries); the use of such repression by Revolutionary Tribunals and People's Courts in the quickest and, *for the revolution, most effective* manner; the compulsory organization of a number of *model* trials (which will stand model as regards the explanation of their significance to the masses of the people by the court and in the press) in Moscow, Petrograd, Khar'kov and other major centres; the influencing of People's Judges and of members of the Revolutionary Tribunals by the party, with the purpose of improving the work of the courts and of intensifying repression; — all this must be taken in hand systematically, resolutely and with determination.

Lenin said that a series of 'noisy, *educative* model trials' must be held in various centres, and must be accompanied by plenty of 'tumult' in the press. After all, trials had an 'enormous educational significance'.

In Lenin's opinion, the judges at these trials should not reach their opinion independently on the basis of written laws. They must conform to the needs of the Communist Party, taking as their point of departure such criteria as 'the *spirit* of our communistic legislation' and *'our revolutionary sense of justice.'*[18]

Lenin's instructions, which were intended for internal use, were rewritten by the Soviet lawyer, Iakov Brandenburgskii, in a form suitable for the public at large, and published in *Pravda* on 23 March. 'The courts must pass severe judgements on the enemies of the Soviet regime', Brandenburgskii wrote, referring to the Mensheviks and the Socialist Revolutionaries, 'and in doing so must take all necessary steps to ensure that information about these trials can penetrate right through to the masses of the people, that the workers and the peasants in the land can hear about the trials, and above all, that they can understand them.'[19]

In the line of thought followed by Lenin and the other Bolshevik leaders, therefore, the trial of the Socialist Revolutionaries was intended not to bring the truth to light but to arouse public opinion against the Socialist Revolutionaries.

The Bolsheviks had already gained some experience with this sort of trial in preceding years; for example, that of the 'Tactical Centre' in August 1920 and that of the Central Committee of the (independent) Ukrainian Socialist Revolutionary Party in May 1921, although these trials had had nothing like the magnitude and significance which that of the Socialist Revolutionaries was to have. They had been more in the nature of try-outs.

What part did the statements signed by Semenov and Konopleva play in all this? It may safely be assumed that Dzerzhinskii was aware of their contents, and even that in all probability the statements were originally inspired by his political police. It seems likely that Dzerzhinskii suggested to the Central Committee on 28 December 1921 that the statements should be used. This was necessary because the opposition pursued by the PSR during the last few years did not provide sufficient basis for a major political trial of its leaders at which severe sentences could be passed. The party had exercised armed resistance only in 1918 and its leaders could not be persecuted on those grounds, at any rate not if the 1919 amnesty was of any consequence. The desired dramatic effect of a political trial of the Socialist Revolutionaries could only be expected if they could be linked with *capital crimes* such as the attempted murder of Lenin. That linkage was provided by Semenov and Konopleva in their statements, which formed an initial step towards the Indictment. This was undoubtedly also the reason why the trial could not be announced before the statements were published in February 1922.

The statements by Semenov and Konopleva, however, were not only intended to prepare public opinion for a major political trial. They also enabled pressure to be brought to bear on the members of the PSR. Semenov made a clear distinction in his pamphlet between the leaders on the one hand, described by him as weak, indecisive, cowardly, secretive, faithless and untruthful, and on the other hand those of their followers who had indeed made mistakes, but who had seen the error of their ways and only needed to find the courage to break with the party.

It was obviously the intention to force the adherents of the PSR to break with the party. For this purpose, an appeal was made on the one hand to their 'sincere revolutionary convictions' and on the other hand also to their less altruistic feelings. After all, everyone could see that the members of the Central Committee were imprisoned and had been *handed over* to the court, while Semenov and Konopleva — not the least guilty, according to their own words — were at liberty and had been *asked* if they would kindly appear before the court. It was thus not without reason that Semenov had published such a detailed list of 'guilty' in his pamphlet. These were now forced to make a choice: either support the Central Committee and be persecuted, or follow the examples of Semenov and Konopleva and go free. Because, although Semenov and Konopleva were in the dock during the trial, as we shall see, they were not really among the accused. Their task was to confess their crimes and to declare that these had been perpetrated on the instructions of the Central Committee of the PSR.

THE TRIAL AND THE
INTERNATIONAL SOCIALIST MOVEMENT

During the night of 24-25 February, i.e. before the announcement of the trial, the members of the Central Committee of the PSR were transferred from Butyrki Prison to the 'Inner Prison' (*Vnutrenniaia tiur'ma*) in GPU headquarters on the Lubianka, where they were shut up in strict isolation. According to the journal of the Menshevik Party, *Sotsialisticheskii vestnik*, they were told by a high-ranking official of the GPU that this was because they were among the 140 accused who were to be put on trial, starting on 20 March. During the next few days numerous arrests were made in Moscow and elsewhere, not only among those Socialist Revolutionary activists who were still at liberty, but also among former members and helpers of the PSR.[20] A press campaign against the PSR broke out at the same time, based on the 'revelations' by Semenov and Konopleva.

A counter-campaign was soon under way. The Central Bureau of the PSR immediately issued a statement, on 28 February, in which it showed its disquiet. Since there was no possibility of holding a campaign in Russia itself, however, the work had to be done abroad. Its focal point was Berlin, the basis of the Foreign Delegation of the PSR. This was the party's official representation outside Russia, and consisted at that time of Viktor Chernov, Il'ia Rubanovich, Nikolai Rusanov, Vasilii Sukhomlin and Vladimir Zenzinov (who had dropped his opposition to the official party line). The paper *Golos Rossii*, which was edited by Socialist Revolutionaries, was also published in Berlin.

On 9 March the Foreign Delegation of the PSR appealed to all socialist parties in the world to prevent the Bolsheviks from settling accounts with their political adversaries with the aid of a framed trial.[21] Earlier, on 7 March, the Socialist Revolutionaries in Berlin had formed a committee to organize an international campaign against the trial. Time seemed to be short: no official announcement had been made regarding the starting date of the trial, but unofficially the date of 20 March had been bruited. The committee started to organize the defence of the threatened party comrades. It also kept the socialist parties of the world informed about the state of affairs, a work in which it could call on the help of groups of Socialist Revolutionaries in various European capitals.[22]

The intention of the Socialist Revolutionaries was to bring pressure to bear on the international socialist movement which at that time was severely divided. In addition to the Second International, which had been resurrected after the world war, and the newly established Third or Communist International (the Comintern), the International Working Union of Socialist Parties had been formed early in

1921 by centre socialist parties who had left the Second International in protest against its 'reformism'. This was known as the 'Vienna Union' after the site of its headquarters, and in the Comintern was described derisively as the 'Two-and-a-half' International. The Vienna Union did not seek to further divide the international socialist movement, however, but on the contrary to reinstate one all-embracing International which would be neither reformist nor communist.

At the end of 1921 the Comintern launched its 'united front' strategy, aimed towards cooperation with the non-communists in the international socialist movement. One important reason for this step was that the Soviet government was seeking support with an eye to the conference with the Western Powers that was soon to be held in Genoa. Therefore, when the Vienna Union took the initiative in January 1922 of calling a general International Congress of Workers' Parties, the Comintern agreed to cooperate. The Second International also agreed to send representatives, but on condition that three items would be put on the agenda of the congress: the question of Georgia — an independent socialist-governed state which had been annexed by Soviet Russia with the use of military force in 1921; the question of the political prisoners — particularly the Russian socialists; and the question of communist cell-formation in socialist trade unions.

Finally, both the Comintern and the Second International agreed that a preparatory conference of the three Internationals should be held in Berlin early in April 1922, at which the organization of such a general congress should be discussed.

The Socialist Revolutionaries now tried to persuade the socialists of the Second and Vienna Internationals that their attitude towards the Comintern's united front strategy should be made dependent on the state of affairs at and surrounding the Moscow trial of the Socialist Revolutionaries. At that time the PSR was not itself a member of any of the Internationals. In March 1920 its Central Committee had decided to withdraw from the Second International and to seek contact with other seceded centre socialist parties in an effort to restore what was called a really revolutionary and socialist International.[23] When the Vienna Union was founded, the Central Committee had therefore requested that the PSR be admitted as member.[24]

There were problems, however. The Vienna Union was in fact far less uncompromising than the PSR towards the regime that had been established in Russia by the October Revolution, even though it had serious criticisms of certain Bolshevik practices. As a result, the Vienna Union was not overly anxious to admit the PSR as member, a party which in the past had used force against 'the revolution' – which the Bolsheviks represented, notwithstanding all else – and which had not always shown complete rejection of 'the counter-revolution'. Quite a few Socialist Revolutionaries, particularly among the political emigrés, therefore felt little enthusiasm about joining the Vienna Union.

The members of the Central Committee who were incarcerated in Russian prisons shared the criticism of what they called 'the half-hearted and ambiguous attitude' of the Vienna Union towards the Bolshevik regime,[25] but considered that the PSR should nevertheless become a member. They therefore insisted that the Foreign Delegation should take the necessary steps towards realizing that membership. So far, however, repeated appeals by the Central Committee and also by the Central Bureau[26] had not achieved the desired result, due both to the reservations shown by Vienna and to those of many Socialist Revolutionaries abroad.

The Socialist Revolutionaries were more successful in their effort to start an international campaign against the trial. The Foreign Delegation's appeal on 9 March brought a wave of response, particularly from Second and Vienna International circles. It was clear from these reactions, however, that the two Internationals held different positions.

The Second International stood up for the Socialist Revolutionaries almost unreservedly and gave as its unequivocal opinion that a judicial show whose objective was to suppress socialist opposition in Russia was unacceptable. It was able to do this without difficulty since it viewed the Comintern's efforts towards rapprochement with some scepticism.

The Vienna Union took a different view. It strongly objected to the Bolshevik persecution of the left opposition, which had also victimized several of its own Menshevik and Left Socialist Revolutionary members, but on the other hand it was anxious not to shut the door in the face of the Comintern.

This ambiguity was characterized by the appeal which Friedrich Adler, the Austrian Secretary of the Vienna Union, made to the Comintern on 17 March with reference to the forthcoming trial.

Adler emphatically dissociated himself from the policies followed by the PSR since the October Revolution and refrained from giving any opinion about the trial. He urged the Soviet government by way of the Comintern, however, to make it plain that it was not its intention to terrorize a socialist party, but to bring the truth to light by means of a strictly fair legal procedure. The trial should be held in open court and, before the sentence was carried out (there was serious concern that the Socialist Revolutionaries would be sentenced to death), the Internationals should be given the opportunity to investigate whether the Socialist Revolutionaries had actually perpetrated counter-revolutionary crimes.[27]

The Foreign Delegation of the PSR protested sharply against this letter, which torpedoed a proposal which it had earlier made to the effect that the trial should be held before a court formed by the three Internationals.[28] It accused Adler that his 'diplomatic' letter sanctioned the Bolshevik jurisdiction and impaired the international protest campaign.[29] The journal *Sotsialisticheskii vestnik* of the Menshevik Party, which was itself a member of the Vienna Union, found this fierce attack to be politically inadvisable but also had its criticisms. It considered that Adler should not have dissociated himself from the Socialist Revolutionaries in a letter whose primary objective was to save them from the terror.[30]

In a talk with Sukhomlin, a member of the Foreign Delegation of the PSR, Adler nevertheless adhered to what he had written in his letter. In his view the Soviet government had the right to try the Socialist Revolutionaries. It could only be asked to do so in a trial that would be open to the public and held before an independent tribunal which would guarantee the accused all facilities for their defence. If, in the investigation to which Adler had referred in his letter, the Internationals should reach the conclusion that the sentence passed had been unjust, then they would be able to demand that that sentence not be put into effect. In any case, Adler doubted whether the Socialist Revolutionaries would be given the death sentence.[31]

With the Berlin conference in the offing, the communists also were apparently not keen to force the issue of the contradictions. Their initial reaction to the international protest campaign was fairly mild. They even made a few concessions, although non-officially and in somewhat scornful terms. On 23 March the Bolshevik commentator,

Lev Sosnovskii, wrote in *Pravda* that the Socialist Revolutionaries might avail themselves of the best defenders they could find and that representatives 'of the yellow International and of the European bourgeoisie which sympathizes with the Socialist Revolutionaries' could, if they so wished, attend the trial (in communist circles the Second International was frequently referred to as the 'yellow' International, in analogy to the 'yellow trade unions', i.e. employer-controlled trade unions).[32] A statement by the Soviet Russian representation in London, published on 25 March in the French communist paper *l'Humanité*, said that the trial would be held in open court. The French communist, Charles Rappoport, who was then in Russia, also wrote in *l'Humanité* on 30 March that he had heard from an authoritative source that the trial would be held in public and that there could be no question of a death penalty ('il ne peut pas s'agir de la peine de mort'). The next day the French communists, Boris Souvarine and Louis Sellier reported in similar vein in a telegram from Russia which was also published in *l'Humanité*.

A far less reassuring voice made itself heard at the Eleventh Congress of the Russian Communist Party, which started at the end of March. Lenin declared at that Congress that the criticisms of the Socialist Revolutionaries and of the Mensheviks must be punished by the revolutionary tribunals with the death sentence. 'Permit us', these critics should be told, 'for these reasons to stand you up against the wall.'[33]

The twentieth of March, the day on which the trial ought to have started according to some rumours, passed without even the mention of a date for its commencement. Nevertheless, the Foreign Delegations of the PSR and the RSDRP (the Russian Social-Democratic Workers Party, i.e. the Mensheviks), decided to hold a preparatory meeting in view of the forthcoming conference of the three Internationals in Berlin.

The Mensheviks and the Bolsheviks had originated in the same Marxist party, but since 1917 the Mensheviks' position had been far closer to that of the Socialist Revolutionaries. Both parties formed part of the socialist opposition to the Bolshevik regime and both were victims of Bolshevik persecution. This did not alter the fact that serious differences of opinion occurred between the Mensheviks and the Socialist Revolutionaries, both with regard to theoretical and to political-strategical matters. A discussion of these differences does not fall within the scope of the present book. Suffice it to say that the Mensheviks belonged to the Vienna Union and that they had partly inspired that organization's criticisms of the PSR.

Nevertheless, Bolshevik propaganda commonly lumped the Mensheviks and the Socialist Revolutionaries together. This was sufficient reason for the Mensheviks in Russia to increase their reservations against the Socialist Revolutionaries. The announcement of the trial was thus somewhat of an embarrassment for them. The Menshevik Central Committee needed a great deal of brain-racking before it could establish a course of action that, on the one hand, would not leave the threatened Socialist Revolutionaries to their fate, but which, on the other hand, would give no-one cause to sweep the Mensheviks together with the Socialist Revolutionaries.[34]

The Foreign Delegation of the Mensheviks in Berlin, whose leading members included Iulii Martov, Fedor Dan and Rafail Abramovich, had more freedom of movement. Although they, too, had never concealed their criticisms of the PSR, they felt that the trial was another matter altogether. With the Foreign Delegation and its official journal, *Sotsialisticheskii vestnik*, setting the example, Mensheviks living outside Russia immediately dedicated themselves to organizing the defence of the threatened Socialist Revolutionaries, without impairing their attitude by prejudice of any sort. On 14 March, for example, the Foreign Delegation called upon the international socialist movement to intervene immediately and as strenuously as possible, 'to prevent the crime that is being prepared.'[35]

The Mensheviks made it clear that, if the accused were to be put to death, the formation of a united front with the communists would be out of the question. The significance that they attached to the matter was thus made obvious in that they were strong advocates of such a united front, thus differing from the Socialist Revolutionaries who had no real faith in a united front.[36]

As a result, at their meeting in Berlin on 27 March, the Foreign Delegations of the PSR and the RSDRP were unable to reach agreement regarding a joint policy at the forthcoming conference of the three Internationals.[37] Both parties agreed that the question of the persecution of the socialists in Russia and of the trial in particular must be discussed at the conference, but their opinions differed as to how this should be done. According to the Socialist Revolutionaries, the Bolsheviks should from the outset, as they put it, be told what the score was. The Mensheviks wanted to prevent a break with the

Comintern, however, and considered that ultimata should not be presented before a general congress of workers' parties had been held. The conference should suffice with issuing a statement in which, *inter alia*, the question of the persecution of the socialists in Russia would be brought to the fore. Martov, the principal spokesman of the Mensheviks, felt that one demand at least should be put before the Comintern as ultimatum: the death penalty must not be carried out on the accused Socialist Revolutionaries (Martov spoke of 'not carrying out the death penalty' and not of not passing the death sentence; apparently he did not appreciate that compliance with this demand could be interpreted in such a way that death sentences could be passed provided they were not put into effect). His political colleague, Dan, also thought it advisable that the guarantee that this would not be done should be sought in private discussion with Karl Radek, the leader of the Comintern delegation, rather than during the public session of the conference.[38]

Once it had become evident that joint action with the Mensheviks was not possible, the Socialist Revolutionaries took their own steps towards telling the Bolsheviks 'what the score was'. In a memorandum to the parties which had gathered for the Berlin conference, the PSR's Foreign Delegation discussed the Bolshevik terror in detail, and labelled Bolshevik efforts towards a united front as an insincere strategical manoeuvre. If the policy of rapprochement towards the communists was to be continued, the latter would need to satisfy a number of preconditions: the Bolshevik terror must be stopped; political prisoners in Russia must be released; the five members of the Central Committee of the PSR who had been appointed delegates to the General Congress of Workers' Parties[39] must be given permission to leave the country; and the forthcoming political trial must be cancelled. If it should nevertheless be held, so stated the Foreign Delegation, then the Socialist Revolutionaries knew their duty. They would appear before the tribunal 'not as accused but as accusers' and would 'unmask the farce of Bolshevik justice.'[40]

On 1 April, the day before the opening of the Berlin conference, the Internationals each held introductory discussions. The Executive Committee of the Second International resolved that the Comintern should be set the following demands: the communists must desist from undermining the socialist trade unions; the Soviet government must withdraw the occupying troops from Georgia; and it must put an end to the persecution of the socialists. In particular, the Comintern must be required to hand over the investigation into the activities of the Socialist Revolutionaries to an international committee of socialists. If the Comintern was not prepared to do this, then the Belgian socialist Emile Vandervelde should be given permission to act as defending counsel for the accused at the trial. The Socialist Revolutionaries Sukhomlin and Zenzinov, who had been invited to attend the meeting, presented two more demands which they were anxious to have granted: that the trial should be held in public, and that no death penalty should be carried out (Sukhomlin and Zenzinov also spoke of 'not carrying out the death penalty'). It is not known whether the Executive Committee took any decision to this effect.[41]

The Executive Committee of the Vienna Union agreed with a Menshevik proposal that the Comintern should not be faced with ultimata, but that a declaration should be issued to the effect that the persecution of the socialists in Russia was in conflict with the notion of a united front. The Executive Committee also decided to inform the Comintern that enforcement of the death penalty on the Socialist Revolutionaries would make it impossible to hold a General Congress.[42]

The Conference of the three Internationals met in the Reichstag in Berlin from 2-5 April, and the chances of organizing a General Congress of Workers' Parties were discussed. The positions of the parties were in strong contrast to each other. Emile Vandervelde and Ramsay MacDonald, on behalf of the Second International, laid before the Comintern the aforementioned three preconditions to the holding of a General Congress. These were rejected forcefully by Karl Radek, the leader of the Comintern delegation. Radek accused Vandervelde *et al.* that their own hands were soiled with the blood of Rosa Luxemburg and Karl Liebknecht and that they themselves in Germany held proletarian fighters (i.e. communists) captive. He repeated a suggestion that the Bolsheviks had earlier made in the press,[43] i.e. that 'the Russian terrorists whom you have canonized' should be exchanged for these imprisoned communists. The Vienna Union had to play a difficult intermediary role to prevent the united front effort from stranding there and then. Its spokesmen, Paul Faure and Otto Bauer, voiced the agreed criticisms of the communists, but also upbraided the Second International. In their opinion, the General Congress must not be abandoned because of stipulations that had been set in advance.

The Comintern was anxious to continue the discussions, however, partly because of the forthcoming Genoa conference, and Radek consequently showed some degree of accommodation. With regard to the trial of the Socialist Revolutionaries, the spokesmen of the Second International had demanded that the right of the accused to a proper defence should be guaranteed and that the Internationals should be allowed to exercise supervision. Radek refused to discuss this latter demand but did not object to MacDonald's proposal that Vandervelde should be admitted to the trial as defending counsel (although he also said that he would prefer to welcome Vandervelde as one of the accused). Furthermore, Radek agreed that representatives of the Internationals should be allowed to make stenographic reports and to study the documents of the case. Faure of the Vienna Union announced that 'the carrying-out of death penalties' would put an end to all attempts towards rapprochement; as we shall see, Radek was ultimately prepared to make concessions on this point as well.[44]

The discussions were continued by a smaller committee whose members finally agreed on the text of a collective statement which was accepted by the entire conference on the evening of 5 April.

According to that statement, the three Internationals would co-equally constitute a committee of nine members to maintain contact among the parties. The Second International did not consider it possible to hold a General Congress in April, according to the statement, but the conference had agreed in principle that the Congress should be called 'as soon as possible'. Since a General Congress could not be held in April, combined labour demonstrations must be organized on an international scale either on 20 April, when the Genoa conference would start, or on 1 May.

Finally, the statement gave particular attention to the trial of the Socialist Revolutionaries:

The conference has noted the announcement by the representatives of the Communist International that in the trial of the 47 Social Revolutionaries all defending counsels chosen by them will be admitted, and that the imposing of the death penalty is excluded, as has been stated in the Soviet press prior to the conference. In view of the fact that the trial will be held in public, representatives of all three Executive Committees [i.e. of the Internationals] will be allowed to attend as observers; they will also be permitted to make stenographic records of the course of the trial in order that they may report back to the parties associated with the Executive Committees.[45]

The number of 47 accused had been mentioned here and there in the press but was not official. The phrase 'as has been stated in the Soviet press prior to the conference' was added at the request of the Comintern delegation and referred to the concessions announced in the communist press regarding the trial, which have been discussed earlier in this chapter.

The exegesis of the Berlin resolution provided certain problems. The text was drafted in German and subsequently translated into other languages. The Russian translation proved to deviate slightly from the German original, a significant difference appearing precisely in the passage regarding the death penalty. According to the German text, the 'Verhängung von Todesstrafen', i.e. the 'imposition of the death sentence', was out of the question; according to the Russian text, the 'primenenie smertnoi kazni', i.e. the 'carrying-out of the death penalty' would not be permitted.[46] On the basis of the Russian formulation it would be possible to condemn the accused to death provided that the sentence would not be carried out, e.g. by the granting of a reprieve. On the other hand, the German text was the original one and had been accepted by the conference.

The concessions made by the Comintern delegation in Berlin were quite far-reaching. All defending counsels chosen by the accused were to be admitted; the trial would be held in public; it could be attended by representatives of the three Internationals who would be allowed to make stenograms; and, above all, no death penalties would be imposed. These concessions by the Comintern delegation were ratified on 19 April by the Executive Committee of the Comintern. In principle, this was also binding on the Russian Communist Party.

Although the socialists had not been able to persuade the communists not to hold a political trial of the Socialist Revolutionaries in Russia, it seemed that they had nevertheless managed to gain a number of not insignificant advantages for the accused.

It now remained to be seen whether the communists would keep their word, since the 'Berlin Agreement' had not been favourably received in communist circles. Even before the resolution had been accepted by the conference, Bukharin had voiced the opinion within the Comintern delegation that Radek had overstepped his authority in making those concessions, and that he had embarked upon matters that were the sole prerogative of the Soviet government.[47] Bukharin's opinion was quickly endorsed by Lenin in an article with the expressive title 'We have paid too high a price', published in *Pravda* and *Izvestiia* on 11 April. Lenin considered that the Comintern delegation should not have conceded that the Soviet government would not enforce the death penalty (he thus based himself on the Russian text of the agreement) and that representatives of the Internationals would be admitted to the trial, particularly since these concessions were made without corresponding concessions by the other side ('the reactionary bourgeoisie'). Nevertheless, in Lenin's opinion, the agreement should not be broken. 'The mistake made by Radek and Bukharin is not a big one', he finished his article with demagogic irony. 'At the most we face the risk that the enemies of Soviet Russia, encouraged by the results of the Berlin conference, will perpetrate two or three attacks, perhaps with success. Because they now know in advance that they can shoot at the communists with the chance that a conference such as that of Berlin will prevent the communists from shooting at them.'[48]

Notwithstanding his criticism, Lenin thus intended to honour the Berlin Agreement, with the sanction of the Politbureau which had approved his article.[49] But in doing so, he based himself on a version of the contents which was not entirely correct. An interview with the People's Commissar of Justice, Kurskii, published by *Pravda* on 19 April, showed even more clearly which interpretation had received Bolshevik approval. According to Kurskii, the agreement was not binding for the Russian judiciary and committed only the Communist Party to ensuring that the death penalty would not be carried out. If the court should pronounce the death sentence, according to Kurskii, the VTsIK, as highest Soviet authority, would therefore have to grant a reprieve. On 22 April, in the German communist paper, *Die Rote Fahne*, Radek also stated that the Soviet government was not committed by the Berlin Agreement. The Comintern delegation, according to Radek, had spoken not on behalf of the Soviet government but only on behalf of the Executive Committee of the Comintern.

From the strictly formal viewpoint these Bolshevik spokesmen were in the right, and the Soviet government and Soviet judicature were not bound by the Berlin Agreement. In view of the fact, however, that the Russian Communist Party had the dominant voice in the Comintern (particularly on a point such as that under consideration) on the one hand, and in the Soviet government and the Soviet legal institutions on the other hand, their reasoning was fallacious.

However much they probably regretted it after the event, the Bolsheviks could hardly deny that they were committed by the agreement of the Comintern, even though in their view this meant merely that no death penalty might be *carried out*. That they were very unhappy about this concession in particular is shown by the fact that they thought of every conceivable way of getting out of it. In his interview Kurskii remarked that the agreement would lose its validity if the other side should resort to methods of armed struggle. Radek in turn emphasized that the Comintern delegation had made its concessions on the basis of the knowledge that the Soviet government had no intention of punishing '*these* crimes' (i.e. the crimes perpetrated by the Socialist Revolutionaries in 1918) with the death penalty at this time. From this it could be deduced that if '*new* crimes should come to light' which implied that the PSR had also used 'methods of armed struggle' in more recent times, the guarantee concerning the death penalty could perhaps lapse.

On 9 May, Radek's colleague, Bukharin, went so far as to tell the Executive Committee of the Comintern in his report on the Berlin conference, that the Comintern delegation in Berlin had *not* promised 'that no death sentences would be imposed.' According to Bukharin, they had merely drawn attention to the announcements in the communist press that the lives of the accused were not in jeopardy.[50]

We have seen that the General Congress of Workers' Parties, discussed at the Berlin conference, could not be held in April due to the Second International but should, in the opinion of the conference, be convened as soon as possible. A committee of nine had been assigned by the conference to keep the consultations going in the intervening period. The Comintern urged that this committee should meet immediately in April. The Vienna Union agreed, but the more reticent Second International said that it would not have time until later in May. This gave rise to a protest in the German Communist Party's paper, *Die Rote Fahne*, on 5 May. The paper posited that the Comintern delegation had made its concessions 'on condition that a general congress be convened immediately.' If the meeting of the Nine were not to be held and the General Congress was to be delayed for an indefinite period then, according to *Die Rote Fahne*, 'the Soviet government would be mad to adhere unilaterally to an agreement which the other side has violated.'[51]

The conference, however, had not decided that the General Congress must be convened 'immediately'. Moreover, as Lenin had at once remarked, the fulfilment of its concessions by the Comintern was not made dependent in the agreement on the fulfilment of concessions by the other side. The article in *Die Rote Fahne* was one of many attempts by the communists to evade their concessions (Radek was later to allege that the Comintern delegation had promised merely to exercise its influence to get only Vandervelde admitted to the trial). Adler wrote to Radek on 13 May, however, that the Second International had agreed that the Nine should meet on 22 May.[52]

It is questionable whether the overture towards the socialists meant anything more for the Bolsheviks than a short-lived tactical manoeuvre. Even during the Berlin conference, on 3 April, the Central Committee of the Russian Communist Party had decided to launch 'a counter-agitation campaign' against the people outside Russia who stood up for the Russian socialists.[53] In Berlin, the Comintern delegate Bukharin instructed Victor Serge, who was present as a journalist, to ensure that the communist press would fiercely attack the European socialists.[54]

After the Berlin conference, and in total accord with the decision of the Central Committee of the Russian Communist Party, the Comintern leadership drafted a resolution according to which the communists must make use of the Berlin Agreement to 'attack the opponent', i.e. the socialist Internationals, 'on each weak point.'[55] Lenin, who commented on the draft on 11 April, found that it did not go far enough. In his view, the resolution should make it clear that the leaders of the socialist Internationals were 'identical' to the Russian socialists who, in turn, had a 'de facto relationship' with 'the joint front of the landlords and the bourgeoisie.'[56]

In that draft resolution the Comintern also decided to make use of the demonstration of 20 April, which had been called by the Berlin conference, in order to criticize the socialist Internationals. In this way the demonstration was not the show of unity that had been intended. The socialists of the Second International and the communists refused to march through the streets together. And it was no better with the 1 May demonstration. The Menshevik Boris Dvinov even reported having seen a banner with the slogan 'Death to the bourgeoisie and to social democracy' at the 1 May demonstration in Moscow.[57]

After the Berlin conference, the Socialist Revolutionaries in exile continued their campaign to save their party comrades in Russia. On 8 April the Foreign Delegation of the PSR decided to take steps to turn the forthcoming trial into 'an international manifestation.'[58]

In the first place the Socialist Revolutionaries, with the aid of the European socialists, must ensure that the Bolsheviks adhered to the concessions made by the Comintern. For this purpose they formed a special committee to undertake the organization of the defence of the accused. On 7 April they had already asked Adler, who was then in Vienna, to use his influence with the communists to ensure that the Socialist Revolutionaries Sukhomlin and Kobiakov would be able to travel to Moscow as defenders of the accused. Adler then sent a telegram to Radek (who was still in Berlin) asking for visas for the two men. At the same time he asked whether it was true that the trial was to start on 20 April. He had heard a rumour to this effect from MacDonald who considered that this would be an infringement of the Berlin Agreement in that it would leave insufficient time to organize the defence.[59] After consulting Moscow, Radek told Adler that the date of the trial had not yet been fixed and that it would be determined in such a way that execution of the Berlin Agreement would be guaranteed.[60]

Radek reacted to Adler's request for visas for Sukhomlin and Kobiakov by asking for a complete list of defenders. At Adler's request, the aforementioned committee of Socialist Revolutionaries, which in the meantime had approached a number of people, telegraphed him a list of defenders. The list included ten names: Vandervelde, Wauters and Haden Guest of the Second International; Paul-Boncour, Theodor Liebknecht and Rosenfeld of the Vienna Union; Modigliani of the Italian Socialist Party (which at that time was not associated with any of the Internationals); and Sukhomlin, Kobiakov and Gurevich of the PSR.[61] The next day, Adler passed this provisional list on to Radek.[62]

Immediately after the list had become known, the communist press started a campaign against the persons named. Vandervelde, who during the war had been a member of the Belgian Government of National Defence and had been a co-signatory to the Versailles Treaty in 1919, was now charged with both these facts. Although he had long since left the government, he was referred to as 'Royal Belgian Minister'. The name of the Englishman, Haden Guest, was sometimes misunderstood and one of the leaders of the socialist

International Federation of Trade Unions, the Dutchman Jan Oudegeest, was attacked in his stead. The other people listed also had to suffer, including the German representatives of the Vienna Union, Liebknecht and Rosenfeld.

Theodor Liebknecht was the brother of Karl Liebknecht who had been murdered in 1919 and was venerated as a martyr by the communists. Theodor Liebknecht belonged to the USPD, whose position was to the left of the SPD, and moreover, to the left wing of the USPD.[63] His nomination as a defender of the opponents of the Bolsheviks was therefore an unpleasant surprise to the communists and, as a result, Liebknecht became the target of hostile articles. *Die Rote Fahne* stated on 3 May that he was a man 'who feels no shame at defiling the name of his great brother with his actions.' This caused Liebknecht to tell the Socialist Revolutionaries that in his view, if the Soviet government were to take the same position, there would be little sense in his going to Moscow: in such a case his presence would only help to cover up a legal sham.[64]

Kurt Rosenfeld also stood to the left in the USPD. He had expressed himself positively on various occasions regarding the prevailing system in Soviet Russia and had advocated closer relations with Moscow and the Comintern. He had frequently acted as defending counsel for communists, including Radek when he was arrested in Berlin in 1919.[65] Nevertheless, he now also became the butt of communist propaganda. It then appeared that the Socialist Revolutionaries had made no attempt to ensure themselves of Rosenfeld's cooperation, and this brought them a serious reprimand from Adler, who moreover considered that to have Rosenfeld taking part in the defence in addition to Liebknecht was rather too much of a good thing. Adler had all the more reason for this opinion because, as he told the Socialist Revolutionaries, Rosenfeld's nomination had roused Radek to great fury since Radek had hoped to 'realize the united front with Rosenfeld's help'. It was Adler's impression that Radek no longer intended to cooperate in fulfilling the concessions made in Berlin. As a result, the Socialist Revolutionaries decided on 6 May to send Chernov and Zenzinov to Rosenfeld, with instructions that if the latter should prove unwilling, they were not to be too insistent.[66]

Also on 6 May the Presidium of the Executive Committee of the Comintern agreed that the ten people nominated as defending counsels should be admitted to the trial, although Boris Souvarine of

France and Karl Kreibich of Czechoslovakia voted against admission of the three Socialist Revolutionaries.[67] Two days later, Clara Zetkin passed this decision on to Adler and at the same time told him that the trial would commence on 23 May.[68]

It is clear from the utterances of the communists that the three Socialist Revolutionaries were particularly unwelcome. On 9 May, Zinov'ev told the Executive Committee of the Comintern, of which he was chairman, that although the ten defenders would be admitted to the trial, they could not be treated as friends since they included 'avowed counter-revolutionary Russians.' They would have complete liberty to carry out their duties as defenders, but for the rest would have to be kept under observation. In view of the fact that the socialist Internationals, according to Zinov'ev, had seized upon the trial as motive for a campaign against the Comintern, he suggested that a number of foreign communists should also be invited. For this purpose, according to Zinov'ev, Frossard and Sadoul of France, Zetkin of Germany, Bordiga of Italy, and Šmeral and Muna of Czechoslovakia had already been invited.[69]

Since first the European socialists had sprung to the defence of their threatened fellow-socialists in Russia and then the communists — who saw this as an attack on themselves — had replied with counter-actions, it began to look as though the forthcoming trial would gain international significance and would be directed not only against the Russian socialists but against socialists in general.

An anonymous correspondent in Russia reported in *Golos Rossii* about a speech which Zinov'ev had held in secret on 13 May for members of the Communist Party in Petrograd. Zinov'ev was reported to have said that the Central Committee of the Communist Party originally had no wish to hold the trial. Now that they were committed to it by the Berlin conference, however, the communists would not shun the fight and would try to bring a crushing moral defeat to the PSR and its defenders in the Second and the Second-and-a-half Internationals.[70]

The French communist, Charles Rappoport, writes in his memoirs that the Bolshevik leaders wanted to turn the trial of the Socialist Revolutionaries into a trial of the counter-revolution 'which, in the name of the opportunist socialists, tried to stab the first revolution in the back.' At a meeting, probably of the Executive Committee of the Comintern, at which the attitude to be shown towards the foreign defenders of the Socialist Revolutionaries was discussed, only Souvarine (whom we have just seen as an extremist) and Rappoport expressed disapproval of the baiting of the defenders. Rappoport, who mentions this in his memoirs, calls this campaign 'hardly correct and in conflict with the good name and the interests of the Soviet government.'[71]

CHAPTER 3

PREPARATIONS FOR THE TRIAL

THE PRELIMINARY INVESTIGATION

In Russia in the meantime preparations for the trial continued, partly behind the scenes and in secret, partly in the open and with a good deal of publicity.

Until 1 April the preliminary investigation was carried out by the GPU, which had put Iakov Agranov in charge. Agranov was a Chekist who had already featured in a number of important political affairs and enjoyed some notoriety among political prisoners. From the many Socialist Revolutionaries who were arrested after the transfer of the members of the Central Committee to Lubianka Prison, Agranov selected a number whom he considered suitable to appear either as witnesses or as accused at the forthcoming trial and, with them, started the preliminary investigation. The others were either released, detained in provincial prisons, or banished to far distant parts of the country, without any form of trial.[1]

After 1 April the conduct of the preliminary investigation was taken over by Nikolai Krylenko, chairman of the Supreme Revolutionary Tribunal, which was then Russia's highest judicial institution. Krylenko's wife, Elena Rozmirovich, chairwoman of the Supreme Tribunal's Investigatory Committee, was formally in charge, but the actual work was done by Krylenko, who was also to act as public prosecutor at the trial.[2]

For as far as we are able to judge from the scanty data at our disposal, the preliminary investigation was not directed towards the principal accused, i.e. the members of the Central Committee and a number of faithful PSR members, who in any case refused to cooperate in any way. It was directed rather towards a group of people whom it was anticipated would be able to make damaging statements against the first group. In his pamphlet Semenov had named a number of people who had been involved in his activities. As many as possible of these were tracked down and pressure was brought to bear to persuade them to make confessions that would be incriminating for the leaders of the Socialist Revolutionaries. The GPU also sought out other people whom it considered qualified for this role.

A few succeeded in evading the GPU. For example, the author Viktor Shklovskii, who had been named by Semenov, got wind of his impending danger in time and escaped to Berlin. In 1919 Shklovskii had been given a personal amnesty and since then had kept out of politics. He had no wish, he wrote at the time, to make any statements against his former comrades.[3] Vladimir Rikhter, former member of the Central Committee of the PSR, even managed to go underground for the duration of the trial.[4]

Not all those who were arrested were prepared to help the GPU. Aleksandr Perkhurov, a former officer who, in July 1918 under orders from Boris Savinkov had organized an uprising in Jaroslavl', flatly refused to declare that the Socialist Revolutionaries had been involved in that uprising. It was not true, he said.[5]

Others, however, did eventually succumb to pressure, for example Filipp Fedorov-Kozlov, a worker whom Semenov had named as a member of his terrorist group. According to a cell mate, Fedorov-Kozlov at first (in March or April 1922) resisted the pressure that was put on him during talks in which Semenov, who had meanwhile returned to Russia, also took part. But in Moscow's Lubianka Prison Fedorov-Kozlov felt lonely and deserted. His wife and children lived in Petrograd and, unlike his cell mates, he never received any parcels. When one day he was offered a parcel that had been sent either by Semenov or by Konopleva, he accepted it after some hesitation. And at that moment his attitude started to change.[6]

Faina Stavskaia, also named by Semenov as a member of his group and arrested in connection with the trial,[7] was given different treatment. Earlier in 1922 she had submitted a request for admission to the Communist Party. It was now proposed to her that she should testify against the leaders of the PSR by way of entrance examination, and she agreed.[8]

Harsher methods were also used, however. The former Socialist Revolutionary Sergei Pashutinskii, for example, was first condemned to death on 2 May 1922, with the annotation that the sentence should be put into effect within 48 hours. Shortly after, a newspaper even carried an announcement that the execution had taken place. Subsequently, however, he proved to be still alive, and probably owed this fact to his ultimate willingness to testify against the Socialist Revolutionary leaders.[9] But Aleksandr Perkhurov who, as we have seen, was not prepared to testify in this way, was executed after the death sentence was passed on him in July 1922.[10]

Only in a few cases do we have any further knowledge about the way in which people were persuaded to make statements. General Verkhovskii, for instance, was talked into it by Agranov who deluded him into believing that his statements were not to be used for the prosecution but would serve solely to throw light on the historical role of the PSR.[11] The witness Snezhko-Blotskii was tackled in quite a different manner. He was pulled in by five armed soldiers, apparently from his home, for a nocturnal interrogation. Notwithstanding the fact that he was ill, he was subjected to brutal questioning for five hours and then forced to sign a statement which gave a twisted version of his words.[12]

Whereas the preliminary investigation was principally occupied with compiling damaging material against the leaders of the Socialist Revolutionaries, the press concurrently published statements that were intended to discredit the PSR as a whole, in line with the example set by the public statements made by Semenov and Konopleva. On 18 March *Izvestiia* printed a letter submitted by a certain Paevskii, and on 12 April *Pravda* published an open letter which had been written by a man called Keller. Both were former Socialist Revolutionaries and both had been named by Semenov. Keller was then serving in the Red Army. Paevskii 'revealed' that the PSR had accepted money from the French embassy. On 25 and 27 May, *Pravda* published two articles by the former Menshevik Ivan Maiskii, who was later to become a wellknown Soviet diplomat, about the activities of the *Komuch* with which he had closely involved. Paevskii and Maiskii both declared in these publications that they were prepared to give evidence at the trial. Keller expressed in his letter the hope that 'the forthcoming trial of the PSR will open the eyes of workers in the whole world to the miserable part which it has played during the revolution, and will thus ease the shift to the revolutionary camp of all those among its present or former members who, for one reason or another, still hesitate.'

As we have seen, the members of the Central Committee of the PSR refused to cooperate in the preliminary investigation. They were isolated from the outside world and from one another for the duration of that investigation, first in Lubianka Prison and later in

Lefortovo Prison. They were told that they would not be allowed to get in touch with one another or to become acquainted with the evidence against them until 23 May, the day on which the preliminary investigation would come to an end. In the meantime it had been made known that the trial was to start on 1 June, and the prisoners protested against this decision, saying that it left them insufficient time in which to prepare their defence. On 17 May, apparently after consulting each other by knocking on the walls of their cells, they started a hunger strike[13] about which nothing is known other than that it lasted four days.

The preliminary investigation was indeed brought officially to a close on 23 May. Four days later the Indictment was ratified by the Supreme Tribunal, but was not given to the accused until 31 May. Meanwhile, the opening of the trial had been postponed until 6 June.[14]

THE INDICTMENT

The 'Indictment in the affair of the Central Committee and of certain members of other organizations of the PSR' totalled 117 pages. The defendants were accused of armed struggle against the Soviet regime, of having organized murderous assaults and raids, and of having maintained treasonable contacts with foreign states.

The Indictment started with a survey of the history of the PSR since the October Revolution, which made up almost half the text. In that time, the PSR had taken the side of the bourgeoisie against the workers and the peasants. It had first undertaken a series of more or less clandestine attempts to overthrow the Soviet regime and later had conducted open civil war against that regime. In doing so, the PSR had cooperated with bourgeois and White Guard organizations and with the Allies from whom it had received financial and other support. In this way, the PSR had caused large parts of the country to fall into the hands of the White generals and of the Allied occupiers. Beaten on all sides, the PSR had at last acknowledged its faults at the 'conference of repentance' in February 1919. It soon appeared, however, that the decision to refrain from armed struggle against the Soviet regime was a temporary measure only. The PSR carried full responsibility for the 'counter-revolutionary' rebellious movement which had manifested itself in 1920. It had been involved in the preparation of revolts in Tambov, in Siberia, and in the Black Sea region, and had been in contact with the Kronstadt rebels.

In itself this was sufficient reason for criminal prosecution of the Central Committee of the PSR, according to the Indictment. But it had now been augmented by Semenov's revelations regarding the party's terrorist activities. With respect to the use of terror by party members, the Central Committee had taken the position of 'silent approval and official denial', a position which individual Committee members had subsequently and 'even more ingeniously "intensified" and "developed".' These members of the Central Committee had been 'the actual leaders' of terrorist activities, particularly of those perpetrated by Semenov and his group.

Finally, the Indictment enumerated the persons involved. First, it listed those who would not appear as accused at the trial. These were divided into two groups. The first group comprised those whose cases had been suspended (*vydeleno proizvodstvom*). These included a number of political notables who had emigrated abroad: Socialist Revolutionaries such as Chernov, Avksent'ev and Zenzinov, but also Mensheviks such as Martov, Dan and Abramovich; a Popular Socialist like Nikolai Chaikovskii, and even Kadets. This group also included people who had successfully evaded arrest, such as Shklovskii and Rikhter. The second group comprised those against whom charges had been dropped (*prekrashcheno proizvodstvom*). These included a number of people who had signed statements to the effect that, since the 1919 amnesty, they had taken no part in 'the counter-revolutionary activities' of the PSR (e.g. Snezhko-Blotskii, Sviatitskii, Keller, Paevskii and Verkhovskii) and a few others of whom, even though they had not signed such a statement, the Indictment considered participation in terrorist activity not proven (e.g. Rakitnikov, Burevoi and Vol'skii).

Then followed the names of the accused. The Indictment commented that the activities of the Central Committee were not covered by the 1919 amnesty because it had continued after the amnesty to prepare for an armed overthrow of the Soviet regime; neither did the amnesty cover terrorist activities carried out prior to February 1919.[15] The members of the Central Committee were accused that, from the October Revolution until the time of their arrest and even thereafter while in prison, as leaders of these activities they had done everything in their power to overturn the Soviet regime. A number of past and present members of the PSR were accused that, in accordance with the directives of the Central Committee, they had engaged in counter-revolutionary activities, including in some cases terrorist activities, from the time of the October Revolution until that of their arrest, with the intention of overthrowing the government.

The Indictment was signed by Rozmirovich, but she seems to have had nothing more to do with its editing than she had had to do with the actual conduct of the preliminary investigation. On 10 April Trotskii suggested to the Politbureau that the Indictment of the Socialist Revolutionaries should be made into 'a finished political product' setting out the entire activity of the PSR, and that its editing should be put into the hands of Lunacharskii, Krylenko and Kurskii.[16] It is not known whether this trio did in fact produce the document.

One thing that is certain is that the Indictment, in accordance with Trotskii's wishes, was more of a political pamphlet than a legal document. Four thousand copies were printed. Also in agreement with Trotskii's wish, its character was frequently more of an accusation against the PSR as a whole than of one against the individual accused.

The PSR, so ran the Indictment, had not only fought the Soviet regime in 1918 by force of arms, but it had continued the fight since then. It had been guilty of collaboration with the bourgeoisie at home and abroad (soglashatel'stvo) and of duplicity against the Soviet regime (dvurushnichestvo): it had pretended merely to practice political opposition, but had clandestinely organized murderous assaults and revolts.

The Indictment sought to forestal any appeal to the February 1919 amnesty by construing the latter in a way that was not mentioned when it was promulgated. According to the Indictment, the amnesty covered only those Socialist Revolutionaries who, after the amnesty, had no longer taken part in 'the counter-revolutionary activities' of the PSR and who had confirmed this in a written statement. In actual fact this meant that only those who had left the party after the amnesty could lay claim to indemnity because the Indictment considered all activities of the PSR to be counter-revolutionary.[17]

The Indictment listed 34 accused who could be divided into two groups, although this was not done in the document. The first group included the real accused, 22 in all: 12 members of the Central Committee and 10 active party members. The 12 Central Committee members were: Dmitrii Dmitrievich Donskoi, Florian Florianovich Fedorovich, Mikhail Iakovlevich Gendel'man, Lev Iakovlevich Gershtein, Abram Rafailovich Gots, Nikolai Nikolaevich Ivanov, Mikhail Aleksandrovich Likhach, Sergei Vladimirovich Morozov, Dmitrii Fedorovich Rakov, Evgeniia Moiseevna Ratner, Evgenii Mikhailovich Timofeev and Mikhail Aleksandrovich Vedeniapin. By the time the trial commenced, all of these had been imprisoned for one to three years. The other 10 members of the first group were: Vladimir Vladimirovich Agapov, Arkadii Ivanovich Al'tovskii, Nikolai Ivanovich Artem'ev, Efrem Solomonovich Berg, Grigorii Lavrent'evich Gor'kov, Elena Aleksandrovna Ivanova, Aleksandr Vasil'evich Liberov, Mikhail Ivanovich L'vov, Vladimir L'vovich Utgof and Pavel Vladimirovich Zlobin.

Various factors seem to have played a role in the composition of the first group. The primary intention was to strike at the most prominent members of the party, and this explained the presence in the dock of the twelve members of the Central Committee. But a number of important prisoners were not ranged under the accused, and some of them went so far as to protest against this fact.[18] On the other hand, the accused comprised a number of people who were far less prominent, such as Berg, Gor'kov, Liberov, L'vov and Zlobin, who were probably included in order to show the rank-and-file Socialist Revolutionaries that they would also come to grief if they did not break with their leaders. The inclusion of Ivanova was probably due to the intent to show that a linkage existed between the members of the Central Committee and Semenov's terrorist group: Semenov after all had declared that Ivanova had taken part in the murderous attacks that he had organized. Finally, the presence of a left-wing figure such as Vedeniapin could have been due to an effort to shatter the solidarity of the group.

The second group consisted of the following 12 defendants: Iosif Samoilovich Dashevskii, Fedor Timofeevich Efimov, Filipp Fedorovich Fedorov-Kozlov, Vladimir Ivanovich Ignat'ev, Lidiia Vasil'evna Konopleva, Iurii Vital'evich Morachevskii, Pavel Nikolaevich Pelevin, Grigorii Moiseevich Ratner, Grigorii Ivanovich Semenov, Faina Efremovna Stavskaia, Konstantin Andreevich Usov and Fedor Vasil'evich Zubkov. Eight of these had been members of Semenov's terrorist

group. Their task now was to confess their crimes and to incriminate
the accused of the first group. In addition, the members of the
second group, as former PSR adherents, were under orders to renounce the party and its leaders and to sing the praises of the Soviet
regime. The second group also included Ignat'ev, not a former PSR
member but of the small Party of Popular Socialists.[19] Like Semenov, he had earlier in 1922 published a pamphlet in which he made
'revelations' about the activities of the Socialist Revolutionaries.

According to the Indictment, the accused had been guilty of activities that were punishable under the Penal Code. Now it so happened
that this Penal Code did not exist when the accused perpetrated the
activities in question or even at the time of their indictment, although work on it had been in progress for some time.[20] The agenda
of the meeting of the VTsIK which started on 12 May 1922 included
a discussion of the draft of the Penal Code. A particular point at
issue was whether or not the combating of 'counter-revolutionary
crimes' (under which the activities of the Socialist Revolutionaries
were deemed to fall) was the task of the judiciary, and, consequently, whether or not the appropriate norms should be laid down in the
Code. It was decided that they should be so recorded but that they
should be given broad definition.[21]

On 17 May, shortly before he was incapacitated for a time through
illness, Lenin suggested 'a politically truthful and not only a juridical-
ly narrow' definition, in his words. This had to make it possible, in
effect, to punish any oppositional political activity with the death
penalty by linking the activity in question with 'the international
bourgeoisie and its fight against us.' In saying this, Lenin had the
activities of the Socialist Revolutionaries and of the Mensheviks in
mind. The courts, according to Lenin, should not eliminate terror,
but should 'give it a legitimate basis, principled, clear, without
hypocrisy or adornment.' The formulation must be 'as broad as
possible', for only 'the revolutionary sense of justice' and 'the revolutionary conscience' would provide the conditions for a 'wider or
narrower application in each case.'[22] Lenin's proposal was used in
the framing of the definitive text of the paragraph 'On counter-
revolutionary crimes' in the Code.[23]

The Penal Code came into force on 1 June 1922, a week before
the start of the trial of the Socialist Revolutionaries. That the latter
were tried on the basis of laws which were non-existent at the time

of the crimes with which they were charged was palpably in conflict with the traditional principle of *nullum crimen sine lege*.

In addition to the Penal Code, the VTsIK concurred with the draft of the Code of Criminal Procedure. This was not to come into force until 1 August 1922, however,[24] so that the 'Regulations for Revolutionary Tribunals' (*Osnovnoe Polozhenie o revoliutsionnykh tribunalakh*) remained valid for the trial of the Socialist Revolutionaries.

THE DEFENCE

In the meantime, negotiations among the three Internationals regarding a united front had come to a dead end. The Comintern's attitude grew steadily more aggressive, strengthening the reservations that already existed in the Second International with regard to the united front aspirations. Even the Vienna Union began to show some scepticism with respect to the chances of cooperation with the Comintern.

At a meeting of the 'Nine' in Berlin on 23 May, MacDonald observed that although the Comintern had so far honoured some of its promises with regard to the trial, it otherwise evinced anything but conciliation towards the socialists. On behalf of the Second International, he repeated the three conditions that had earlier been set for the holding of a general congress. In particular, he wished to await the outcome of the trial.[25]

Radek rejected MacDonald's reproaches and gave as his opinion that the Comintern had more than acquitted itself of its obligations. The Comintern would break off negotiations if the decision to hold a general congress was not quickly taken. Even in that case, however, he guaranteed that the Socialist Revolutionaries would retain their right to a defence and that the trial would be held in open court.[26]

Adler's attempts to bring the parties closer to one another were unsuccessful, and Radek ultimately announced that the Comintern was withdrawing its delegation. Under these circumstances, the foreign defenders of the Socialist Revolutionaries could hardly count on a friendly reception in Moscow.

Early in May the Comintern had made it known that the ten defenders named on the list submitted by Adler would be admitted to the trial. Some of them dropped out, however. The three Socialist Revolutionaries withdrew at the request of the Central Bureau of the

PSR in Moscow[27] in order to avoid creating the impression that the defence had political intentions.[28] Moreover, some of the foreigners eventually proved unwilling or unable to take part in the defence. In the end, the only ones left were Vandervelde and his fellow countryman and party associate Arthur Wauters of the Second International, and Rosenfeld (who had finally declared himself willing to go to Moscow as defender) and Theodor Liebknecht of the Vienna Union.[29]

On 15 May Vandervelde and Wauters joined Rosenfeld and Liebknecht in Berlin. Radek visited Vandervelde in his hotel.[30] The four defenders submitted a protest to the Soviet Russian representative in Berlin, Nikolai Krestinskii, about the hostility shown towards them in the communist press.[31] They then left by train for Russia.

In the night of 24 May they crossed the frontier at Sebezh. On Sebezh station and at the following stations along the line, the western socialists were treated to a series of demonstrations. Aggressive crowds abused them for scoundrels and murderers; at one station a revolver shot was fired and the window of Liebknecht's compartment was broken. Angry travellers forced their way into the carriage which the Soviet authorities had put at the disposal of the defenders, venting their anger at the fact that the foreigners had an entire carriage to themselves. The biggest demonstration was held in Moscow on their arrival late in the afternoon of 25 May. A crowd of some thousands of people had gathered in front of the station. They carried banners with such inscriptions as : 'Down with the traitors to the working class!', 'Cain, Cain, where is your brother Karl!',[32] and 'Shame on the defender of the murderers of his brother, Karl Liebknecht';[33] and chanted doggerels such as 'It is a pity, friends, that we cannot hang him [Vandervelde] here.'[34] The crowd broke through the police cordon when the defenders left the station, and they were able only with difficulty to reach the waiting car. Rosenfeld, whose face was spat at by one of the demonstrators, was able to ascertain that the demonstration was organized by none other than Bukharin, who even whistled through his fingers at him.[35]

The foreign defenders were lodged on the Vorontsovo estate, twelve kilometers from the centre of Moscow, but were also given an office in the centre of town. Their freedom of movement was severely restricted and their escorts never left their side.[36] On 27 May they visited the People's Commissariat of Justice in order to regulate the formalities of the defence. They submitted a statement to the effect that they had come to Moscow solely to defend the accused Socialist Revolutionaries and not for a political demonstration. They therefore protested against the press campaign directed against them and the accused, and asked the Soviet government to put an end to it.[37] Kurskii rejected their protest: in Soviet Russia there was no freedom of the press in the bourgeois meaning; the press served the true interests of the working class and it was therefore unnecessary for the government to restrict it in any way. In his view, the statement made by the foreign defenders was nothing but a 'continuation and expansion' of their 'political campaign against the Russian revolution surrounded as it is by world imperialism.'[38]

The foreigners were allowed to visit Lefortovo Prison almost daily, however, in order that they might discuss the defence with the 22 accused of the first group, who had accepted them as their defenders. Abram Gots acted as principal spokesman for the group. They greeted the western socialists as political associates, but made it clear that they did not see their task as being a strictly legal one, as did their defenders, and that the preclusion of a death sentence was not their primary concern. The Socialist Revolutionaries did not accept that the Bolsheviks had any right to try them, and they therefore intended during the trial to attack rather than to defend, i.e. themselves to become accusers. They saw the trial as a means in their political struggle against the Bolsheviks, 'a platform on which, in the eyes of workers in the whole world, to unmask the anti-socialist and counter-revolutionary character of Bolshevism.'[39]

Like the Bolsheviks, therefore, the Socialist Revolutionaries regarded their trial as a political affair. Just as the Bolsheviks wanted to use it to make propaganda against them, so they wanted to use it to make propaganda against the Bolsheviks. The Socialist Revolutionaries had therefore decided to adopt the same attitude towards their communist judges as the revolutionaries of old Russia had shown towards their Tsarist judges, and from their position in the dock to broadcast to the world an accusation against the ruling order. The weak point of their stand, however, was that the communist regime had a far greater grasp over the press and over opinion forming in Russia than the Tsarist regime had ever had, so that their accusation had very little chance of getting through to the public.

The western defenders were also given the opportunity to meet their Russian colleagues, because, apart from the representatives of the Socialist Internationals, the 22 arraigned Socialist Revolution-

aries were defended by a number of Russian lawyers, i.e. S.A. Gurevich (not to be confused with the Socialist Revolutionary V.Ia. Gurevich mentioned in Chapter 2 above), Kariakin, N.V. Kommodov
(who later withdrew), Lipskerov, N.K. Murav'ev, M.A. Otsep, G.B.
Patushinskii, B. Ratner, A.S. Tager and V.A. Zhdanov.[40] On 8 June,
Pravda called them 'corrupt professional lawyers' and 'died-in-the-
wool perverters of justice'. In fact they represented a choice selection
of members of the traditional Russian bar. Some of them, particularly Murav'ev, Tager and Zhdanov, had already won fame as radical
lawyers before 1917, and had pleaded in political trials both before
and after the revolution.

The accused and their defenders encountered great problems in
the proper preparation of their defence. The accused were kept in
isolation until 23 May; prior to that date they were cut off from the
outside world, including their defending counsel. In view of the fact
that the Indictment was not handed to the accused or, in all probability, to their defenders, until 31 May,[41] it was hardly surprising
that *Izvestiia* was able to announce, one day previously, that no
requests had been received for permission to call witnesses for the
defence. By then, the witnesses for the prosecution had long been
subpoenad.

Later, during the sitting, the accused Likhach declared that the accused had been given only 24 hours in which to study the evidence,
which consisted of many volumes. The historian Mikhail Pokrovskii,
who appeared as prosecutor during the trial, later denied this, saying
that the accused had in fact had ten days in which to study the evidence.[42] Even if this were true, however, the time was extraordinar-
ily short in view of the scope of the accusation.

The attempt was also made to have some Mensheviks take part in the
defence. We have seen earlier that the Mensheviks in Russia found it
difficult to determine their standpoint with regard to the trial. They
thought it their duty to help the accused, but were in doubt as to
whether, at the same time, they should not dissociate themselves
from the politics of the Socialist Revolutionaries. Finally, on 28
April, their Central Committee suggested to the party's Foreign
Delegation that one of its members should be added to those defenders appointed by the Vienna Union. Although Martov then seems to
have conceived the plan of going to Moscow himself as one of the
defenders, nothing eventually came of this intention.

The Menshevik Central Committee thought it advisable not to send its own representatives to the trial, saying that this would cause trouble to both the accused and the Mensheviks. The 'Right' opposition in the party protested, arguing that the trial was just as much an affair for the Mensheviks. In May, two of its members, Mark Liber and Anatolii Diubua, asked permission to accept a request from the Socialist Revolutionaries that they act as defenders. The Central Committee found them unsuitable, however, because as members of the opposition (Liber at that time did not even belong to the party) they would not be able to present the party's position correctly. When, in a letter dated 31 May, the accused Socialist Revolutionaries also asked that the Mensheviks should participate in their defence, the Central Committee finally delegated Boris Ber, Isaak Rubin and Semen Vainshtein as defenders, on condition that they would be allowed, during the trial, to make the Menshevik Party line known and thus to dissociate themselves, if necessary, from the position of the Socialist Revolutionaries.[43]

In principle, the admittance of the defenders was the responsibility of the Supreme Tribunal, which devoted a number of sessions to regulating the procedure to be followed. Under Article 17 of the 'Regulations for Revolutionary Tribunals', defenders at a trial might include members of 'the college of defenders and prosecutors by the Soviets', 'associates or relatives' of the accused, or 'persons who enjoy the complete confidence of the tribunal.'[44] Although, during the sitting on 27 May, the Tribunal gave as its opinion that the representatives of the socialist Internationals and some of the Russian lawyers did not meet any of these norms, it admitted them to the trial 'by way of exception to Article 17'.[45] In this way, the Tribunal made it clear that the defenders in question did *not* enjoy its confidence.

The request that the three Menshevik defenders should be admitted, on the other hand, was rejected on 2 June. From the fact that their request was supported by 'an anonymous paper, signed by the Central Committee of the RSDRP', the Tribunal had decided that their action had 'counter-revolutionary objectives'. It passed the Menshevik statement on to the GPU for investigation.[46] Liber, who had also submitted his name, was accepted in the first instance. On 6 June, however, the Tribunal reversed this decision at the request of the GPU. According to the GPU, Liber had given the undertaking in 1919 never again to engage in political activity.[47] In reality, according to *Golos Rossii*, the *Cheka* had asked Liber to sign a statement to that effect when he was released from prison in 1919, but Liber had refused to do so.[48] The Tribunal thus considered participation in the defence of the Socialist Revolutionaries to be counter-revolutionary political activity, and the four Mensheviks were quickly put under arrest.[49]

Just as there were two groups of accused, so there were two groups of defenders. The Russian defenders of the second group included: A.A. Bitsenko, N.I. Bukharin, S.B. Chlenov, R.P. Katanian, N.N. Ovsiannikov, I.N. Stukov, M.P. Tomskii, V. Veger, A.A. Znamenskii and S.S. Zorin. In contrast to the defenders of the first group, all of these were political figures, Bukharin and Tomskii even being among the top leadership of the Bolshevik Party. In *Izvestiia*, on 3 June, these defenders dissociated themselves from the accused of the first group and their defenders, dubbing the latter 'enemies of the revolution and of the proletariat'. They considered it their 'revolutionary duty', however, to devote themselves during the trial to 'the moral rehabilitation' and to 'the political defence' of those accused who had seen the error of their former ways. In the end, Znamenskii and Zorin did not feature at the trial, their place being taken by P. Shubin.

The Comintern also deputed a number of western communists to appear at the trial; a few of these, as we have seen, had already been invited at the beginning of May. On 6 June, the Presidium of the Executive Committee of the Comintern appointed Jacques Sadoul of France and Feliks Kon of Poland as defenders (of the second group). A day later, the Executive Committee added Antonio Gramsci of Italy to the defenders,[50] but Gramsci in actual fact did not carry out the task assigned to him.

The Supreme Tribunal also approved the appointment of N.V. Krylenko, A.V. Lunacharskii and M.N. Pokrovskii as members of the Public Prosecution at the trial. All three were distinctly political figures, Lunacharskii and Pokrovskii even being members of the Soviet government, as People's Commissar and Deputy People's Commissar of Education respectively. Of the three, Krylenko was to feature as the true legal prosecutor.

In this case, too, the Comintern delegated a number of foreign communists. In addition to those mentioned above, the Presidium of the Executive Committee appointed on 6 June Clara Zetkin of Germany, Alois Muna of Czechoslovakia and Dezsö Bokányi of Hungary as prosecutors. Furthermore, the Presidium appointed the Secretary-General of the French Communist Party Louis-Olivier Frossard, the Czechoslovakian communist leader Bohumír Šmeral, Thomas Bell of England and Iordan Iordanov of Bulgaria as witnesses and 'political experts', whose task was to be to incriminate western governments as well as the western socialists. Like Gramsci, however, Bell and Iordanov did not in fact fulfil the function assigned to them. Boris Souvarine of France was given the task of organizing the activities of the western communists who appeared at the trial.[51]

The court before which the trial was to be held was finally made up of G.L. Piatakov as president; A.V. Galkin and O.Ia. Karklin, members; and N.M. Nemtsov and Ozol as reserve members. All these were members of the Communist Party, Piatakov even belonging to the Central Committee.

The trial started on 8 June. On its eve, the GPU rounded-up some of the remaining active Socialist Revolutionaries who were still at liberty in Moscow and Petrograd,[52] and also arrested a number of witnesses.[53]

According to one of the accused, their treatment was improved just before the commencement of the trial in order that the worst of the traces left by their lengthy imprisonment and their recent hunger strike might be effaced.[54]

At the start of the trial it was uncertain how long it would last. Kurskii told the western defenders that he expected it to last one or two weeks; the Russian lawyer Murav'ev thought it would be three weeks.[55] In the event it was to last for more than eight.

CHAPTER 4

THE TREATMENT OF THE ACCUSED,
DEFENDERS AND WITNESSES DURING THE TRIAL

CONFLICT WITH THE WESTERN DEFENDERS

The trial, which started on 8 June, was held in the Empire-style Pillar Hall of the House of the Trade Unions in the centre of Moscow. This was the former ballroom of the Nobles Club, in which the bust of the Tsar had been replaced by one of Lenin.[1] At the front of the hall hung a large poster representing a worker who crushed a snake with a hammer, accompanied by the words: 'The proletarian court is the shield of the revolution.'[2] The court sat on a dais under the portrait, with the accused and their defenders on the right, and the prosecutors on the left. The hall, which could seat about 1500 people, was guarded both inside and out, and the accused were surrounded by soldiers, presumably to give the impression that dangerous criminals were on trial. For the rest, everything in the hall was very informal.[3] People smoked, and wore their everyday working clothes, with the exception of Vandervelde who appeared in a morning coat.

It was a selected public, admission being restricted to those who could show cards which had been distributed through official channels. The public was entirely on the side of the communists and had plenty of opportunity to show this in noisy demonstrations: applauding the communists who took part in the trial, and jeering the accused Socialist Revolutionaries and their defenders.[4]

The court sat six days a week, including Saturdays, from twelve noon to five in the afternoons, and in the evenings from seven until about midnight. The evening sittings were justified with the argument that the workers had to have the opportunity to attend the trial after their work. This was a very heavy programme for the 22 accused of the first group who, when not in the courtroom, had to spend their time in the prison on Kisel'nyi pereulok.[5] The twelve members of the second group, on the other hand, had their liberty and during the trial showed very amicable relations with the communists.[6]

The first days of the trial were dominated by a conflict between the court and the western defenders with regard to the procedure to be followed, basically due to differing interpretations of the agreement signed in Berlin by the three Internationals.

In the first place, the accused and their defenders were of the opinion that the court did not meet the impartiality requirement since it was made up entirely of members of the Communist Party. With the support of the prosecutors, the members of the second group and their defenders, and with the noisy approval of the public, the court rejected the charge, declaring that justice in the Soviet Republic did not stand above classes. It, the court, as subordinate organ of the Soviet regime, was partial as regards the protection of the safety of the Soviet regime, but was impartial in its investigation of the facts in the indictment.[7]

The defence then protested against the fact that only very few admission tickets had been granted to the accused, considering this to be seriously detrimental to the openness of the trial. This protest was also rejected by the court.

The third point brought forward by the accused and their defenders concerned the scope of the defence. As we have seen in the previous chapter, the court had refused to accept four Mensheviks who had notified their willingness to take part in the defence. It had also refused to allow a whole series of witnesses to be summonsed for the defence. The court answered that it had not admitted the four Mensheviks as defenders because they did not enjoy the court's confidence, and that this decision had been in complete accord with Article 17 of the 'Regulations for Revolutionary Tribunals'. With regard to the witnesses for the defence, the court made a very minor concession which, as we shall see, made almost no difference. It also refused to give the defence the right to consult documents in the State Archives, as the prosecution was allowed to do.

The western defenders based their protests not only on Soviet law and on generally accepted legal norms, but also on the Berlin Agreement. As a result, Radek took the witness stand to report that the socialists themselves had violated the Berlin Agreement by refusing to cooperate in the convening of an international congress. Apart from that, he said, the Comintern delegation could only enter into commitments on behalf of the Comintern and not on behalf of the Soviet government and the Soviet judicature. The delegation had promised to intercede to get Vandervelde admitted as one of the

defenders, but only Vandervelde.[8] Vandervelde, however, with the
Berlin Agreement in his hand, proved that this was not true: the
Comintern delegation had promised to admit all the defenders requested by the accused. And with regard to the question of whether
or not the Berlin Agreement was binding on the court, he argued that
representatives of a state that did not acknowledge any separation of
powers could hardly maintain that it was not binding on the court.[9]

The differences of opinion regarding the Berlin Agreement came
to a head around what was in fact a fairly insignificant matter of
reporting. The court could not, or would not, supply the defendants
betimes with the official stenogram of the previous sittings. The accused were unable to get the hang of the trial without a stenogram,
however, and they therefore asked permission to make their own.
This was refused by the court on the pretext that there was insufficient space for extra stenographers. Vandervelde then repeated the
request on behalf of the Second International, basing himself on the
Berlin Agreement which, after all, had given the representatives of
the Internationals the right to make their own stenograms.[10] This
request was also rejected by the court, however, with the argument
that it was not bound by the Berlin Agreement. In the discussion on
this point, Bukharin even went so far as to contend that the Berlin
Agreement was no longer valid.[11]

Towards the end of the first week of the trial, the western defenders
began to doubt whether their presence at the trial was meaningful.
Every request made by the defence had been rejected. The court
regularly deprived or denied the accused and their defenders the right
to speak. The western defenders themselves were continually ridi-
culed and intimidated. They were jeered by the public. They were
overwhelmed by a stream of hostile resolutions submitted by factories and institutions, some of which were even handed to them in
the courtroom. People like Jacques Sadoul regularly addressed Vandervelde as 'Royal Minister'. Bukharin constantly referred to Vandervelde's Second International as the 'yellow International', ranking it
together with Pinkerton's Agency, so notorious in the circles of the
left, which in the USA had been held responsible for strike break-
ing.[12] When Vandervelde, who was hard of hearing, did not hear an
interruption by the president of the Tribunal, Piatakov, due to the
noise in the hall and thus continued with his speech, the court
threatened even to bar the western defenders from the trial if such

behaviour should be repeated.[13] One of the communist defenders told them that it would be better if they went.[14]

In the morning of 14 June the socialist defenders met together with the accused, who considered that the defenders should no longer sanction this 'parody of justice' with their presence. After the afternoon session, at which the western defenders did not appear, they met again to draw up a statement. Then followed an emotional leave-taking, at which the Socialist Revolutionaries bade farewell to their defenders with the singing of 'the Internationale'.[15]

In the statement, the western defenders listed the points on which they considered the Berlin Agreement to have been violated: the court had not admitted four defenders; it had not given the defence permission to make its own stenogram; it had threatened to exclude the western defenders from the trial; and some communist participants in the trial had declared that the Berlin Agreement was not binding on the court and, moreover, that it had been invalidated. The defenders stated, however, that they would continue at the disposal of the accused and would act in accordance with their wishes.[16] That same evening the accused submitted the statement to the Tribunal, saying that the arguments expounded therein had their support. They had thought that the presence of their western defenders would guarantee that their rights would be respected. Now that this had proved not to be the case, they endorsed the decision of their defenders to lay down their task.

The Tribunal next day gave ample consideration to the statement, disposing of the action of the western defenders as a political demonstration:

The western defence has from the beginning taken an incorrect attitude towards the Tribunal and has tried to cast doubt on its objectivity and impartiality by comparing it with anti-proletarian bourgeois courts in capitalist states. On the basis of the facts, however, it has had to conclude that the trial is being carried out with all guarantees for a genuine defence of the accused and for a genuine clarification of each person's individual guilt, and that the scope for a political demonstration is steadily decreasing. This defence, therefore, merely sought a pretext for leaving the trial now that participation in it has clearly become politically disadvantageous.

The court made one concession: the defence might make its own stenogram. The admittance of stenographs was an affair for the superintendent of the courtroom and not for the court, according to the Tribunal, and the president had given the superintendent orders to meet any request that the defence might make for stenographers.

But this concession was quite insufficient for the western defenders. To them, the stenogram question was merely the last straw. They wanted to know whether the Berlin Agreement was valid, yes or no. The answer to this question was particularly significant because the lives of the accused could depend on it. On that point, however, the Tribunal refused to budge. It repeated that it had nothing to do with the Berlin Agreement and that any questions in that connection should be submitted to the Soviet government.[17]

When the spokesman of the accused, Mikhail Gendel'man, wanted to discuss the court's statement after it had been read out, he was silenced by president Piatakov with the words: 'Accused, you have repeatedly used your "right to defence" to make accusations against the Tribunal, to bring discredit to the highest court of the Workers' and Peasants' Republic.'[18]

The western defenders left Russia on 19 June. Surprisingly enough, the communists made every possible effort to prevent their departure, and they were only able to obtain their visas to leave Russia after a 24-hour hunger strike. The representatives of the Comintern, in particular, tried to persuade them to resume the defence. The defenders declared that they would be prepared to do so if the communists would state unequivocally that there would be no question of the death penalty. The German communist Heinrich Brandler, however, demanded that they should first persuade their clients to make a statement to the court to the effect that they would cease their struggle against the Soviet regime. This proposal was rejected by the defenders. 'People's lives are dealt with there as though they were merchandise', Rosenfeld said later.[19]

The socialists ultimately departed, to continue their task abroad. 'We are still the defenders of the Socialist Revolutionaries', wrote Vandervelde.[20] Why the communists tried to persuade them not to leave is not entirely clear. Perhaps it was because these western socialists helped to surround the trial with an illusion of objectivity, and simultaneously formed an easy target for communist polemics against international socialism in general.

THE DEMONSTRATION ON 20 JUNE AND THE RUSSIAN DEFENDERS

The trial of the Socialist Revolutionaries was not an isolated affair, but formed part of a considerable propaganda operation. The propaganda campaign around the trial will be discussed in a separate chapter. One event in that campaign, however, was so narrowly interwoven with the progress of the trial that it needs to be discussed here.

One of the charges brought against the Socialist Revolutionaries was that, on 20 June 1918, they had murdered the Bolshevik People's Commissar for Press Affairs, Moisei Volodarskii. The fourth anniversary of that murder occurred during the trial, and the Bolshevik leaders decided to take the opportunity for a major demonstration against the Socialist Revolutionaries. Starting on 15 June, the Communist Party appealed to the population through the press to take part in this demonstration.[21] Leading Bolsheviks went to the factories to incite the workers to cooperate.

On 20 June, therefore, the newspapers were crammed with articles in memory of Volodarskii and attacking 'his murderers', the Socialist Revolutionaries and their colleagues. Starting at noon, after a shortened working day, groups of demonstrators gathered in Moscow at points which had been indicated by the organizers, to march from there to the Red Square which had been decorated with flags and banners. At 4 o'clock the presidium of the mass meeting climbed onto the platform that had been erected in the square: the chairman of the meeting Kamenev, the president of the Tribunal Piatakov, the prosecutors Krylenko and Zetkin, the defenders of the second group, Bukharin, Kon and Sadoul, and other Russian and western communists, including Radek, Šmeral, Souvarine and the American Bill Haywood. At the same time, the demonstrators began to flow in from the surrounding streets to fill the square which, until then, had been cordoned off by soldiers.[22]

A division of soldiers first marched into the square to the music of the Dead March. Behind them, in compact rows and accompanied by martial bands, came the demonstrators — 300,000, according to our principal source of information, i.e. reports in the Soviet press. They carried banners on which the Socialist Revolutionaries were denounced as 'agents of the foreign capitalists' and as culprits for the civil war and all its victims, demanding that they be shot: 'Death to the traitors of the revolution!', 'Death to the Social Democrats!', 'For the blood of our leaders, for the blood of our husbands, sons and brothers, we demand a severe punishment!'; and 'Mercy for those who are penitent!', referring to the accused of the second group. They carried a cardboard likeness of Vandervelde, whose arms

and legs, operated by strings, moved wildly up and down in time
with the music, to the great hilarity of the demonstrators. 'Vandervelde, dancer for the king', was its text. They also carried a sort of
icon on which the Socialist Revolutionary leader Viktor Chernov
was depicted as 'Village Mother of God among the hosts of the White
generals', an image which was frequently to be seen during the action
against the Socialist Revolutionaries.[23]

The leaders on the platform were loudly cheered by the demonstrators, particularly Krylenko and Piatakov, the latter of whom had
brought the afternoon sitting of the trial to an early close in view of
the demonstration. Taking the stand as first speaker, Piatakov assured the demonstrators that the court would watch over 'the interests and the peace of the working class' and would mete out 'right-
eous and severe' punishment on the accused for that which would be
brought to light by the investigation. Krylenko asked the demonstrators to support and approve the sentence which he would demand at
the trial, i.e. the death penalty for the accused. 'A worker' who was
added to the list of speakers, was of the opinion that the court did
not need to devote much time to the Socialist Revolutionaries:
'Death to the traitors, death to the murderers!', he finished. 'Long
live the proletarian court, death to the Socialist Revolutionaries!' replied the crowd. Radek stigmatized the 'flight' of the western defenders. Bukharin was loudly applauded by the demonstrators for his
defence of Semenov and consorts.[24] 'Let our enemies bow the head
to us, and if anyone refuses, let him lose it', said Kamenev according
to *Golos Rossii.*[25] He asked the demonstrators if they had faith in
the court. 'We do, we do!', they cried, and loudly cheered the people
on the platform.[26]

The demonstration was something betwixt a meeting and a procession. Between and after the speeches the demonstrators filed past
the dais, sometimes giving petitions to Piatakov in which they
demanded that the Socialist Revolutionaries should be given short
shrift. Military bands played fighting songs (such as the 'Internationale') alternated with funeral marches. People sung the Marseillaise,
the 'Za vlast' Sovetov' ('For the power of the Soviets') and special
compositions ('To the barricades / No mercy for the Socialist Revolutionaries'). Orators at various points in the Red Square fervently
demanded death for 'the murderers of the heroes of the Revolution'.
'Workers poets', who had held a competition for the best anti-
Socialist Revolutionary poems, held up boards showing their pro-

ducts.[27] In addition to male and female workers, many children took part in the procession. Notwithstanding the bloodthirsty tenor of the slogans, it seems that the demonstrators were in cheerful mood.[28]

The demonstration lasted several hours and ranged as far as the House of the Trade Unions (where the court was seated), which is not far from the Red Square. At about seven o'clock the accused were forced to appear on the balcony so that they might be jeered by the demonstrators.[29] Orators accused the Socialist Revolutionaries that they had murdered 'workers leaders'; that they had been the 'executioners' of 'thousands of workers and peasants' who had been 'tortured to death' by them; that they were 'railway saboteurs' and 'instigators of a new civil war'. The demonstrators expressed their approval loudly. The procession even included a couple of lorries laden with invalids who carried a banner with the text 'Death to the Socialist Revolutionaries who mutilated us!'. While the accused looked on, two women workers waved a broom and spade, loudly cheered by the crowd. 'Everyone understands', according to the report in *Bednota*. 'The face of the Soviet Republic must be swept clean, must be purified of the Socialist Revolutionary traitors.'[30] The crowd took no notice when it suddenly started to rain, and the whole affair lasted until almost eight o'clock.

If, during the daytime, the president of the Tribunal and the Public Prosecutor had taken part in a street demonstration against the accused, in the evening demonstrators were admitted into the courtroom. The sitting was rather late in starting and the public was more restless than usual. At about 10 o'clock Piatakov announced that two delegations of 'representatives of the proletariat of Moscow and Petrograd' had asked permission to make statements before the court. He asked the parties what they thought of this request.

Krylenko was of the opinion that the request should be met, although it was not provided for in law nor legal practice. His reasoning conformed with the instructions that Lenin had given during the preparations for the trial. According to Krylenko, the proletarian administration of justice should not be guided solely by 'formal requirements'; it should also be guided by 'the essence and the spirit' of the proletarian state.

Bukharin agreed, saying that the court should hear 'the voice of the workers'. The defender of the first group, Murav'ev, on the other hand, adhered to what *Pravda* called 'a strictly formal position'. He thought that the request should be rejected since the people concerned had nothing whatsoever to do with the case being tried. The court decided that the request should be met, however, because 'the opinion of the working masses' was of 'fundamental importance' to it. The Tribunal added that its judgement would be taken 'completely independently of the influence of individual groups'.[31]

On this, a couple of dozens of 'workers delegates', with 'heated, severe and concentrated faces' (according to an eye witness) stormed into the courtroom.[32] They took turns in denouncing the Socialist Revolutionaries as 'enemies of the working class', 'deadly enemies of the great revolution', 'paid agents of the Entente', etc. The accused had not only murdered 'workers leaders' but also — according to 'a representative of the working women of Moscow' — 'our husbands and children'. The delegates demanded that the court should give the accused 'the highest punishment', i.e. the death sentence. They lent force to their words by submitting petitions with countless signatures. The enthusiastic public cheered each speaker and screamed slogans such as 'death to the murderers'.[33]

The 'representatives of the workers' abused the defendants in this way for two and a half hours, after which they were thanked by the president of the Tribunal, Piatakov. Piatakov said that the demonstration in the Red Square and the performance of the workers delegates in the courtroom had proved that 'the proletarian court is in close contact with the workers'. But, he added, they were not concerned with a meeting but with a trial, in which they had to conduct a scrupulous investigation as to who was guilty and who was innocent. At last, at two o'clock in the night, he brought the sitting to a close, thus bringing an end to the defendants' 'Golgotha', as the Menshevik Dvinov has called this exhibition.[34]

The next day the Russian defenders of the first group came into action. Since the departure of the western defenders, they had had to carry the entire burden of the defence, and they now protested against the events of the previous day. Those events, in the opinion of Murav'ev, had made a mockery of the Soviet law of criminal procedure. He called what had happened a catastrophe. He asked for the stenogram of the session of 20 June and asked that the sitting be adjourned for some considerable time in order that the defence might deliberate on its further course of action. Krylenko opposed this request, Murav'ev's colleagues and the defendants of the first group supported it. In the end Piatakov announced a break of some hours, and gave orders that the stenogram should be given to the defenders as soon as possible.[35]

During the evening session on 22 June, Murav'ev made a statement on behalf of the defenders of the first group regarding the events of 20 June. In his opinion, these events had 'completely infringed the existing legal framework on which we depend.' Workers delegates had been allowed to make statements in court. Their statements had had the character of depositions; with their demand that the highest punishment should be meted out, they had exercised pressure on the judges; and they had said insulting things about the accused and their defenders. Moreover, the president of the Tribunal and the Public Prosecutor had taken part in a political demonstration on the streets, and had made speeches to the demonstrators. All this was an infringement of the law of criminal procedure. Murav'ev cited Article 8 of the 'Instructions for the Courts of Appeal of the Supreme Tribunal regarding reasons for annulment of sentences' (*Nakaz Kassatsionnym Kollegiiam Verkhovnogo Tribunala o povodakh k otmene prigovorov*). Article 8 stipulated that when people were allowed to take part in a lawsuit who were not named in the rules that applied to the Tribunal, i.e. other than the members of the court, the accused, the prosecutors and defenders, the witnesses, the experts, this was 'unconditional' reason for annulment of the sentence.[36] The admittance of the workers delegates, according to Murav'ev, had in advance deprived the sentence of its legality. Continuation of the trial was therefore meaningless, in his opinion. A trial was a struggle between two parties for the opinion of the judges, 'strictly within the framework of the existing laws.' Those laws had now been violated and, in the opinion of the defenders, justice could now only take its correct course if this trial was brought to an end and a new one opened, with a new court and a new prosecutor.[37]

Krylenko answered that Murav'ev's objections regarding what had happened outside the courtroom were irrelevant. As regards events in the courtroom, 'from a formal point of view' the law indeed did not provide for such cases, but on the basis of 'the spirit and the essence' of the Soviet state and of the Soviet jurisdiction, the appearance in court of representatives of the working masses was 'completely legitimate'. The statements made by the workers delegates would not influence the sentence. The Tribunal would investigate all facts in order to ascertain the guilt of each accused individually. On that basis it would determine the severity of the punishment, in accordance with the law and with its conscience. The sentence was thus not predetermined and no outside influence was brought to bear upon it. As regards the article of law referred to by Murav'ev, Krylenko said that according to the law a sentence could only be annulled if it could be proven that intervention in the case by outsiders had influenced the conscience of the judges. The defence had not been able to prove that the actions of the workers delegates had influenced the judges, and their request that the trial be closed was therefore to be rejected.[38]

On behalf of the defenders of the second group, Feliks Kon also contested any dissolution of the Tribunal. In his opinion, the defenders of the first group were measuring by double standards. It was not the workers delegates who had first tried to bring influence to bear on the sentence, but Vandervelde and his colleagues who, by referring to the Berlin Agreement, had introduced politics into the trial. But the defenders of the first group had not protested against that. 'Vandervelde has left but his spirit is still here in the courtroom! The remaining defenders are saturated with it.' According to Kon, it was illogical first to say, as the accused had done, that they only recognized the pronouncement of the proletariat, and then to protest when the workers in the courtroom pronounced their judgement. And it was equally illogical that the defence had protested that the workers had abused the accused, but had not done so when the accused of the first group had abused those of the second group.[39]

In his reply, Murav'ev continued to appeal to the law. 'Woe to the country, woe to the people, who show contempt for the law and who mock those who defend the law.'

'Go, get out! You are insulting the Russian people!', called the public according to *Pravda*. 'I call you to order and censure you for contempt of the Russian people', said Piatakov.[40]

During the sitting of 23 June, in answer to Murav'ev's arguments of the previous day, Piatakov read a statement on behalf of the Tribunal to the effect that Murav'ev's request that the Tribunal should dissolve itself could only be explained by his 'complete ignorance' and complete misunderstanding of human and legal relationships. The Tribunal acted on the basis of its 'revolutionary conscience', and of 'a revolutionary conception of proletarian law'; it had thus consciously admitted the workers delegates to the courtroom and had itself attended the demonstration outside the court. Proletarian law had not been violated by these actions. 'Under the cloak of legal argumentation', Murav'ev and his colleagues were pursuing 'a deliberate political fight' against the sentence of the Tribunal. The idea that a court could only reach its sentence in splendid isolation could only emanate from a 'dyed-in-the-wool bourgeois manner of thinking'. Judges were after all human beings who could not be isolated from the community that surrounded them. The important thing was the way in which they reacted to events. The court categorically denied that the statements made by the workers delegates had any significance as evidence. They could have no influence whatsoever on the sentence that would be pronounced. The court was not interested in the statements for their factual information. The intention of the demonstration of 20 June and the appearance in the courtroom of the workers delegates had only been to establish that the working masses of Moscow and Petrograd gave their full support to the Soviet regime and the proletarian court. If the workers delegates had insulted the accused, it should be remembered that they had not been through any law school and were not familiar with customary court behaviour. Moreover, far greater insults had been uttered during the trial against the Soviet Republic, the working masses and the Tribunal.

It was 'hypocritical' to pretend that jurisdiction could stand above classes and aloof from class conflict, as though it could pass verdicts with 'a sort of supernatural impartiality'. In this respect, each court was partial and defended the interests of a certain class. This particular court defended the interests of the proletariat. But it was impartial in establishing a punishable offence, in the qualification of that offence, and in determining the severity of the sentence. The admittance of the workers delegates into the courtroom had not violated trial regulations in any way because it was not forbidden by any law; the statement by the defence must therefore be rejected as being without foundation.[41]

During the evening session, Piatakov announced that he had received a written statement from the defenders, but that he could not read it out in its entirety 'because it contains criticisms of the Tribunal'. He therefore confined himself to reading the concluding part of the statement in which the defenders, also on behalf of the accused, asked to be relieved of their task because it had been made impossible for them to carry out that task in a proper manner.[42]

The reading of the statement by the defenders led to a debate regarding whether or not the defenders had the right to withdraw. Krylenko pointed out that, according to the proletarian concept, the defence was 'a public law obligation' and the defenders must therefore continue with their work. Tager countered this by saying that the Tribunal's statement, which had included such phrases as 'the complete ignorance' and the 'dyed-in-the-wool bourgeois manner of thinking' of the defenders, had made it obvious that the defence did not enjoy the confidence of the court. Their further participation in the trial would therefore serve no purpose whatsoever. Gendel'man concurred with this on behalf of the accused. The Tribunal replied that its faith in the defence was not the subject of discussion. It accepted Krylenko's reasoning, and rejected the request of the defence.[43]

Next day (24 June) during the evening sitting, the debate over the defenders' right to withdraw flared up once again. Gendel'man reiterated that the accused had released their defenders from their obligations and that the accused would now carry out their own defence. Krylenko called the decision by the defenders to pull out a political deed that was against the law. He therefore asked the Tribunal to apply to the Moscow Soviet, as being the institution which determined the composition of the College of Advocates, with the proposal that those defenders who had resigned their task should be deprived of the right to practice law. In his opinion, the People's Commissariat of Justice should investigate whether these counsels should not be prosecuted for their refusal to carry out the public task which they had taken upon themselves. These suggestions won Krylenko applause from the audience in the courtroom. Notwithstanding his threats, however, the defenders persisted in their refusal to continue their task.[44]

After deliberation, the Tribunal declared that the request that the defenders be relieved of their task had been made in the first instance not by the accused but by the defenders themselves. Only then had it received the support of the accused. It was obvious, therefore, that the defenders 'are hiding behind the backs of their clients in their attempt to withdraw from participation in the trial'. In addition, the motives which the defenders gave for their request were completely unfounded. The Tribunal had therefore decided to submit details of the defenders' behaviour to the People's Commissar of Justice. It demanded that each defending counsel and each of the accused should declare in writing that he resigned his task or renounced the services of his defender.[45]

The defenders were still in attendance at the afternoon sitting of 26 June, apparently in order to submit the required written declarations. Only Murav'ev was not present. According to *Golos Rossii*, more attempts were made to make them reconsider their decision, but these were unsuccessful and the defenders did not appear at the evening sitting,[46] at which Piatakov announced that he had received the required statements from the accused and the defenders. The Tribunal then decided that the defence should be relieved of its obligations and that the case should be submitted to the People's Commissar of Justice.[47]

Bukharin called the departure of the defending counsels 'a flight from the battlefield', saying that he had the impression that the step formed part of a well-thought-out plan to disturb the normal trial procedure. First, the 'social-opportunist' defenders had departed, then the 'bourgeois' (*burzhuazno-tsenzovye*) lawyers, and now he supposed that the accused would want to leave. The defenders and the accused formed 'a coalition of two shades', whose objective it had been to draw back from the investigation now that the trial was to deal with the most serious crimes, in order 'to play the injured innocent'. On behalf of the second group, Bukharin demanded the guarantee that the trial would follow its normal course. The accused of the first group replied that they had not the slightest intention of withdrawing.[48]

The threats to the Russian defenders were no mere rhetoric. Although official confirmation of this point cannot be found, it may be assumed that items in the Russian underground press and in the emigré press were correct. Murav'ev, Tager and Zhdanov are said to have been arrested after laying down their task, to have been imprisoned for some months, and then to have been exiled to other parts of Russia. Kariakin, Lipskerov and B. Ratner are also said to have been subjected to persecution.[49]

The attitude of the communists towards the Russian defenders was just as ambiguous as that which they had shown to the western defenders. While on the one hand it was made impossible for them to carry out their task properly, on the other hand every effort was made to keep them at the trial. Here, too, it seemed that the illusion had to be maintained that the trial was genuine.

THE WITNESSES

In the first paragraph of this chapter we have seen that, at the start of the trial, the accused and their defenders had protested against the refusal of the Tribunal to subpoena a large number of witnesses for the defence. After some rather uneasy palaver back and forth,[50] the Tribunal made a small concession on this point.

As against 58 witnesses for the prosecution, the accused had asked for 40 witnesses to be called for the defence. Twenty of these were approved by the Tribunal.[51] The names of the other 20 who were not accepted are not all known. The majority, it seems, were Socialist Revolutionaries who were then in prison: Mikhail Tseitlin, a member of the Central Committee who, for one reason or another, was not included among the accused; Iurii Podbel'skii, who could have told more about the Tambov uprising; Vladimir Merkhalev, who had sat on the Military Committee together with Semenov; and someone called Eremeev who in 1918 had been a member of the Petrograd Committee of the PSR and who, according to the accused, could have given details of the background of the attack on Volodarskii.[52] It seems reasonable to assume, therefore, that the 20 witnesses who were rejected by the Tribunal would have been able to give evidence that was relevant to the investigation.

In the end, only nine witnesses for the defence were heard of the 20 who were accepted by the Tribunal.[53] More than three-quarters of the witnesses wanted by the defence therefore had no chance to speak. In view of the purpose of the trial, however, this is actually less surprising than the fact that nine witnesses for the defence were allowed to give evidence. This was also undoubtedly due to the efforts made to present the trial to the world as genuine.

The witnesses who were heard at the trial can be divided roughly into three groups: the witnesses for the defence; the witnesses for the prosecution, who endorsed the indictment; and a centre group, also of witnesses for the prosecution, who refused to fall in completely with the demands of the prosecutors. In the following survey we shall examine how these people were treated in connection with the trial.

The witnesses for the defence included: V.N. Filippovskii, A.P. Gel'fgot, B.S. Ivanov, I.P. Kashin, S.A. Kudriavtsev, V.P. Shestakov, F.D. Sorokin, E. Tiapkin, and a ninth whose identity cannot be determined with any certainty on the strength of the sources available. It might have been N.P. Smirnov who, in that case, did not belong to the 'centre group' of witnesses in which he is placed in this overview. Apart from Kashin, who had left the PSR, these were all imprisoned Socialist Revolutionaries, some of whom held prominent positions in the party. During the trial some of them tried to declare their solidarity with the accused, also in the name of other Socialist Revolutionary prisoners, but Piatakov gave them no opportunity to do so. In view of the fact that the witnesses for the defence refused to make the sort of statements that the communists expected of them, the Tribunal decided that two of them, Ivanov and Gel'fgot, should be prosecuted.[54] The former Socialist Revolutionary, Ivan Kashin, was a particularly fitting target for intimidation owing to the fact that, according to the Indictment, the case against him had been suspended. Supported by Chlenov, the defender of the second group, Krylenko insinuated that Kashin had made false statements, not neglecting to point out that the question was still pending whether the witness himself would have to be put on trial.[55]

On the other side stood those witnesses who supported the charges. The majority were former Socialist Revolutionaries (the initials of some are not known): I. Alekseev, Alekseeva, Berman, S.A. (?) Bessonov, A.S. Bogoliubskii, M.A. Davydov, B.M. D'iakonov, Ia.S. Dvorzhets, Gorodskii, K.S. Iudin, Kandelaki, K.A. Keller, S.E. Kononov, A.A. Krakovetskii, Kudria, Paevskii, S.N. Pashutinskii, M. Rakitin, V.K. Reizner. This group also included a few former members of other Russian socialist groupings: I.M. Maiskii, M.G. Rafes and A.F. Merinov; and the western communists Louis-Olivier Frossard, René Marchand and Pierre Pascal of France, and Bohumír Šmeral of Czechoslovakia. The Bolsheviks Gerasimov, Mazalov and Karl Radek appeared as experts.

The majority of these witnesses were the 19 former Socialist Revolutionaries whose performance at the trial in fact differed little from that of the accused of the second group. Gendel'man said in his address that all of them had been arrested during the preparations for the trial and had made their statements under the threat that they would themselves be tried and sentenced.[56] It is impossible to verify Gendel'man's words for each of the witnesses, but we have already seen in chapter 3 that force was indeed used during the preliminary investigation.

Finally, there was a group of more neutral witnesses: K.S. Burevoi, Ia.T. Dedusenko, A.B. El'iashevich, A.Iu. Feit, N.D. Kondrat'ev, A.P. Perkhurov, N.I. Rakitnikov, N.P. Smirnov, Snezhko-Blotskii, N.V. Sviatitskii, A.I. Verkhovskii, Zakgeim. With the exception of Perkhurov, all were former members of the PSR.

These witnesses were not prepared to fall in with all the wishes of the communists. Feit was the most stubborn of the witnesses for the prosecution, declaring himself in absolute sympathy with the accused.[57] Perkhurov who, during the preliminary investigation, had refused to make the statements demanded of him, continued to refuse during the trial.[58] El'iashevich refused to name people when this was demanded of him.[59] Snezhko-Blotskii, Dedusenko and Burevoi dissociated themselves from the versions of their own statements which were given in the report of the preliminary investigation.[60]

Some of these witnesses were subjected to intimidation. It is said that Perkhurov was treated as an accused rather than as a witness,[61] while Burevoi, notwithstanding his illness, was kept in the witness room almost as a prisoner for the entire month of June, not being called to give his evidence until 6 July.[62] All this probably applied also to a greater or lesser degree to the other witnesses. El'iashevich was reprimanded by Piatakov for his refusal to give names. Krylenko charged Dedusenko with making statements that were intentionally mendacious.[63] *Izvestiia* accused Burevoi of making 'confused and insincere' statements with the intention of 'justifying' his former comrades,[64] and Kondrat'ev of giving evasive answers.[65] Verkhovskii was reasonably compliant;[66] nevertheless, he did not want to entirely corroborate the charges and the Tribunal therefore decided that he should be prosecuted.[67]

As in the case of the defenders, these were no empty threats. Burevoi, Rakitnikov, Smirnov and Sviatitskii, all former members of the *Narod* group, had already been arrested during the preparations for the trial, as had been the political leader of the *Narod* group, Vladimir Vol'skii. But other than Vol'skii, one of the witnesses for the defence who were not heard, they had later been released. After the trial, however, Burevoi and Rakitnikov were again arrested and put for some time in the prison of Nizhnii-Novgorod.[68] Kondrat'ev was also arrested in the hunt for 'counter-revolutionary' intellectuals which was started immediately after the trial.[69] Zakgeim also landed in prison, to be exiled subsequently to a far distant part of the country.[70] Perkhurov was sentenced to death and executed in the night of 24-25 July.[71] Verkhovskii escaped prosecution by declaring publicly that he greatly regretted 'the misunderstandings' that had arisen in relation to the trial.[72]

THE ACCUSED

The Bolshevik accusers were keen to make the trial of the Socialist Revolutionaries seem genuine. The accused of the first group, on the other hand, took the position that it was not, and could not be, a genuine trial. What was happening in the courtroom, said Gendel'-man after the events of 20 June, showed merely some outward resemblance to a trial. In reality, it was a form of political struggle against the PSR. It was not up to a Bolshevik Party court to judge the political activity of the Socialist Revolutionaries, but only to 'the Russian working class, the international proletariat, and history'.

Krylenko answered this with the characteristic words:

A state which, for five years and in unbearable pain and sorrow, has conducted an uninterrupted fight against its enemies, which has conquered those enemies, has consolidated its power, and has even forced the capitalist states to respect it, such a state has the right to summons before the court all those who have hindered it in its genesis and its development.... A state which has laws at its disposal, has the duty to call to account all criminals and transgressors of those laws, notwithstanding when those deeds were committed, unless they are covered by an amnesty or are superannuated. Gendel'man says that history will pass judgement on us. The five years of the existence and uninterrupted fight of the Soviet regime, with the powerful support of the entire Russian proletariat and of the Russian peasantry, have shown on whose side history stands. History has already judged us. It has passed its sentence, and not in your favour.[73]

It is obvious that the accused of the first group held very different opinions about the nature of their trial to those of their defenders. The accused saw it not as litigation but as a political debate with the communists. The defenders, on the other hand, tried to benefit from the Bolsheviks' attempts to give the illusion that a genuine trial was being held in order to conduct a proper legal defence.

This difference showed up clearly in the debate about the events of 20 June. On the strength of those happenings, defender Murav'ev demanded that the Tribunal be disbanded. On the same occasion Evgenii Timofeev declared that the accused had from the first repudiated the court on political grounds, and therefore could not subscribe to its repudiation on legal grounds.[74]

The defendants declared that they did not regard themselves as accused and did not consider the court competent to judge over them. They said that they owed accountability only to their party and to the working class in Russia and in the world. To emphasize their repudiation of the court, the defendants refused to stand up when the Tribunal entered the courtroom at the beginning of each sitting, being the only ones not to do so. They fastened on the trial in order to defend Socialist Revolutionary policies and to impeach those of the Bolsheviks.

At the beginning of the trial Gendel'man declared, on behalf of the accused, that the court which had arrogated to itself the right to judge them represented the Communist Party dictatorship — in their view an illegitimate government — and that for that reason they considered themselves 'no accused at this trial'. They had only appeared in court because they hoped 'that within certain limits we shall be able to speak freely and, as against your charges, shall be able to hurl our own charges in your faces.'[75] Others said similar things.[76]

It was not made easy for the accused to carry out their purpose. Their requests were constantly rejected and their statements interrupted by Piatakov who commented that the trial was 'of the PSR and not of the communists', and that they were not to criticize the Communist Party or accuse its representatives.[77]

The accused of the second group, on the other hand, agreed that the Tribunal was competent to sit in judgement on them. They endorsed the charges and, during the trial, took the side of the communists against that of the Socialist Revolutionaries. In the propaganda campaign with which the trial was accompanied, Zinov'ev declared that the second group 'is not being tried', but 'in effect acts as accuser'.[78] Gendel'man, notwithstanding the outraged response that he evoked, was thus justified in calling them 'accusers' and 'second-rate Krylenko's'.[79] Not all members of the second group, however, played their part with the same enthusiasm as Semenov and Konopleva. As we saw in the discussion of the preliminary investigation, some of them had merely succumbed to the pressure that had been brought to bear on them. That was why Gots declared that, although the second group contained a few proven traitors and *provocateurs*, it also included a number of people whom the defendants had no wish to insult: their consciences would give them qualms enough in the future.[80]

Their instructions required that the members of the second group should react indignantly to such utterances, and they did so with the boisterous support of the public. In Konstantin Usov's words, from the point of view of 'bourgeois morals' they were perhaps traitors, but then traitors to 'the interests of the bourgeoisie'.[81]

The 'ideologue' of the second group was Grigorii Ratner, brother of Evgeniia Ratner of the first group. He called her his 'former sister' and repudiated any idea of 'family sentiment'.[82] Such things belonged to 'a narrow-minded petty bourgeois morality'. If the revolution demanded it, there were no family relationships: 'If the revolution requires it, a man should be able to send his own sister to the scaffold'.[83]

The Tribunal naturally protected the second group in every conceivable way. It thus refused to allow any investigation into the background of the activities of Semenov and Konopleva.[84] When Gendel'-man interrogated him, Semenov, with the agreement of the Tribunal and loud approval of the public, was thus able to reply that he would not give details of how his pamphlet came about to 'agents of the Entente'.[85]

We have seen that the accused of the first group, in contrast to those of the second, were lodged in prison while they attended the trial. At one session, according to *Sotsialisticheskii vestnik*, Mikhail Likhach protested on behalf of the accused against the treatment they were given. The evening sessions never ended before midnight, said Likhach, so that the accused had to spend twelve hours per day in the court building and did not return to the prison until about one o'clock at night. They were transported to and fro in a small lorry with barred windows, known in prison language as the 'dog's van' (*sobachii furgon*), which had insufficient seats for the 22 defendants. On arrival at the prison they were frisked roughly by sometimes drunken soldiers, which had already given rise to a scrap on more than one occasion. Moreover, during their absence, the GPU searched the cells of the prisoners and took away documents that were necessary for their defence.[86]

Krylenko replied that it was the duty of the GPU to search the trial papers of the prisoners.[87] And Piatakov added that, according to the GPU, it was not the soldiers but the prisoners who had behaved badly while being searched. It was necessary to frisk the accused because they were able to meet their relatives in the courthouse.

Piatakov had therefore decided that such meetings should be stopped until the case had been sorted out. In protest against this decision the accused went on hunger strike,[88] but no information is available on the course and result of that action.

CHAPTER 5

THE JUDICIAL INVESTIGATION

The judicial investigation was concerned with all the activities of the PSR since October 1917. A great many affairs were therefore discussed during the two months that the trial lasted, and it would be going too far to try to deal with all of them. It is possible to form a good impression of the character of the judicial investigation, however, by examining the ways in which some of the most important issues were handled: the attack on Lenin, the Tambov uprising, the activities of the Socialist Revolutionaries abroad, contacts with the Union for the Regeneration, and contacts with the Allies.

THE ATTACK ON LENIN

Before the February Revolution of 1917, the PSR had considered the use of terror to be an acceptable method in the fight against the autocracy. According to the concepts that then applied, although acts of terror could not replace the people's movement, they could provide it with the necessary impetus. The carrying out of an attack required the permission of the highest party authority, and the party had publicly to claim responsibility for the attack. After the October Revolution a number of attacks were perpetrated on Bolshevik leaders. The Bolsheviks could not very well accept that these attacks were the work of a few individuals, and were inclined to hold the PSR responsible, particularly in view of its hostility towards the Bolshevik regime and of its terrorist tradition. The PSR, however, had persistently denied having anything to do with the attacks, and the Bolsheviks now wanted to prove during the trial that it had of course been responsible. Their charge was that at the end of 1917 prominent Socialist Revolutionary leaders such as Viktor Chernov and Abram Gots had already alluded to the chance that the party would make use of terror if the Bolsheviks were to prevent the meeting of the Constituent Assembly. Abram Gots, for example, had written in a letter to the Fourth Party Congress that in such a case the party would remember 'its old well-tested tactics'.[1] According to the charges, the matter was also discussed in the Central Committee, which was said to have turned down a proposal that the use of terror should be rejected as a matter of principle, and to have accepted another one which left open the possibility of using terror. The Indictment consequently described the attitude of the Central Committee to the use of terror against the Bolsheviks as one of 'tacit approval and official denial'.[2]

The defendants replied that the Central Committee of the PSR had indeed never taken a principled decision to refrain from possible use of terror against repressive governments, amongst which it included the Soviet government, but that in practice it had always rejected the use of terror against the Bolsheviks. Gots and Chernov, they contended, in those statements made at the end of 1917, had not had terror in mind but a mass uprising in defence of the Constituent Assembly.[3] During the first half of 1918 the Central Committee had occasionally discussed the use of terror, but never in the form of a debate over the two alternatives which were mentioned in the Indictment. As a result of those discussions it had taken a position that amounted to prohibiting the use of terror against the Bolsheviks because, said Timofeev, the fight 'was not against individuals but against the Soviet regime as a whole': 'We didn't want to make martyrs of the Russian communists. We were far too convinced that you would founder in your own filth and in the blood that you have spilt.'[4]

The statements made by the accused seem quite plausible. Moreover, they were confirmed during the trial by the witnesses Burevoi and Rakitnikov, who had been members of the Central Committee of the PSR. According to Rakitnikov, the Central Committee had taken the position that, in a revolutionary period, 'when the masses have come into action, individual terror is inadmissible.'[5] Other sources that have been preserved from that time also indicate the accuracy of the version given by the defendants.[6] Some doubt is perhaps justified only with regard to the statements made by Chernov and Gots late in 1917, but if they had indeed had terror in mind, then it seems that they very soon reconsidered.

After this preliminary interrogation of the accused as to their general beliefs, the Tribunal passed on to discussing the acts of terror for which the Indictment held them responsible. According to accusations, they had organized the successful attack on Volodarskii on 20 June 1918, and the unsuccessful attempt on Lenin on 30 August 1918; in July or August 1918 they had tried to kill Reingol'd Berzin, a Red Army commander in the Urals; they had prepared attacks on the train which was to bring the Council of People's Commissars from Petrograd to Moscow in March 1918, on Lenin (a second time), and on Trotskii. Leonid Kanegisser's successful attack on Moisei Uritskii, head of the *Cheka* in Petrograd, on 30 August 1918, was admittedly not the work of the Socialist Revolutionaries, but they had planned such an attack on him and also one on Zinov'ev. They had also organized a series of expropriations.

The most important items in the Indictment were concerned with the activities of Semenov's terrorist group, and the greatest attention was given to Fania Kaplan's attack on Lenin on 30 August 1918.

In this affair the Indictment depended almost entirely on statements made by members of the second group, in particular on that by Semenov, whose story was more or less the following. In May 1918, in Petrograd, he had approached Central Committee members Gots and Donskoi, and proposed that a terrorist group should be formed. They had received the suggestion with enthusiasm, and Semenov had subsequently organized such a group, the party's 'central fighting division' (*tsentral'nyi boevoi otriad*), as he called it. Its members included a number of the accused of the second group and a few others, among whom had been Elena Ivanova of the first group. Together with these people, Semenov had started to prepare attacks on Bolshevik leaders, for which he had had the approval of Gots and Donskoi.[7]

In July 1918 Semenov's group had transferred its activities from Petrograd to Moscow. There, at the end of July, Semenov had twice visited Gots who was staying in Udel'naia, close to Moscow. According to Semenov, Gots had then assured him that the Central Committee now considered an attack on Lenin to be essential and, at the second visit, had given Semenov his 'word of honour' that the Committee would claim responsibility, on behalf of the party, for an attack made on Lenin by Semenov's group. Fania Kaplan, who had long planned to make an attempt on Lenin, was then admitted into the group by Semenov, who had also designated her one of the candidates for carrying out the attack. In the latter half of August he had introduced her to Donskoi in that capacity. Donskoi had agreed with the choice of Kaplan, but had insisted that, in the event of arrest, whoever carried out the attack should conceal the fact that it had been on the instructions of the party. On 30 August Kaplan had shot Lenin and seriously wounded him. Two days later, and notwithstanding the promises made to Semenov, the Central Committee had issued a statement that none of the party organizations had had anything to do with the attack.[8]

The accused of the first group dismissed Semenov's story. Some of its ingredients were correct, but the rest was mere fabrication. In the period in question, Semenov had been an organizer of party *druzhinniki*, i.e. members of *boevye druzhiny* (fighting groups) employed by the party. In that capacity he had indeed had meetings with members of the Central Committee, including Gots and Donskoi. At those meetings, as a man who was inclined towards the use of terror, he had more than once asked whether, in the meantime, the attitude of the Central Committee with regard to the use of terror had not changed, in view of the altered circumstances. Gots and Donskoi, however, had always replied that the Central Committee still disagreed with the use of terror, and had never given him instructions to form a terrorist group or to organize attacks on any Bolshevik leaders, including Lenin.[9] Semenov had indeed introduced Kaplan to Donskoi one day when they met in the street, on which occasion she had spoken of her intention to make an attempt. That she had earlier said the same thing to a few other Socialist Revolutionary leaders, Donskoi did not know at the time. According to Donskoi, he had advised her not to do it, and told her that she would place herself outside the party if she carried out her plan. Later, when Donskoi had heard that she had after all made an attempt on Lenin, he had thus felt justified in issuing a statement, on behalf of the Central Committee, to the effect that the PSR had had nothing to do with it.[10]

Ivanova declared that, owing to the fact that at the time she had also worked with the party *druzhinniki*, she had been in touch with Semenov and with members of his group, but she had not been a member herself, neither had she taken part in the terrorist activities described by Semenov.[11]

The accused of the first group also pointed out a series of inconsistencies in the behaviour of, and statements by, those who endorsed the charges. Why, for example, had Semenov not informed the other members of the Central Committee, whom he had met at the time, about his terrorist activities? This applied in particular to Timofeev and Evgeniia Ratner, who had then managed the party's activities in Moscow and without whose permission Semenov should not have carried out his plans at all.[12]

What evidence was there to support the version propagated by the accused Socialist Revolutionaries and what was there against it? The Indictment rested chiefly on Semenov's statements and only on very few points was given essential support by statements by other members of the second group who, after all, had been Semenov's subordinates and therefore could tell little more than what he had told them earlier, i.e. that the group had acted with the approval of the Central Committee. Kaplan had been executed shortly after her assassination attempt and was therefore unable to testify. The court had the report on her interrogation during which she had declared that she had acted 'on her own initiative' and to belong 'at present to no party at all'.[13] Even though Semenov said that she had made this statement in accordance with Donskoi's instructions, it did not militate against the accused but rather in their favour.

Moreover, in 1919, Vladimir Zenzinov, a member of the Central Committee of the PSR, had written that, in the spring of 1918, Kaplan had suggested to him via an intermediary that she should make an attempt on Lenin's life, but that the Central Committee had rejected this suggestion.[14] Zenzinov's words, written long before there was any threat of a trial, also seemed to argue that Kaplan had not made the attempt on behalf of the PSR.

Vladimir Vol'skii, a former party member, declared during the preliminary investigation that he had met Kaplan twice in May 1918, when she had told him that she wanted to commit terror against the Bolshevik leaders.[15] During the trial, a statement by Vol'skii was read to the court but we have only slight knowledge of its contents, gleaned from the address by the defender of the second group, Shubin. In that statement Vol'skii mentioned a talk that he had had later with Semenov, in which the latter had told him that the attacks were not only perpetrated without the knowledge of the Central Committee, but also without the knowledge of Gots and Donskoi.[16]

A member of Semenov's group who was out of the country at the time of the trial, a certain Mikhail Tislenko, wrote in *Golos Rossii* on 23 March 1922 that after the attempt on Lenin's life he had been in touch with members of the Central Committee, and that he had then become convinced that Semenov had never had the permission of the Central Committee for the attacks and that he had lied about this to the other members of the group.

The witnesses Burevoi and Rakitnikov, former members of the Central Committee of the PSR but now no longer party members, both declared that they had known nothing of Semenov's terrorist activities and that, in their opinion, the other members of the Central Committee had been equally uninformed. They considered it inconceivable that one or two members of the Central Committee would have kept such a thing secret from their colleagues.[17]

Two accused of the second group, Filipp Fedorov-Kozlov and Fedor Efimov, who had been members of Semenov's group, declared that they had not known that Ivanova had also been a member of the group.[18]

All these details were known to the Tribunal, and can now be complemented by two more facts. Firstly, there is the fact that Viktor Chernov, in a letter dated 25 December 1918 written to the poet Valerii Briusov, had surmised that the attack on Lenin had been the (foolish) work of the Left Socialist Revolutionaries.[19] Chernov probably based his assumption on the fact that Kaplan had been a member of Mariia Spiridonova's circle. In any case, the fact that Chernov was able to voice such a supposition militates against any complicity of the Central Committee of the PSR, of which he was a member.

In prison, about ten years after the trial, the Socialist Revolutionary Ekaterina Olitskaia met one of the accused in the 1922 trial, Aleksandr Liberov, who had also met Kaplan before she made her attack. According to Olitskaia, Liberov told her that the party leadership had turned down Kaplan's suggestion that she should shoot Lenin, but he thought nevertheless that 'no sufficient measures were taken to keep Kaplan from her deed.'[20]

In his address to the court, the defender of the second group, Chlenov, quoted from the report of a committee of inquiry which the Socialist Revolutionaries had set up in 1909 to investigate the affair of the traitor Azef.[21] According to Chlenov, it was evident from that report that terrorist groups in the PSR were accustomed to work autonomously, receiving only general directives from the Central Committee. The leader of a terrorist organization maintained contact with only one member of the Central Committee. Semenov, therefore, if he had received a terrorist assignment from a particular member of the Central Committee, had not needed to have this confirmed by other members of the Central Committee, at least according to Chlenov.[22]

Krylenko referred to the evidence of a former official of the *Okhrana*, Aleksandr Spiridovich. Spiridovich had written a book on the history of terrorism in Russia, a censored version of which had been published in 1915 in a limited edition.[23] In that book Spiridovich had also discussed the trial of a Socialist Revolutionary 'fighting group of the Central Committee', which had been accused of planning an assassination attempt on Tsar Nicholas II. The Central Committee had always declared that it knew nothing of this fighting group and that this entire plot was nothing but provocation on the part of the *Okhrana*. According to Spiridovich, however, the Socialist Revolutionary disclaimers conflicted with the truth, and party members had later admitted that the PSR had in fact known about it. It had denied any foreknowledge only for tactical reasons.[24] According to Krylenko, this proved that, even before the revolution, the Socialist Revolutionaries had been accustomed to deny their complicity in murderous assaults, and that there was therefore no reason to assume that they were now speaking the truth.[25]

Everything that has come to light about the attempt on Lenin's life indicates that Fania Kaplan was not acting on instructions from the Central Committee of the PSR, and that the charge against the Socialist Revolutionaries of the first group was therefore unfounded. But they were not entirely innocent. They did not oppose the use of terror on principle, even when it was directed against the Bolsheviks. When Kaplan told them of her intention to attack Lenin, they did not find it necessary to inform the police (i.e. the *Cheka*),[26] apparently because they had greater objections to the police and the regime than to attempted murder. In effect, they considered the Bolsheviks themselves to be responsible for attacks such as those on Volodarskii and Lenin, and saw these attacks as spontaneous expressions of the people's anger against the criminal policies of the Bolsheviks.[27]

Another point that should be considered was the tolerance shown towards those who had been involved in assassination attempts. There was naturally nothing more to be done about Kaplan, but Volodarskii's murderer, the party *druzhinnik* Sergeev, had not even been expelled from the party. As Gots said, he had after all sacrificed himself for a revolutionary ideal, although he might have done it in the wrong way, and expulsion would have delivered him into the hands of the *Cheka*.[28] Neither had disciplinary measures been taken against Semenov, although it must long have been clear what sort of a man he was. After the attempt on Lenin's life, Semenov himself had told Donskoi that he had given Kaplan her revolver. Nevertheless, Semenov was able to continue his work with the *druzhinniki* as though nothing had happened. True, the majority of the Central Committee members had not been aware of the help that Semenov had given Kaplan, and sanctions no longer had any purpose when they were eventually told because by then Semenov was in prison and he later joined the *Narod* group, but all the same, the impression made by all this is not very favourable.

On the other hand, the chaotic conditions in which all this took place should not be forgotten. A civil war was in progress in which the Socialist Revolutionaries and the Bolsheviks were on opposite sides; in Bolshevik territory the PSR was illegal; the Central Committee was dispersed in all directions; and many leading figures were in the Volga region.

The greatest likelihood seems to be that Semenov invented his story that he had acted on instructions from the Central Committee of the PSR, firstly in order to bind the members of his group to himself, and later to oblige the Bolsheviks who wanted to accuse the leaders of the PSR of having been responsible for the attack on Lenin. It seems certain that those leaders did not give such instructions. But they tolerated the presence of people like Semenov in the party and could do little against their irresponsible craving for action. To that extent, the leaders carried some degree of accountability, but that was nothing as compared to that of Semenov himself.

Prosecutor and Tribunal did not concentrate on that which could be proven, however, or on that which seemed feasible. In effect, they simply adopted Semenov's accusations. Krylenko said in his speech for the prosecution that the members of the terrorist group led by Semenov had worked according to instructions given by the accused of the first group and that their principals had later dissociated themselves from them. Krylenko saw 'this repudiation' which, according to him, the legal investigation had also proven for a series of other activities, as 'the best proof' of the guilt of the accused. In Krylenko's opinion, Kaplan had been 'incited' to carry out the attack by Donskoi and the other accused. Ivanova was lying about her share in the terrorist activities. Krylenko concluded from his summing-up of the Kaplan case that 'the link with the Central Committee and in particular the part played by Ivanova' was 'proven unconditionally'. He also considered it quite proven that Gots had had 'the direct leadership of the fighting group and of its terrorist activities.'[29]

In pronouncing judgement, the Tribunal adopted Krylenko's conclusions. It gave as its opinion that the attempt on Lenin's life had been made by 'the fighting group of the Central Committee of the PSR' (*boevaia gruppa pri TsK PSR*), i.e. by Semenov's group. That group had received instructions for its terrorist activities from the Central Committee members, Gots and Donskoi, while Ivanova had been a member of the group and its liaison with members of the Central Committee. It had been proven that the group 'did not operate independently but according to the instructions of the Central Committee or of a group of members of the Central Committee'. Gots and Donskoi 'had taken part in the organization of terrorist attacks', while some other members of the Central Committee 'were at least partly informed about these activities'. Gots and Donskoi had 'led the activities' of the terrorist group which had carried out the attempt on Lenin's life.[30]

That the Tribunal made no attempt really to examine the issues is shown by its treatment of the attack on Lenin and also of that on Volodarskii. It gave almost no attention to the actual deed, to the identity of its perpetrator and to his or her motives, or to the possible involvement of others than the Socialist Revolutionaries (e.g. Boris Savinkov, for whose organization the accused suspected that Semenov had worked at the time).[31] This applied to an even stronger degree to the attack on Berzin in which, in the opinion of the Tribunal, the accused Lev Gershtein had been involved, in a similar manner to Gots and Donskoi by the attack on Lenin (Gershtein denied such involvement). No attempt was made to elucidate when, where, by whom, under which circumstances and with what result (Berzin had certainly not been killed, but had he been wounded?) the attack had been carried out. The accused even doubted whether the attack had actually been made.[32] Neither was it made clear when the alleged attack on Trotskii had been attempted, in which Ivanova was said to have played a part. At any rate, Ivanova denied having had anything to do with such an affair.

THE TAMBOV UPRISING

The Socialist Revolutionaries were charged with having undertaken a series of attempts to overthrow the Soviet regime. In 1917 they had resisted the October Revolution; they had planned a number of uprisings early in 1918 including one on 5 January, the opening day of the Constituent Assembly. Later the same year they had taken up the armed struggle against the Soviet regime in earnest. All this meant that they were responsible for the civil war and for its countless victims, for the Allied intervention, and for the developing power of the Whites. Even after 1919, according to the charges, the Socialist Revolutionaries had continued these activities. They had planned uprisings in Tambov, in Siberia, and in the Black Sea area, and to some extent had been involved in the revolts in Kronstadt and Karelia.

The Bolsheviks thus also wanted to demonstrate during the trial that the PSR was responsible for the rebellious and, according to the Bolsheviks, counter-revolutionary peasants movement which had made its appearance in Russia after the close of the civil war and which had manifested itself most strikingly in the Tambov uprising in 1920-1921. On this matter the prosecutors were less dependent on the accused of the second group. Although there were differences of opinion on some of the facts, there was agreement on most of them, and the point at issue was the way in which those facts should be interpreted. According to the prosecutors, the Socialist Revolutionaries had not really abandoned the idea of armed struggle against the Soviet regime in 1919; as in the question of terrorist activities, they had left their options open.[33] The accused replied that the PSR indeed had never decided in principle to renounce the right to use weapons against the Soviet regime but that, since the end of 1918, it had in practice always rejected the idea of using arms in such a manner.[34]

With regard to the Tambov uprising, let us first consider those facts about which no difference of opinion existed. In May 1920 the Central Committee of the PSR had distributed a circular in which it urged that political agitation among the peasants should be intensified and that non-party peasants unions should be set up.[35] The Socialist Revolutionaries in the province of Tambov had followed these instructions issued by the party leadership.[36] In that same province an uprising had broken out in 1920, led by Aleksandr Antonov, a man who called himself a Socialist Revolutionary and who used Socialist Revolutionary slogans, but who was not a member of the party. It was also known — as we have seen in chapter 1 — that at a conference in September 1920 after the start of the uprising, representatives of local PSR organizations (including a representative from Tambov) had pointed out the inevitability that the PSR would renew the armed fight against the Soviet regime at some time in the future.

According to the prosecutors, the PSR was responsible for the Tambov uprising. With its circular of May 1920 the PSR had created an atmosphere in which local peasant uprisings were unavoidable. The September conference, in effect, had endorsed the rebellious movement. The activist tone of that conference had been completely in accord with the instructions of the Central Committee. With their agitational activities in Tambov and the formation there of a peasants union, the Socialist Revolutionaries had provoked the Tambov uprising. They had been in touch with Antonov. The uprising had been supported by organizations of the Tambov peasants union and the rebels had made use of Socialist Revolutionary slogans. Having unchained the revolt, however, the PSR had deserted it in midstream, leaving its leadership in the hands of 'the adventurer', 'the bandit' Antonov.[37]

The accused, on the other hand, held that Bolshevik policies had been responsible for the uprising.[38] They pointed out that the Central Committee of the PSR had always warned its adherents against isolated uprisings. According to the accused, the September conference had taken a far more activist attitude than that of the Central Committee. Neither the national nor the local Tambov organization of the PSR (the latter of which had been heavily affected by arrests of its members in August 1920, i.e. shortly before the start of the uprising)[39] had been involved in the uprising.[40]

On the basis of available data, what opinion are we able to form about the responsibility of the Socialist Revolutionaries for the Tambov uprising? The witness for the prosecution, A.S. Bogoliubskii, who was Antonov's brother-in-law and had until recently been a Socialist Revolutionary, said during the trial that there had been a relationship between the peasants union and the 'cells' of Antonov's movement.[41] The Socialist Revolutionary Iurii Podbel'skii, who had not been accepted as a witness, had earlier denied this in a publication dated March 1921. According to Podbel'skii, the uprising had broken out spontaneously, independent of and unanticipated by the peasants union, whose leadership had always been opposed to the idea of an immedate uprising. Podbel'skii had also written, however, that the rank and file of the union had not agreed with their leaders on that point.[42] According to Bogoliubskii, the uprising had started in those places where the Socialist Revolutionaries had formed the strongest branches of the peasants union.

Bogoliubskii said that the Tambov organization of the PSR had still been in touch with Antonov after the outbreak of the uprising. According to the Indictment, Ivan Ishin, a Socialist Revolutionary from Tambov who had been executed some time before the trial, had declared that in November 1920 they had been informed that Chernov approved the uprising.[43] That the Central Committee of the PSR had been implicated in the uprising, however, was denied by the Bolshevik Vladimir Antonov-Ovseenko, who had taken part in the violent suppression of the uprising. In July 1921, in a report on the revolt, he wrote that local Socialist Revolutionaries had been involved but that there had been no link with the Central Committee.[44] Podbel'skii, like the accused, denied that the local party organization had been involved. It had merely asked Antonov — in vain — either not to call himself a Socialist Revolutionary or to subject himself to party discipline, i.e. to stop his insurgent activities. Podbel'skii admitted, however, that the uprising had made use of Socialist Revolutionary slogans and that the rebels had assumed that the uprising was supported by the party. Mikhail Fomichev, himself one of the rebels, also writes in his remembrances of the uprising that the PSR organization had been averse to the uprising but that some members and adherents of the party had joined the rebels, under the impression that the movement was backed by the party.[45]

In its judgement, the Tribunal posited that the PSR was responsible for the Tambov uprising. The party had provoked and prepared the revolt, laying down its 'plan' in its May 1920 circular. That the PSR had not placed itself officially at the head of the movement was due to 'political duplicity', to 'fear' of taking responsibility for a movement which, although kindled by the Socialist Revolutionaries, was clearly heading for defeat. The Tribunal considered that 'the organizational link' between the PSR and the uprising, and the party's 'inspirational role' were proven beyond any doubt. Therefore, it considered the party also to be responsible for the victims of the uprising.[46]

Was this judgement well-founded? The conclusion of the American historian, Oliver Radkey, who has specialized in the Tambov uprising, is that the uprising was spontaneous and that the PSR can only indirectly be held responsible. By its agitational activities and by setting-up the peasants union, it had contributed to the revolt. Local Socialist Revolutionaries had taken part in the uprising. The leadership of the PSR, however, had refused to give its endorsement, both before and after the uprising.[47]

Since 1919 the objective of the PSR had been to pursue political opposition to the Soviet regime. Loyalty towards the regime, in its view, was inconceivable because this would entail acceptance of the regime and in practice would mean that the party would have to abandon its independent politics. Violent opposition to the regime was also infeasible in that it might cause senseless bloodshed and 'reaction' might win the day. Under the regime that had been established by the Bolsheviks, however, purely political opposition had proven impossible. In practice, political opposition meant that the party leadership adopted what was mostly a wait-and-see attitude without taking the fundamental decision to reject the use of political violence against the Bolsheviks. This not only doomed the PSR to impotence, but laid it open to reproaches of double-dealing, because the party had insufficient control over its adherents to prevent political violence on their part.

According to Radkey, the Socialist Revolutionaries were guilty not so much of 'conspiracy' as of 'confusion',[48] a conclusion that is better founded than that of the Bolsheviks, who declared that the Socialist Revolutionaries were guilty of conspiracy.

THE SOCIALIST REVOLUTIONARIES ABROAD

During the trial, the Bolsheviks also raised the matter of the activities of those Socialist Revolutionaries who were out of the country, stating that they continued their efforts for a violent overthrow of the Soviet regime. They demanded, therefore, that the accused should dissociate themselves from their political associates abroad.

The principal evidence for the Public Prosecutor's statement that the Socialist Revolutionary emigrés continued to strive for a violent overthrow of the Soviet regime was provided by the reports of an organization known as the 'Administrative Centre'. These reports were not produced by Krylenko until 7 July, well after the start of the trial, neither did he clarify how he had managed to get hold of the documents. It has been established that they were stolen from the archives of the Administrative Centre in Paris some time in the middle of June 1922. The Socialist Revolutionaries were fairly positive that the culprits were Russian monarchists. Nevertheless, the papers surfaced in Moscow three weeks later at the trial of the Socialist Revolutionaries.[49]

The contents of these documents are not known to us. According to the Bolsheviks they showed that the Administrative Centre had been an organization of Socialist Revolutionaries abroad which had existed in 1921-1922, and whose objective had been to overthrow the Soviet regime with the aid of the Allied powers and of international capitalism. With this aim in view, the Centre had sent agents to places along the entire western frontier of Soviet Russia and into the country itself. It had been in touch with rebellious elements in Soviet Russia, including the Kronstadt rebels, to whom it had offered aid.[50]

The accused refused to defend themselves against the accusation, being of the opinion that the matter should not be handled in the courtroom. They said that they had never heard of the Administrative Centre and that they did not trust the documents, whose authenticity they could not verify.[51]

The accusations could thus only be answered by the Socialist Revolutionary emigrés who declared that the Administrative Centre had been at the head of an organization which had called itself the 'Non-Party Association' (*Vnepartiinoe Ob"edinenie*). This organization, which was not linked to any party, had been set up in the summer of 1920 in order to inform public opinion and to make propaganda. The association had its own agents through whom it tried to maintain contact with Russia, but had not planned any armed revolt in Russia although it had sympathized with revolts such as that of Kronstadt. The organization had been disbanded in the autumn of 1921 because it had proved impossible to maintain regular contacts with Russia.[52]

The Socialist Revolutionaries outside Russia thus admitted that the Administrative Centre had existed, but denied that it had been oriented towards a violent overthrow of the Soviet regime. New light was thrown on the affair in 1929 as a consequence of a rupture in the PSR's Foreign Delegation. The question of the Administrative Centre was among the questions discussed in a memorandum about the party quarrels which the left minority wrote to the Labour and Socialist International. The writers of that memorandum, who included Viktor Chernov, reproduced a good many of the accusations made by the communists in 1922. The Administrative Centre, according to them, had been set up by right-wing Socialist Revolutionary emigrants whose objective had been to overthrow the Soviet regime by means of armed revolt, notwithstanding the fact that such a strategy had been rejected by the Central Committee. The Centre had tried (unsuccessfully) to make contacts with Russia without the knowledge of the party organizations.[53] In his own memorandum to the International on behalf of the majority of the Foreign Delegation, however, Vasilii Sukhomlin maintained the version given by the Socialist Revolutionaries in 1922.[54]

On the basis of the now known facts it is not possible to establish which of the two parties tampered with the truth. But even if the Bolsheviks were in the right in 1922 with their characterization of the Administrative Centre, it can still be taken as certain that the accused, who had been in prison since 1920, had had nothing to do with it. They resisted vigorously, therefore, any examination of the affair during the trial: the accusations, after all, did not concern themselves or any representative organ of the party and, in addition, could not be verified by them. The prosecutors replied, through Krylenko, that they could only consider excluding the affair from the trial if the accused would dissociate themselves from the Socialist Revolutionary emigrés, whose activities were in question. This the accused refused to do. They said that they could not dissociate themselves from the Administrative Centre without knowledge of all the facts.[55]

Even the Tribunal did not consider a link between the accused and the Administrative Centre to be proven. It certainly mentioned the activities of the Administrative Centre in its judgement, but without saying that the accused were responsible for those activities. This did not hinder the propagandists from taking the linkage for granted, however. One of the defenders of the second group, P. Shubin, for example, wrote in September 1922 that the Tribunal had had to declare the Central Committee responsible for the activities of the Administrative Centre.[56]

It seems reasonable to assume that the Bolsheviks were anxious to discuss the Administrative Centre affair during the trial partly because they wanted to drive a wedge between the accused and their party associates abroad.

A similar intention was undoubtedly also present in the examination of another affair.

A conference of members of the Constituent Assembly had been held in Paris in January 1921 and attended by both Socialist Revolutionaries and Kadets. The conference had appointed an Executive Committee, whose members also included both Socialist Revolutionaries and Kadets. Viktor Chernov had been critical of the whole enterprise which, in his view, could be construed as the forming of a coalition between Socialist Revolutionaries and bourgeois politicians. He refused to attend the conference but nevertheless took part in the deliberations of the Socialist Revolutionary fraction of the conference in order that, according to what he said later, they could get out of the business with as little political damage as possible.

A month later, in February 1921, the conference was denounced by the Central Committee of the PSR in Russia. The Central Committee demanded of those who had joined the Executive Committee of the conference that they resign from that Committee, on pain of expulsion from the party.[57]

This decision caused a reaction by Chernov, laid down in a letter which fell into the hands of the Bolsheviks. In that letter Chernov urged the Central Committee to reconsider its decision, as otherwise there would be the danger of a rift, not only with the right wing of the Socialist Revolutionary emigrés, but also with the centre (Chernov himself belonged to the left wing).[58] A group of Socialist Revolutionaries who had taken part in the conference also protested to the Central Committee against its decision.[59]

Shortly after, the arrest of its last members to be at liberty meant that the Central Committee ceased to function. From their prison, however, members of the Central Committee made it known that they adhered to their decision,[60] and the Central Bureau, which had taken over the daily management of the party, confirmed that decision yet again in October 1921.[61]

According to the Indictment, those Socialist Revolutionaries who had attended the Paris conference had, by their presence, violated the prohibition laid down by the Ninth Party Council of the PSR regarding the formation of coalitions with bourgeois parties. The prosecutors confronted the accused with Chernov's letter in which he had asked the Central Committee to reconsider its position of complete rejection towards those party members who had taken part in the conference. On the basis of that letter, the prosecutors demanded that the accused should publicly denounce Chernov — one of the most influential leaders of the PSR — before the Tribunal.

This the accused naturally refused to do, from which the prosecutors concluded that the accused must be held responsible for the activities of the party's right wing. 'Avksent'ev is shielded by Kerenskii, Kerenskii by Chernov, and Chernov by you', exclaimed prosecutor Lunacharskii.[62] *Pravda*, on 28 July, was even more outspoken: 'Either you endorse the activities of Kerenskii, Avksent'ev, Zenzinov and Chernov', *Pravda* addressed itself to the accused, 'in which case we are trying a branch of the French-Czechoslovakian intelligence service, or you must say: "that branch, Chernov, Zenzinov, that is not us, that is our foreign delegation, and we break all our connections with them".'

This shows once again that the Bolsheviks tried to induce the accused to criticize their party associates abroad in the hope of thus turning the Socialist Revolutionaries abroad and at home against each other. The accused resisted the attempt strongly. We shall not let ourselves be divided, said their spokesman Gots, however much you would like to separate us from our representatives abroad. And he added: 'There is not one political grouping which would not have to pay for an overture towards you with its political death.'[63]

In addition, it is difficult to avoid the impression that the Bolsheviks could not understand the tolerance shown for minority opinions within the PSR. Reacting to *Izvestiia*'s publication of his above-mentioned letter, Chernov wrote that expulsion of the right minority was contrary to the tradition of the PSR, which was accustomed to tolerate minorities as long as they accepted party discipline.[64] Such a conception of the character of a political party aroused contempt and suspicion among the Bolsheviks who prided themselves on the monolithic nature of their party: contempt because it was not fitting, and suspicion because it could not really be the truth, it could only be an act, and there must be some purpose behind it. That was the reason for Krylenko's fulminations against the hypocrisy, the deceit and duplicity of the PSR.[65] This side of the matter will be discussed further in the following chapter.

THE UNION FOR THE REGENERATION

During the trial the Bolsheviks also wanted to hold the Socialist

Revolutionaries responsible for the activities of organizations with which they had been in contact in one way or another. For example, the fact that representatives of the Socialist Revolutionaries had had informative contacts early in 1918 with the anti-Bolshevik organization of a certain Ivanov, which was rightist and pro-German, was construed by Krylenko as the formation of 'a political bloc with German spies'.[66] Modelling itself on Krylenko, the Tribunal asserted in its judgement that the PSR had formed 'an objective bloc' with 'undisguisedly Black Hundreds elements such as the organization of Ivanov, who was an immediate and direct agent of Hohenzollern Germany.'[67] It undoubtedly gave the Bolsheviks great satisfaction to be able to accuse the Socialist Revolutionaries of having been in contact with a pro-German organization at the same time that Lenin was accused of being a German agent. This was only one of a number of cases, however, in which they held that the PSR was responsible for activities against the Soviet regime which had been perpetrated by other organizations, for the simple reason that the PSR had not opposed or clearly dissociated itself from such activities.

Another example of this guilt by association is formed by the PSR's contacts with the 'Union for the Regeneration of Russia' (*Soiuz Vozrozhdeniia Rossii*), an organization of leftist liberals and rightist socialists which had been formed in the spring of 1918. Prosecutors and accused more or less agreed on the facts. The target of the Union for the Regeneration had been to establish a democracy in Russia and it had exercised some influence on the formation of the Ufa Directory. Its intention had been to fight Germany and the Bolsheviks; it had been in touch with representatives of the Allies and had also received financial aid from them. Some right-wing Socialist Revolutionaries had joined the Union, not as representatives of the party but on an individual basis. At first the Central Committee of the PSR had tolerated this, but in October 1918 it had prohibited membership of the Union which, in its opinion, had adopted a policy that was too independent. According to the prosecutors, Gots had also joined the Union. This was contested by the accused, according to whom no member of the Central Committee had belonged to the Union. Nevertheless, the Tribunal accepted the prosecutors' statement that Gots had been a member.

The defence put up by the accused had its weak spots. In 1918 the activities of the PSR and of the Union for the Regeneration had in fact been intertwined to some extent. Even after October 1918 a few

Socialist Revolutionaries had still been members of the Union, without this being reason for their expulsion from the party. It was of little consequence to the less well-disposed observer, whether the Socialist Revolutionaries had accepted money from the Union for 'national tasks' only, as Gots said, and not for the work of the party.[68]

But how did the prosecutors handle these facts? In Krylenko's opinion, the Central Committee was responsible for the political activities of all party members, i.e. including the activities of those members who had joined the Union for the Regeneration and, therefore, those of the Union itself. He spoke of 'a political bloc with the bourgeoisie on the basis of combating the Soviet regime'. There had been 'a united political front' running from the Allies and the reactionary Russian officers on the right, up to and including the Socialist Revolutionaries on the left, linked together by 'the closest ties that exist in the capitalist world, those of gold.'[69]

The accused members of the Central Committee of the PSR were thus held responsible by the prosecutors not only for the activities of the official party organs, but also for those of the representatives of the party's right wing, who had often pursued a fairly independent policy. Nor was that all. They also found that the Central Committee was responsible for the activities of those with whom members of the right wing of the party had cooperated, and were within an ace of holding them responsible for the deeds of the associates of their associates as well. Indeed, the witness Nikolai Kondrat'ev who, as Socialist Revolutionary, had been a member of the Union for the Regeneration between the summer of 1918 and the end of 1919, declared that there had been a committee for informative contacts between the Union and the 'National Centre' which stood to the right of the Union; a committee which had become known as the 'Tactical Centre'. Krylenko drew the conclusion from Kondrat'ev's words that there had thus been a 'bloc', made up of the Union for the Regeneration and the National Centre.[70]

CONTACTS WITH THE ALLIES

According to the Indictment, the PSR in 1918 had maintained contact with representatives of the Allied governments from whom they had received financial and other assistance. The party was also charged with co-responsibility for the Allied intervention in Russia in 1918.

Prosecutors and accused were agreed that the Socialist Revolutionaries had been in contact with representatives of the Allies in 1918. The accused defended themselves by pointing out that their contacts had been with other people than those named in the Indictment, and that the latter did not give a correct representation of the reasons for those contacts. Prior to the formation of the *Komuch* they had been in touch only with the socialists Charles Dumas and Jean Ehrlich, with the sole purpose of using them to publicize in other countries the endeavours of the PSR. The fact that Dumas and Ehrlich had worked for the French mission had not been a factor. Only later, after the forming of the *Komuch*, had they sought contact with official representatives of foreign powers on behalf of that government.[71]

This was far from being the strongest point in the defence of the accused. There was no denying the fact that Dumas and Ehrlich had been members of the French mission. It was also an irrefutable fact that various Socialist Revolutionaries had been in touch with Allied representatives in 1918, if not in the name of the party then in the name of the Union for the Regeneration.

On the basis of these facts, Krylenko naturally concluded that there had been 'a formal bloc', 'an agreement' between the PSR and the Allies,[72] whereby the Socialist Revolutionaries had sold themselves as mercenaries to the Allied occupiers.

But the prosecutors were unable to prove that the Socialist Revolutionaries had accepted subsidies from the Allies. A number of cases were discussed during the trial in which there was talk of Allied subsidies. The French witness René Marchand, for example, said that he was certain that the Socialist Revolutionaries had received money from the French consulate-general. He had heard this from the consulate's cashier, who 'more than once' had given money to the Socialist Revolutionaries. According to Marchand, he had himself once seen that Ehrlich came to the consulate with 50,000 rubles which he had collected in person from the military mission in order to pass it on to the PSR.[73]

The accused denied ever having received money from the Allies,[74] however, and the assertions of Marchand and others in this respect could in no way be proven. In a pamphlet which he wrote about the trial, even prosecutor Lunacharskii admitted that 'some of the statements made by Marchand during the trial were based on a misunderstanding.' 'The Allies did not offer the Socialist Revolutionaries what you can call money', wrote Lunacharskii. 'Apparently they received it only through the Union for the Regeneration and then only in small amounts.'[75] The charge that the PSR had accepted funds from Allied governments remained completely unproven.

Finally, there was the charge that the Socialist Revolutionaries had induced the Allied intervention in Russia and, in particular, the Allied landing in Arkhangel'sk. In 1918 the Socialist Revolutionaries had cooperated in the formation of an anti-Bolshevik government in Arkhangel'sk; according to the accused, they had done so to prevent that the landing of Allied troops, expected there as part of the fight against Germany, should result in a military occupation. Their efforts had been unsuccessful, however, and they had withdrawn towards the end of September (the forming of the government and the subsequent landing had both taken place early in August).[76] According to Krylenko, however, the Socialist Revolutionaries had been interested only in winning Allied support for their struggle against the Bolsheviks. In Arkhangel'sk they had laid the basis for the Allied occupation and for a takeover by the Whites. As events subsequently took their logical course, however, the Socialist Revolutionaries had pulled out, 'weak and miserable cowards' that they were.[77]

The defence which the accused put up on the question of the Allied intervention was also far from strong. They said that the Socialist Revolutionaries had cooperated with the Allies in 1918 only within the framework of the fight against Germany and not in that of a fight against the Bolsheviks. In fact, of course, these two goals had been interlinked to some considerable extent. According to the accused, the Socialist Revolutionaries had been against intervention in Russian domestic affairs by Allied troops, but then they had made an exception in the case of the soldiers of the Czechoslovakian legion who had supported the *Komuch*: according to Timofeev, those soldiers had formed 'part of the Russian democratic and socialist forces'.[78]

GENERAL CHARACTERISTICS
OF THE BOLSHEVIKS' LINE OF CONDUCT

We have seen in the foregoing that the charges brought against the

Socialist Revolutionaries were formidable, but this gave the Indictment a somewhat paradoxical character. In one way or another, the PSR was said to be responsible for almost all opposition against the Bolsheviks, thus giving the impression that the PSR was an extremely powerful organization. Yet the intention was to prove to the populace that the PSR was nothing but a paltry handful of indecisive cowards, of absolutely no significance. The Socialist Revolutionaries were guilty of 'hypocrisy', 'duplicity', 'opportunism'; they were liars and cowards. Gots had organized a revolt among the 'junkers', i.e. cadets, against the newly-established Soviet regime, and when that had failed, he had denounced the attempt. (Gots refuted this accusation convincingly, but without effect.) The Socialist Revolutionaries were accustomed first to launch a scheme that was bound to fail and, when that happened, to wash their hands of it. They dissociated themselves from activities that were undertaken on their instigation and left others to take the blame. They said one thing and did another. They concealed themselves in a hole-and-corner manner behind deceptive under-cover organizations so that, if the execution of their plans should fail, they could behave as though they had had nothing to do with them. The Administrative Centre and the Union for the Regeneration had been just such organizations.

The trial was not so much concerned with facts that were punishable by law. The Socialist Revolutionaries were denounced for the policy that they had followed since October 1917. But in order to arrive at that denouncement, the Bolsheviks made use of the technicalities of legal argumentation. The PSR was charged with the fact that it had not resigned itself to the situation that had been created in Russia by the October Revolution of 1917 as though that were a crime, and all actions that had derived from that political choice as just as many crimes.

The legal argumentation used by the Bolsheviks during the trial, however, was unsound. The cases were not properly investigated. As we have seen in the discussion of the attack on Lenin, the Tribunal did not concentrate on that which could actually be proven. The material on which it based its judgement was for a large part dubious of character: statements by the accused of the second group and by a series of witnesses who fell into the same category; and documents such as those of the Administrative Centre. The judgement of the Tribunal was not only in all cases tendentious; in many cases the evidence on which it was based was utterly inadequate.

CHAPTER 6

THE SOCIALIST REVOLUTIONARIES
VERSUS THE BOLSHEVIKS

To understand the conflict between the Socialist Revolutionaries
and the Bolsheviks, it is essential to realize that they believed in the
same things, only each in their own way. Both were motivated by
revolution and socialism. The Bolsheviks considered themselves to be
Marxists, but Gendel'man did not speak only for himself when he remarked during the trial that he had 'always been a Marxist and
a Socialist Revolutionary'.[1] Both parties were opposed to 'the
counter-revolution', 'the bourgeoisie', 'the reaction'. Both spoke
about 'class struggle' and the 'dictatorship of the proletariat'. Each of
the two parties considered itself to be socialist and denied the other
the right to so call itself.

The political debate between the Bolsheviks and the Socialist
Revolutionaries burgeoned above all in the addresses by the prosecutors and in those for the defence, the rejoinders and the closing addresses to the court of the accused. It should be remembered, however, that the Bolsheviks did not really want to enter into a debate.
Piatakov, for instance, interrupted Gots when he was making his
speech for the defence, with the remark that 'the *Uchredilka*' — a
pejorative for the Constituent Assembly (*Uchreditel'noe Sobranie*) —
had 'rightly' been dispersed and that Gots should confine himself to
the case. In Russia, the 'dictatorship of the proletariat' was 'an in-
contestable form of government' which was 'not under discussion' in
the courtroom.[2]

THE BOLSHEVIKS

The most important spokesmen for the Bolsheviks in the political
debate were the prosecutors Lunacharskii, Krylenko and Pokrovskii,
and the defender of the second group, Bukharin. Invoking Marxism,
they took a number of axioms as their points of departure: the Com-

munist Party represents the proletariat; the proletariat is involved in a fight with the bourgeoisie; the PSR is a petty bourgeois party which takes the part of the bourgeoisie.

The PSR is neither socialist nor revolutionary, was the *Leitmotiv* of their reasoning. Bukharin thought that he could say 'with absolute certainty' that the PSR 'systematically, day in day out, has betrayed the interests of the working class and the interests of socialism'. According to Pokrovskii, the PSR was 'clearly a bourgeois reactionary party'. Lunacharskii said that the PSR made use of the lack of education among certain strata of the Russian proletariat to tempt them from the 'correct path', the path of political organization on a class basis.

In contrast to other bourgeois reactionary parties, such as the Kadets, Pokrovskii considered that the Socialist Revolutionaries lacked 'a genuine social basis'. Consequently, their party was 'less sincere and more hypocritical' than those other parties. They tried to combine the proletariat with the peasants and the intelligentsia in one party, 'with classes that are vague and highly unstable, both in their ideology and in their strategy', according to Lunacharskii. This had to give rise to eclecticism because the various groupings had contradictory interests. That was why the PSR had to break up into a number of groups which pursued completely contradictory policies, and why it could not have a decent party centre at its disposal.

The lack of clear authority relations within the PSR provoked plenty of comment from the prosecutors. 'We are people who think more crudely about politics', said Krylenko. 'We consider that a party is a party and that a Central Committee is therefore a Central Committee because, once it has taken a decision, the others have to obey and not to speak. But the Socialist Revolutionaries have other ideas on this matter.' Krylenko, and the other Bolshevik spokesmen with him, thought that there was more in this than met the eye, that 'isolated independent activities' of groups and individuals were 'not a coincidence but a system' in the PSR. Bukharin compared the PSR with the Communist Party. The first had its 'currents', the second its 'specialisms'. In his opinion, the PSR formed a hotchpotch of miscellaneous currents with which anything was possible. In the centre was a small oligarchic clique which, as though on a chessboard, advanced first a leftist pawn and then a rightist one. It refused to accept any responsibility itself. Lunacharskii declared that in this way the PSR could allow its left-wing supporters to perpetrate terror whenever this suited it, and could then behave as though it had nothing to do with the terrorists.

A party such as that of the Socialist Revolutionaries which, as the prosecutors thought they had proven with their class analysis, was counter-revolutionary because of its activities and counter-revolutionary in essence, could not be granted the right to be politically active. In Krylenko's opinion, 'the so-called pure democracy' was nothing other than a screen behind which were hidden the interests of the ruling classes. To the communists, political freedom had always been 'only a fighting weapon and certainly not a fetish or absolute value'. The point at issue was whether, seen from 'the interests of the workers as we understand them', it was 'efficient' or, on the contrary, 'detrimental' to 'personally put a weapon into the hands of the enemy'. In this case, in Krylenko's opinion, it was detrimental. Neither the PSR nor any other oppositional grouping could be given political liberty.

The prosecutors saw the efforts of the Socialist Revolutionaries to gain greater political latitude, as was illustrated, for example, by their demand for free elections to the Soviets, merely as 'a manoeuvre'. If that latitude was to be granted, the PSR would misuse it in order to stir up trouble, to 'poison the backward or weary masses' — as Lunacharskii expressed it — and to incite them against the Soviet regime. In this way the PSR hoped to overthrow the Soviet regime. If that should succeed, two things might happen. Either the bourgeois capitalists or the Socialist Revolutionaries would seize power. In the latter case, however, the Socialist Revolutionaries would be forced 'to carry out the ideals of bourgeois capitalists'. They would then 'be assigned the honourable role of gradually organizing the forces of the proletariat, the role which the bourgeoisie offers very politely to all Second Internationals'.

According to the Bolshevik spokesmen, there was only one solution for the petty bourgeois elements in Russia: they had to choose the side of the proletariat, to accept the existing order and to undertake nothing against it. The PSR, according to Lunacharskii, had 'all the repulsiveness and the ludicrousness of a class which is not called upon to take a leading role: green and inexperienced as any hodgepodge, any job lot which thinks of taking up the struggle against spontaneous colossal revolutionary forces.' It was 'harmful' and therefore must be destroyed. That was also the reason for this trial.

Although the PSR did not signify very much, according to Krylenko, it was 'the only political grouping with which can affiliate the oppositional strata of the petty bourgeois democracy which is the avant-garde, the vanguard, behind which advance the heavy pha-lanxes of the international and of the Russian bourgeoisie.' Its exis-tence could therefore not be tolerated. The proletariat had to be pro-vided with maximum security. The communists, according to Bukha-rin, must 'close every flaw, every crack'.

In Bukharin's view, the Communist Party, as the party of the proletariat, was the only legitimate authority in Russia. In 'an iron age' only that party could exist and govern which worked as 'an iron mechanism'. 'Thanks to that mechanism', the Communist Party had defeated all its enemies and would further 'smash' them. In this way the Communist Party carried out the task that had been assigned to it by history: the destruction of capitalism as an economic system and of the bourgeoisie as ruling class, and the establishment of the proletarian dictatorship as 'an iron state power' and of the commu-nist system.

In this, the use of repression and of violence against political enemies were justified. The notion that socialism and violence were in conflict with each other was absurd, according to Krylenko. So-cialism could not even exist without violence. Marx, after all, had said that violence is the midwife when the old order becomes preg-nant of a new order.[3]

THE SOCIALIST REVOLUTIONARIES

The Socialist Revolutionaries were able to play a powerful trump card in their own defence: communist Rosa Luxemburg's opinion of the Bolsheviks. In 1918 Luxemburg had written a pamphlet entitled 'The Russian Revolution', which was published posthumously in 1922, shortly before the opening of the trial. In that pamphlet Luxemburg had condemned the dissolution of the Constituent Assembly by the Bolsheviks. Prior to October 1917 the Bolsheviks had demanded urgently that the Constituent Assembly should be convened. Once they had gained power, however, they had dissolved the Assembly with the argument that it had not kept up with the sentiments in the country. Luxemburg considered that the Bolshe-viks, if this was the view they held, ought to have held elections for a new Constituent Assembly. She acknowledged that democratic institutions have their limitations. But the method used by the Bolsheviks, i.e. the total liquidation of democracy, she considered to be even worse than the evil that it was intended to counteract. Without socialist democracy, i.e. without general elections, a free and unobstructed press, and freedom of speech, association and assembly, the rule of the broad masses of the people was quite inconceivable. 'Freedom only for the supporters of the government, only for the members of one party — however numerous they may be — is not freedom. Freedom can only mean the freedom of those of different beliefs.' If freedom became a privilege, it lost its effect. The bureaucracy had everything its own way, and a dictatorship would come into being. Not a dictatorship of the proletariat, but a dictatorship in the bourgeois sense, of a handful of politicians: a sort of Jacobin rule.[4]

When Abram Gots, in his address for the defence, quoted Luxemburg's opinion in support of his argument, Bukharin interrupted him, saying that she had 'wanted to burn that book'. Gots answered justifiably that that was a fabrication, but that he could quite understand that 'Bukharin would like to burn the book.'[5]

In their defence, the Socialist Revolutionary accused went into the conflict between their own party and the Bolsheviks. In their opinion, it was not the Socialist Revolutionaries, as contended in the Indictment, but on the contrary the Bolsheviks who were to blame for the civil war. In 1917 the Socialist Revolutionaries, by cooperating with the other socialists, had done their best to create the conditions in which socialism could be realized. The Bolsheviks had refused to cooperate, however, because they thought that they would immediately be able to accomplish a socialist revolution. That had proved impossible. As a result, they had fought not against the oppressors but against the other socialists. And behind the contending parties, as a derisive third, stood the bourgeoisie.

Initially, the Socialist Revolutionaries had not shown any particularly powerful resistance to the newly-established Bolshevik regime — in their eyes, an illegal regime. 'We were of the opinion that the Bolsheviks were mere foam on the waves of the revolution, which would disappear automatically', said Timofeev during the debates.[6] They had quickly desisted from any attempt to nullify the October Revolution with the use of arms, especially in view of the danger that threatened from the right. They had then started to direct their efforts towards isolating the Bolsheviks from the proletariat.

But when the Bolsheviks had dissolved the Constituent Assembly — the legal authority, in the eyes of the Socialist Revolutionaries — and had also concluded a separate peace with Germany, the PSR had at last seen no other way than that of violence. In May 1918, therefore, when the masses of the people had started to move (a necessary precondition in its view) in the Volga region, the PSR had decided to take up arms against both the Bolsheviks and the Germans.[7]

The attempt to overthrow the Soviet regime by force of arms, however, had failed as a result of the insincerity of the Russian bourgeoisie who had allowed its protégé Kolchak to inflict a treacherous blow on the party. Under these circumstances the PSR had decided to abandon armed struggle against the Bolsheviks.[8]

The accused then discussed the attitude which the Central Committee of the PSR had shown towards the Soviet regime after the suspension of armed conflict. The PSR, they argued, had not renounced its general right to armed combat. A political and revolutionary organization, in their opinion, could never completely waive its right to insurgency. Under no circumstances would the party support a movement directed against the Soviet regime, which was linked to counter-revolutionary elements, foreign powers, or bourgeois parties. It would be different if a spontaneous mass movement were to break out against the Soviet regime which had nothing to do with such influences. The Socialist Revolutionaries, as implacable opponents of the Bolsheviks, would then not fail to take their place at the head of such a movement.

In reply to Krylenko's question as to exactly what the party would do in such a case, Gots replied: 'In the first instance the PSR will intermediate between the government and the rebels, and in the second instance and in the most extreme case, it will choose the side of the rebels.'[9]

But even if the party had not renounced the right to armed resistance, since 1919 it had in practice found a political struggle more effective. The working class, according to the accused, had been destroyed by the Bolsheviks; the workers were 'de-classed', 'atomized'. The PSR now oriented itself towards 'organizing the broad working masses of town and country', in which the central point was the conquering of 'broad political liberties and democratic guarantees'. The PSR considered that when expression could be given to 'the will of the organized masses', the Bolsheviks would have to 'yield to the principles of democracy'. It was of the opinion that to provoke an armed revolt would only bring harm to the working class. Notwithstanding the persecution to which the party had been subjected under the rule of the Bolsheviks, it had not changed its tactics since 1919.

Agreement between the Socialist Revolutionaries and the Bolsheviks, however, was out of the question. The Socialist Revolutionaries would not be regretful if pressure by the working masses were to cause the fall of the Soviet regime; they were convinced, even, that the Bolsheviks ultimately would suffer defeat. In Gots's opinion, the working class would eventually manage to liberate itself. It would then depend on the Bolsheviks whether this would occur peacefully or violently. He hoped that the Bolsheviks would concede to the workers betimes; otherwise, a new civil war, with all its fatal consequences, would be inevitable. If the criminal terror of the Bolsheviks should cause the political struggle to end in a bloody collision, then they themselves would carry full responsibility.[10]

The accused went extensively into the issue of the totally different notions of the concepts 'freedom' and 'democracy' which, in their opinion, was the basis of their conflict with the Bolsheviks. Gots made grateful use of the criticisms uttered by Rosa Luxemburg against the Bolsheviks. Modelling himself on Luxemburg, he called the dissolution of the Constituent Assembly by the Bolsheviks 'a turning point in the history of the Russian Revolution'. Previously, the Bolsheviks had used the demand that the Constituent Assembly should be convened as a weapon in their attacks on the Provisional Government. They had professed democracy as long as they thought that they would be supported by a majority. Once they had realized that the majority of the workers opposed them, however, they had rejected democracy and had thrown overboard the principle of popular representation. Democracy, as prosecutor Krylenko himself had said, was after all not a fetish or an idol of the Bolsheviks. The same applied to political freedom. The Bolsheviks favoured it, as long as they could use it. But when they no longer needed it, they turned against it.

This was countered by the accused with the opinion held by the Socialist Revolutionaries, namely, that socialism could not be realized without freedom and democracy. And freedom meant freedom for all, not only for a few. Without freedom, without a workers mass

movement, and without self-activity by the working masses, socialism could not exist because, according to Gots, all these things
formed 'the heart of socialism'. The 'emancipation of the workers'
was 'an affair for the workers themselves'. If freedom existed only
for adherents of the government, it became a privilege.

According to Evgeniia Ratner, the Socialist Revolutionaries, 'just
as all European socialism', considered that the dictatorship of the
proletariat should be understood as 'the dictatorship of the majority
over a rebellious minority', and not vice versa. 'The dictatorship of
the working class', in the opinion of the accused, could 'not be expressed in the dictatorship of a party', a dictatorship *over* the working class.[11]

In Timofeev's opinion, the Socialist Revolutionaries advocated a
socialism 'which originates in the free development of the productive
forces in the country'. They rejected 'the military socialism' of the
Bolsheviks, a socialism 'which depends on the gun', which oppressed
the proletariat and thus, in essence, was not socialism. According to
Evgeniia Ratner, they did not consider the Soviet government as a
socialist government because, in their view, a regime of terror and socialism were incompatible.

Efrem Berg referred to the Soviet regime as 'the so-called workers
and peasants regime, which has atomized and ruined all workers in
Russia.' Gots pointed out that, although socialism needed an organized proletariat and a large industrial sector, the Bolsheviks had dis-
organized both industry and proletariat.

The accused turned against the 'false and twisted socialism' of the
Bolsheviks, 'permeated with terror and violence against the working
masses'. They arraigned the Bolsheviks for their policy of suppression
and tutelage of the workers and peasants. According to Arkadii
Al'tovskii, the Bolsheviks had 'altered all Russia into an enormous
forced labour prison for the people'. Mikhail Vedeniapin quoted
Lunacharskii, who had said that 'the communist regime will lead the
nation out of Egypt and through the desert into the promised land.'
According to Vedeniapin, it seemed more as though people had left
Egypt only to get stuck in the desert, where they were doomed to
perish.[12]

The accused also compared the internal structures of the Communist Party and of the PSR. Gots pointed out that in the Communist
Party even the freedom of its own members was not a matter of
course. Evgeniia Ratner drew attention to the fatal effect which

might be achieved by the strict disciplinarity of the Bolsheviks, their party's 'iron mechanism' which they praised so much. At the same time she denied that the PSR was a hodgepodge. It was true that the party, as a democratic non-sectarian party, included a number of currents. A party would die if there were no living exchange of ideas.[13]

Evgeniia Ratner accused the Bolsheviks that they had elevated the twisting of truth into a system, a system based on suppression of the freedom of the press and of speech. They had monopolized the truth and tolerated no contradiction. As example, Ratner named the way in which the Bolsheviks made use of Marx. To them, Marx was 'what the starry sky is to the astrologist, what the holy books are to the charlatan monk: a source on the basis of which theses can be proven even though they are in flagrant contradiction to each other, in which you can read exactly what you want to read.'[14]

The accused also criticized the New Economic Policy (NEP) which had been launched by the Bolsheviks in 1921. They pointed out that the PSR had argued much earlier for such an economic policy which would once again leave a certain amount of latitude to private initiative in trade and industry. But the PSR had also pointed out that the economic concessions made by the Bolsheviks in introducing the NEP, needed to be complemented with political concessions. The Bolsheviks, however, had refused categorically to do so.

The criticisms which the Socialist Revolutionaries uttered with regard to the NEP showed 'leftist' characteristics. The NEP encouraged the rise of a new trading and industrial class. This new bourgeoisie, according to Timofeev, was 'a thousand times more dangerous than the earlier bourgeoisie'. Part of the reason why it was so dangerous was that the working class could not organize itself without freedom and democracy, and therefore could not raise itself out of the decay and apathy in which it found itself. The new bourgeoisie of the NEP could even become a threat to the rule of the Communist Party.[15]

Evgeniia Ratner was prepared to admit that the Bolshevik regime would accomplish things which 'are historically progressive and historically necessary'. A revolution, after all, always advanced the cause of a nation. But that did not make their regime a socialist regime. The Bolsheviks were the first party to attempt to realize 'the ideals of the socialist system ..., about which the socialists have written and spoken for decades.' In this way they had 'gained control of all the socialist capital that the workers movement has amassed in the course of a century-long struggle.' Although from origin, therefore, they were not 'the party of the new Russian bourgeoisie', they were in effect becoming so.[16] Timofeev pointed out that the Jacobins, with whom Bukharin had compared the Bolsheviks in his rejoinder,[17] had brought 'the dominion of petty bourgeois virtues'.[18] But the Socialist Revolutionaries themselves did not compare the Bolsheviks with the Jacobins. They spoke about 'Thermidor', 'Directoire', 'the Eighteenth Brumaire', and 'Bonapartism'.[19] Evgeniia Ratner concluded, therefore, that it was the Communist Party which scandalously committed treason to socialism, because it wasted all the socialist capital over which it had gained control on a 'bourgeois cause.'[20]

Lev Gershtein predicted that the Bolshevik rule would lead 'not to socialism but to the most terrible reaction'. The lack of 'self-activity by the workers' meant that nothing stood in the way of 'the appearance of a general on a white horse'. When he spoke of 'reaction', he had in mind such people as Iurii Kliuchnikov, a former minister in the government of admiral Kolchak and now one of the leaders of the *Smena vekh* (A Changing of Landmarks) movement, which had propagated support to the Soviet regime since the introduction of the NEP. The accused considered that the greatest danger threatened from this particular corner. That was why, according to Gershtein, it made little sense for the Socialist Revolutionaries to fight the Bolsheviks. They should hold themselves ready as 'the revolution's reserve against the coming reaction in the person of Kliuchnikov and worse.'[21]

The Socialist Revolutionaries were not alone in their anticipation that, after the introduction of the NEP, the communist regime in Russia would become more and more bourgeois. Among the Russian intelligentsia of those days the idea of a future 'bourgeoisisation' of the regime was widespread. The accused made use of this during the trial to show that not they but the Bolsheviks were 'tools of the bourgeoisie', that not the Bolsheviks but they were the better socialists.

During the trial the Socialist Revolutionaries stressed their loyalty to the Soviet regime in the field of international relations. In Timofeev's words, as long as a fight for power was in process in Russia, the PSR had agitated against recognition abroad of the Soviet government.

Once the struggle had been determined in favour of the Bolsheviks, however, it had agreed with the recognition of the Soviet regime 'not only *de facto*, but also *de jure*.' According to Gots, the PSR defended 'the interests of Russia as a whole, by whichever government it is administered' against 'international rapacity'. The Socialist Revolutionaries also wanted capitalist Europe to recognize the Soviet government. If that government were not to be recognized − principally through the Bolsheviks' own fault − that would lead to 'the most terrible forms of subjugation of Russia to international capital'. The objective of the Socialist Revolutionaries was to combat all forms of intervention and blockade, including the camouflaged ones, and to cooperate with the Soviet government in the fight against the 'rapacious demands of foreign capital'.[22]

THE SECOND GROUP

'It is time to recognize that the principle of people's sovereignty, that the ideas of democratism, are not bringing us any nearer to the radiant idea of socialism, on the contrary, are alienating us from it, that they cannot guarantee power to the workers and the peasants. The only form of power which can give such a guarantee is the dictatorship of the workers and the peasants.' So wrote the former Socialist Revolutionary, N.V. Makarochkin, in an open letter published in *Pravda* on 12th July 1922. Similar opinions were expressed during the trial by the accused of the second group. In their own way, they also participated in the political debate during the trial. The Bolsheviks had allotted them the role of representatives of the rank-and-file members of the PSR, who were considered to have left the party *en masse* after having realized that they had allowed themselves to be misguided by the party leaders. 'Their teachers', according to one of their defenders, Anastasiia Bitsenko (herself a former Left Socialist Revolutionary) had taught them that 'the Constituent Assembly should be considered as holy', that 'this idol, the Constituent Assembly, must be defended unconditionally when attempts are made to break it', that 'general suffrage is a right that must always be defended.' And they had put their trust in those principles.[23]

But if they had realized that they had been misguided, why had they stayed in the PSR for so long? Grigorii Ratner gave as the principal reason 'the colossal power, the hypnosis exercised by old viewpoints and concepts', from which it was not so easy to dissociate oneself. It was different for the Bolsheviks, according to Ratner. They had never tied themselves down to such concepts as people's sovereignty and civic freedom, had from the beginning considered such things as instruments and not as objectives. For him and his fellow converts, however, the notion of the people's sovereignty had been 'almost a fetish', 'the absolute', which 'was not tied to time or to transitional periods'. The 'hypnotic force of old ideas', further strengthened by 'the hypnosis of the party leaders in whom we believed, whose capability could not be disparaged in our view', had then caused them to remain in the PSR.[24]

For these reasons, too, according to Fedor Zubkov, they had seen the Bolsheviks as 'usurpers', as 'stranglers of the revolution', and had taken up the fight against them at the side of their party comrades in defence of the Constituent Assembly. But when they had later ascertained that 'Kolchak and his band of monarchists' had acted under the PSR flag, they had broken permanently with the party.[25]

Konstantin Usov called the dissolution of the Constituent Assembly 'an act carried out in the interests of the working class', even though he had not understood it as such at the time.[26] The Constituent Assembly had not expressed 'the opinion and will of the revolutionary majority'. 'Only the petty bourgeois' had voted for the PSR, 'elements that did not carry in themselves the spirit of the revolution and which could not make revolutions.' That was why the Constituent Assembly was 'easily dispersed'. That was also why Usov and his fellows had subsequently left the PSR.[27]

According to Semenov, the revolutionary elements had turned their backs *en masse* on the PSR and had chosen the side of the communists. According to Fedor Efimov, the PSR leaders had betrayed their revolutionary principles. Iosif Dashevskii pointed out that the Socialist Revolutionaries and the Populists initially had not wanted a bourgeois revolution, but rather a social revolution of the workers and the peasants against the bourgeois system. In his view, the activities of the PSR since 1917 had repudiated those principles.[28]

At an earlier stage of the trial, Grigorii Ratner also discussed the ideology of the PSR. He compared the activist policies of the party's 'adventurist' elements (e.g. Semenov and his group in 1918) with the 'careful' policies oriented towards the masses, which the Central Committee had advocated, according to the accused of the first group. Ratner pointed out that the Socialist Revolutionaries had always given pride of place to 'the critically thinking individual' and to 'the rights of the leading minority'. If the consciousness of the masses was not given sufficient and clear expression, the PSR had always attempted to arouse and to fashion it through its own actions. Ratner therefore wondered since when the former theory had been exchanged for the 'Menshevik-fatalistic-Tolstoian reasonings' which Gots and his colleagues now expressed. In his view, Semenov and his fellows had acted according to PSR tradition. But the party leaders, double-faced as they were, had in fact always set their heart on armed struggle with the Soviet regime, in cooperation with the rightist elements, said Ratner: 'Because, according to the theory held by the Central Committee, the "order" of the Black Hundreds was far preferable to the "anarchy" of the Bolsheviks.'[29]

SOME WEAKNESSES OF SOCIALIST REVOLUTIONARY POLICIES

The policy followed by the leaders of the PSR since the October Revolution of 1917 was characterized by a certain intrinsic contradiction which hindered their defence of it when they were brought to trial in 1922. That contradiction was the fact that although they condemned the Bolshevik regime in no uncertain terms, they showed great hesitation when it came to actual revolt against that regime.

We have seen that the Bolsheviks blamed the hesitation by the Socialist Revolutionary leaders on their 'duplicity': they had encouraged acts of resistance, but had attempted to conceal this so that they could shirk their responsibility. There seems to be no reason, however, to accuse the Socialist Revolutionaries of insincerity. Apart from feelings of impotence, their doubts were caused by genuine fear of 'the reaction' and by their conviction that the initiative for resistance to the Bolshevik regime must come from the 'working masses', and that the party should abstain from any intervention until those masses had started to move.[30] This attitude was expressed clearly by the witness Aleksandr El'iashevich, who in the past had been a prominent member of the Socialist Revolutionary fraction in the Constituent Assembly. El'iashevich declared that, during the first few months after the October Revolution, the Socialist Revolutionaries had not called for an overthrow of the Soviet regime. Why not? 'Not because we considered the overthrow of the Soviet regime to be an inadmissible act, but because in those days we took the view that a revolt of the masses must come from below, that a fight for the people's sovereignty needed to develop spontaneously from below. The Socialist Revolutionaries merely tried to give a lead to the spontaneous dissatisfaction of the masses.'[31]

The Socialist Revolutionaries gave similar explanations when their policy as regards the *Komuch* came up for discussion. They stated that the *Komuch* had been formed spontaneously by the workers and peasants who had rebelled against Bolshevik policies. But, declared Gendel'man, the people's masses had not sufficiently realized that the system that they had created also had to be defended. That was why the *Komuch* had fallen.[32]

This complaint that the masses had not started to move was not merely an excuse for the failure of their own policies. It was rooted in their belief in the people, in 'the masses' from whom, in the opinion of the Socialist Revolutionary leaders, the initiative for resistance to the Bolsheviks that was to have any likelihood of success, must, and would inevitably, be launched. This belief contributed to the considerable inactivity shown by the Socialist Revolutionaries during the civil war and to what was in many respects an attitude of loyalty towards the Soviet regime.

One of the consequences of this non-interference on the part of the leaders was that many of its adherents turned their backs on the PSR in frustration. On the one hand were those who ignored the warnings of the party leaders and took part in 'isolated' rebellious movements such as that led by Antonov in Tambov, which had actively fought against the Soviet regime. On the other hand, people such as Grigorii Ratner had chosen the side of the Bolsheviks who, other than the Socialist Revolutionary leaders, had not remained inactive.

Not every disappointed Socialist Revolutionary went over lock, stock and barrel to the Bolsheviks, as did Ratner. Many withdrew from politics altogether and worked under the Soviet regime in the service of their country and people. One of these was Nikolai Kondrat'ev, the famous economist, who had been a member of the right wing of the PSR. During the trial Kondrat'ev declared as a witness that he had left the party at that time (early 1920) because he was disappointed with its position. He was 'an evolutionist'; many points of departure in the Socialist Revolutionary ideology were in his view 'utopian', and the party strategy was 'inconsistent and indecisive'. The PSR, according to Kondrat'ev, 'under-estimated the roots of Bolshevism, and its endeavour to overthrow the Soviet regime thus was not sufficiently well-grounded.'[33]

CHAPTER 7

THE VERDICT AND HOW IT WAS BROUGHT ABOUT

THE ADDRESSES FOR THE PROSECUTION AND THE DEFENCE, AND THE CLOSING ADDRESSES BY THE ACCUSED

On 27 July the final phase of the trial started in which the prosecutors held their speeches for the prosecution, the defenders their speeches for the defence, and the accused had the opportunity to give their closing addresses.

As we have seen earlier, there were six prosecutors: three Russians and three foreigners, the latter having been appointed by the Comintern. Of the six, Chief Prosecutor Nikolai Krylenko was the last to speak, preceded by Anatolii Lunacharskii, Mikhail Pokrovskii and Alois Muna on 27 July, and by Dezső Bokányi and Clara Zetkin on 28 July. Zetkin's speech was later published in expanded form under the title *Wir klagen an!*

Clara Zetkin said outrightly that the trial was not 'a purely judicial' but a 'political affair', in which legal formulae could not be the decisive factor. The right of the proletarian revolution in Soviet Russia and in the whole world to defend itself would have to be the decisive factor. In Zetkin's view, the accused were guilty not because of what they had done, but because of the purpose in whose name they had done it. That purpose, the overthrow of the proletarian dictatorship, gave the activities of the Socialist Revolutionaries their 'criminal character'. She considered that the Tribunal, as protector of the proletariat in the international class conflict against the bourgeoisie, was in duty bound to pronounce a severe sentence against the Socialist Revolutionaries.[1]

On 28 and 29 July, Chief Prosecutor Nikolai Krylenko gave his speech for the prosecution which lasted 18 hours. In his own speech a few days later, Bukharin praised 'the really brilliant expressive power' and 'the exceptional revolutionary fervour' with which Krylenko had put forth his arguments.[2] Gendel'man, on the other hand, complained about 'the tragic whisper and the ominous rattle'

brought forth by Krylenko.[3] When Krylenko discussed the attack on
'Vladimir Il'ich', he did in fact give the impression that his feelings
were too much for him. He drew attention to the absolute necessity
of Lenin's 'clear intellect' and 'iron will' for the Russian and the
international revolution, and to the consequences of what he called
the terrible deed of the Socialist Revolutionaries which were still
felt 'up to the present day' — an obvious allusion to the stroke that
Lenin recently had suffered and which had caused him to retire for
some time from political life.[4]

Like the other prosecutors, Krylenko emphasized the demonstrative significance of the trial. It had informed the Russian workers and
peasants about all the secret misdemeanours of the Socialist Revolutionaries, and given the people the opportunity to form their own
opinion regarding the hypocrisy of the Socialist Revolutionaries, in
which they had persisted even during the trial.[5] But although the
trial had shown the Socialist Revolutionaries in their true colours to
the broad working masses of Russia, this could not suffice. Millions
of Russian workers and peasants had had to pay with their lives for
the deeds of the accused, who now had to settle the account for all
that suffering and bloodshed. Proletarian justice was not to be trifled
with, and would not allow itself to be thwarted by the agitation of
the international bourgeoisie and its pseudo-socialist spongers of the
Second International.[6]

The Soviet regime had now been fighting for its existence for five
years, exerting itself to the utmost, and in all that time the accused
had done everything possible to make things difficult for the regime.
The *Cheka* could have got even with them but had not done so, and
the accused had thus been able to get away with it. They had now
been given a trial that was surrounded by all possible legal guarantees. But they had made use of those legal guarantees to declare publicly that in future they would continue their injurious and criminal
activities. People should thus be under no illusion: the Socialist
Revolutionaries would always form a united front with the bourgeoisie against the Soviet regime. The accused had not changed in all
these five years. And with great sarcasm, Krylenko compared them
with Baron von Grünwaldus in Koz'ma Prutkov's[7] 'German Ballad':
the knight of the rueful countenance who, year after year, languished
beneath the window of his Amalia, who had spurned his love. The
Socialist Revolutionaries were just such quixotic knights who, as
Krylenko made it plain, had for years been waiting for the moment

when the people would come to them. But the people had spurned them.

At the end of his long-winded address, in which he once again reviewed all the accusations against the Socialist Revolutionaries, Krylenko urged that the Tribunal, in passing sentence, should not allow itself to be influenced by the thought of what coming generations ('history's court') would say, but only by what was good for the Soviet Republic. To communists, that should be the supreme law, to which all else should be subordinated.

Krylenko then formulated his demands. The other prosecutors had required punishment of the Socialist Revolutionaries only in general terms, but Krylenko had very exact demands for each of the accused. Surprisingly enough, however, he made no demands as regards the accused of the second group who, in his opinion, had been of great help to the Tribunal. In the Soviet legal system, punishment was not intended as revenge, but as a means with which to prevent future crimes. There were thus ways by which the severity of the sentences applicable to the accused of the second group could be reduced. The Tribunal's point of departure must be whether or not socially-dangerous elements were involved.

Krylenko demanded 'the highest penalty' for the accused of the first group. 'There can only be one verdict: the bullet for all without exception, for all the crimes, for all the bloodshed, for all the horrors, for all the suffering, for all the hardships, which we have had to undergo during the last five years and which these people have deliberately inflicted upon the Republic', said Krylenko. In addition to all that, the accused had testified that in future they would continue to exert all their strength in an effort to injure the Soviet regime. 'Through our suffering we have won the right to self-defence and self-protection against our enemies. I demand the highest penalty.'[8] When Krylenko thus ended his speech for the prosecution at two o'clock in the night, loud applause broke out in the courtroom.[9]

The speeches for the defence started on 31 July. In view of the fact that the defenders of the accused of the first group had withdrawn, a few of the accused took upon themselves the task of addressing the court in defence of the group: Mikhail Gendel'man and Evgenii Timofeev on 31 July, and Abram Gots, Evgeniia Ratner and Dmitrii Rakov on 1 August.

In his plea, Gendel'man in turn accused the prosecutors of hypocrisy. Krylenko had demanded the death penalty, with the argument that the Soviet Republic had to be protected against the accused, who did not repudiate rebellion. That was a lie in which the Bolsheviks themselves did not believe. The real reason why Krylenko had demanded the death penalty was that the Bolsheviks wanted to put a spoke in the wheels of the Second International and the Vienna Union, who had sprung to the aid of the Socialist Revolutionaries.[10]

Gendel'man and Timofeev both forcefully rejected all attempts by the Bolsheviks to induce the accused to show repentance, to renounce their political past, and to subjugate themselves to the Soviet regime. The accused were not cowards who deserted in the hour of danger. In that regard, the Bolsheviks might consider them as 'unrepentant recidivists'. 'Your way is not our way', said Timofeev. 'We continue to stand on the side of the people whom you call social traitors.'[11]

Gendel'man and Gots finished their addresses for the defence by drawing attention to the positive aspects of the trial. Gendel'man considered that the trial had offered the imprisoned Socialist Revolutionaries a good opportunity to defend the PSR, socialism and the revolution, and to unmask the Bolshevik dictatorship before the eyes of the Russian and the international working class. Gots was grateful to the Bolsheviks for offering the Socialist Revolutionary leaders whose imprisonment had cut them off from all political activities for more than two years, 'a platform' from which they could address themselves to the working class and to the party. Over the heads of the prosecutors they had used that platform 'to report to the working class about our activities in the past, about the involuntary mistakes that were unavoidable in a revolutionary crisis', and 'to tell them our thoughts about possible ways by which to save the revolution.' If death now awaited the accused then, according to Gots, they would 'die as revolutionaries' and would look death 'straight in the eye, without fear.' If they should stay alive, then they would use all their strength 'to fight further as socialists, on behalf of the interests of the working class.'[12]

Then followed the speeches by the defenders of the second group: on 1 August that by Semen Chlenov, and on 2 August those by P. Shubin, Feliks Kon, Anastasiia Bitsenko, Ruben Katanian, V. Veger, Nikolai Bukharin and Jacques Sadoul. In effect, however, these speeches were more like denunciations of the accused of the first group. Chlenov, for example, started by declaring that he had to deviate from the unwritten rule which forbade defending counsels to plea for their clients at the cost of other accused, because the accused of the first group wanted to shift the blame onto those of the second group. He argued that the accused of the first group saw the Tribunal as a hostile institution and therefore did not consider themselves obliged to tell the truth. Anyone who aimed at being a good party member did not relate 'what has happened', but 'what is necessary to rehabilitate the party and to preserve it from destruction by the *Cheka* and the Tribunal'. Whoever contravened these 'directives' and reported facts that were denied by the Central Committee, was consequently a traitor in the eyes of the Central Committee.[13] Shubin explained that to defend Semenov entailed proving 'that everything written in his pamphlet is the truth' and that the accused of the first group were lying.[14]

Chlenov contested the insinuation that the trial had been stage-managed by the *Cheka* which manipulated the accused of the second group as its pawns. In his view, the very fact that the accused of the first group were able to score 'cheap triumphs' from contradictions in the statements by members of the second group was evidence against such a notion. If the *Cheka* had really wanted to stage-manage a trial then, according to Chlenov, it would have been absolutely watertight.[15]

All defenders of the second group asked for understanding and leniency. They alluded to 'the inner fight' which their clients had had to conduct during the last few years, the 'painful developments' which they had experienced. Chlenov spoke of the 'enormous personal tragedy' of a person such as Konopleva who, for the sake of the revolution, had joined the party against which she had first raised her hand and who, in order to fulfil her duty as a revolutionary, had exposed her former party. Bukharin emphasized that the accused of the second group had done useful work for the international proletarian revolution. With these and similar arguments, the defenders appealed to the Tribunal for acquittal for these accused, who not only were no longer a danger to the revolution but who, on the contrary, would be of benefit to it. According to Bukharin, this was also the desire of the workers who had taken part in the public demonstration on 20 June. The defenders also asked the Tribunal to rehabilitate these accused in their revolutionary honour and to pronounce them worthy to return to the ranks of the proletariat.

Although he did not deviate further from the general trend, Sadoul did strike a somewhat different note on one point. He considered that, although the Tribunal was indeed responsible for the security of the Soviet Republic, it should not be out for revenge. The revolution — synonym for the Soviet regime — according to Sadoul, had 'not established the terror for all eternity'. Blood should not be shed needlessly.[16]

Krylenko was not in entire agreement with the defenders of the second group. In his replication he said that although the law might allow reduced sentences for the accused of the second group, it did not allow acquittal. He maintained his demand against the accused of the first group: 'Wherever you look, you see the same thing. In the future it will be the same as in the past: blood and yet more blood. That is what is so terrible. That is why blood must be shed here in cold blood, so that in the future no blood at all, or at least less blood will flow.'[17]

On 4 August, when the accused of the first group were given the opportunity to make their closing addresses to the court, Piatakov asked them to expound 'how they would act if — in a hypothetical case — they should be released from prison.' According to Piatakov, it was 'exceptionally important' that the Tribunal, in drawing up its verdict, 'should know whether the accused would continue the fight against the Soviet regime, and the manner in which they would do so.'[18]

If it was Piatakov's intention to sow dissension among the accused with this question, then he was not successful. They retained their unity and declared that they would remain faithful to their party and would not subjugate themselves to the Bolsheviks.

In their attempts to create discord among the accused, the Bolsheviks set their hopes in particular on Mikhail Vedeniapin. Judging by his reaction to the conference of the PSR held in September 1920,[19] which was recorded in the files, Vedeniapin was opposed to any armed struggle against the Bolsheviks. The Indictment mentioned this reaction on his part, as did Shubin, Bukharin and Kon in their speeches for the defence. Feliks Kon drew attention to the difference between people such as Gendel'man and Gots, and a man like Vedeniapin. In his closing address to the court, however, Vedeniapin took exception to these efforts to separate him from his fellow accused. 'Bukharin may have my head', he said, 'but I will not allow anyone

ever to throw the slightest blemish on my honour as a revolutionary.'
He declared that he would remain at the side of his comrades 'until
the end'.[20]

A number of the accused discussed the character of the trial in
their closing addresses. In Evgeniia Ratner's opinion, the Bolsheviks
were using the trial to scatter poisonous seed in the hearts of those
whom they liked to call the undeveloped elements. 'The spiritual
rape which you are exercising here under the lable of "the educative
role of the trial" is your greatest crime', said Ratner. She thought,
however, that in the last analysis, the people would not allow itself
to be misled.[21]

Nikolai Artem'ev considered the trial to be an 'historical' event in
two respects. Firstly, because it had brought to light 'the gigantic and
heroic struggle of democracy, led by the PSR in the name of socialism'. Secondly, it was an historical event 'because, for the first time,
the Communist Party has moved towards a bloody settlement with
its socialist opponents by legal means'. With the death penalty that
had been demanded against the accused, the communists were starting 'a new era of bloody violence', an era of legal terror. A militant
revolutionary and socialist must always be prepared for death, according to Artem'ev, who declared that the accused would accept
the death sentence 'with pride'.[22]

As the last speaker of the first group, Abram Gots pointed out
that the Bolsheviks considered themselves entitled to judge the Socialist Revolutionaries because they were the victors. In their turn,
victors were often judged cruelly by 'history's court'. At this
moment, however, the Socialist Revolutionaries could confront the
right of the victor with nothing other than the knowledge that they
had 'moral and political right' on their side. They did not wish to
enter into an 'agreement with the victors' and, as the price for not
doing so, they now had to enter into an 'agreement with death'. With
'the courage of revolutionaries', however, they knew how to look
death 'straight in the eyes'.[23]

The Socialist Revolutionary accused were not really the last to speak
at the trial; that right was given to the accused of the second group
on 5 August. These were far less united than the first group, although
this was not allowed to show externally. In her closing address to the
court, Elena Ivanova of the first group called people such as Semenov
and Konopleva cheaters. In her opinion, however, this qualification

did not apply to Fedorov-Kozlov and Zubkov who merely had submitted to pressure. Zubkov said in reply that he did not accept Ivanova's forgiveness. Fedorov-Kozlov's reaction to Ivanova is not known because his closing address is not to be found in any report of the trial.

In accordance with the image that had to be created, the members of the second group professed, in their closing addresses, the creed of the convert who has settled with the past (although they contended simultaneously that *they* represented the original Socialist Revolutionary principles and that these had been betrayed by the leaders of the PSR).

According to Iosif Dashevskii, ethical norms were not absolute but were linked to class, time, etc. The Central Committee of the PSR had turned away from the revolution and from socialism, and the 'moral obligations' of the former Socialist Revolutionaries to their previous party comrades had therefore had to make way for 'the new ethical categorical imperatives' of socialism and of the revolution. Those imperatives had demanded that Dashevskii and his fellows should tell 'the truth' about the enemies of the revolution and of socialism.[24]

Faina Stavskaia said that the attitude of her former party comrades during the trial had strengthened her conviction that at the beginning of the revolution she had committed 'criminal activities' together with them, that she had been in 'a morass'. But her greatest crime, in her opinion, was that she had not done much earlier what she had now done during the trial, on behalf of the revolution.[25]

Grigorii Semenov considered that he had achieved his objective, the exposure of the PSR. It had been his duty to pursue that goal because for the revolutionary there could be 'only one highest moral', namely, to serve the revolution. He regretted that he had not made his revelations much sooner. His own trial, according to Semenov, had begun far earlier than the trial in which he now took part. That trial, 'the trial of the revolutionary conscience', had started in 1919 when he had realized 'the utter criminality' of his former activities in the PSR. In time, the members of the Central Committee would also have to stand before 'that tribunal' (i.e. of 'the revolutionary conscience'). They would then come to understand 'how difficult, how immeasurably difficult it is for a revolutionary to realize the criminal character of his deeds.' The fact that he was Volodarskii's 'murderer', that he had perhaps shortened the lifespan of 'the leader of world socialism, Il'ich' by many years, would haunt him for the rest of his days. The Tribunal's verdict would not alter the fact that already he was punished severely by his own conscience, which had condemned him.[26]

As we have seen, the last speaker, Grigorii Ratner, declared that, on behalf of the revolution, a man could send even his own sister to the scaffold, by which he referred to his 'former sister' Evgeniia Ratner. He called the trial 'an enormous tragedy' both for the accused of the first group who had had to demonstrate 'the historical death' of the PSR (he referred to the party as a corpse that was already in a state of decomposition), and for those of the second group who, 'with unbelievable pain and difficulty' had had to make a radical break with their past. The latter, according to Ratner, had had no intention of turning this tragedy into 'a vaudeville for lawyers'.

In Ratner's opinion, the accused of the first group were blind. They had surrounded themselves with 'a mist of phrases, words and out-of-date concepts' and consequently had not seen 'the enormous new cultural force' which was making its appearance. They saw only the externalities, only 'those forms of dictatorship which must cause distress to them'. 'And their personal embitterment prevents them from seeing the enormous cultural regeneration of the working class which already shows the radiance of a colossal new culture, a new state and a new spiritual life.'[27]

According to *Golos Rossii*, after the accused had made their closing addresses, Piatakov once again asked the accused of the first group to tell the Tribunal, before this retired to consider its verdict, what their attitude would be towards the Soviet regime if that verdict should exempt them from punishment. Timofeev replied that the accused had explained their position in their closing addresses, and that they stood by that position.[28] Thereupon, on Saturday, 5 August, at eight o'clock in the evening, the Tribunal retired to deliberate on its verdict.

THE VERDICT

On the evening of Monday, 7 August, approximately 48 hours after having retired to deliberate on the sentence, the Tribunal pronounced its verdict. Inside and outside the House of the Trade Unions the guard had been reinforced substantially that evening, ostensibly to prevent any demonstrations by those who sympathized with the accused. A line of soldiers was drawn up between the platform and the public. The accused of the first group were brought into the courtroom, escorted by a strong guard, but were presently taken away again when they refused to stand while sentence was pronounced.[29]

The verdict first listed the names of the accused, emphasizing the fact that many of them were of well-to-do family and had enjoyed a university education. It spoke of the PSR as the 'Party of the so-called "Socialist Revolutionaries".' The PSR was not a socialist but a bourgeois party, 'a counter-revolutionary party of enemies of the people [*vragi naroda*]', which called itself socialist in order to deceive the masses.

The principal Article which the Tribunal wielded against the 22 accused of the first group was Article 60 of the new Penal Code, according to which membership was punishable of any organization whose activities were oriented towards perpetration of the crimes that were listed in Articles 57, 58 and 59. Article 57 described as counter-revolutionary all activities that were oriented towards the overthrow of the Soviet regime, as well as all those that were intended to provide support to that part of the international bourgeoisie which did not acknowledge the equality before the law of the communist system, and which strove to achieve its overthrow by means of blockade, espionage, financing of the press, etc. Article 58 listed as actionable the organization of, and participation in, armed conflict with counter-revolutionary objectives. And Article 59 made actionable the maintaining of contacts with foreign powers or their representatives with the purpose of persuading them to take up arms against the Soviet Republic, as well as the providing of support to foreign powers who were in armed conflict with the Soviet Republic. Articles 58 and 59 as well as 60 provided the death penalty as maximum sentence. In this case the Tribunal considered the PSR as a criminal organization within the meaning of Article 60.

The Tribunal pronounced the death sentence over twelve accused of the first group. With regard to the eight members of the Central Committee among those twelve — Donskoi, Gendel'man, Gershtein, Gots, Ivanov, Likhach, Evgeniia Ratner and Timofeev — the Tribunal applied Articles 57 to 60, and also Articles 65 (sabotage activities) and 76-2 (complicity in expropriations, etc.). With regard to Donskoi, Gershtein and Gots, the Tribunal also applied Article 64 (participation in acts of terrorism on representatives of the Soviet regime); with regard to Ivanov, Evgeniia Ratner and Timofeev, Article 68 (complicity in such actions); and finally, with respect to Donskoi, Article 76-1 (organization of, and participation in, expropriations, etc.).

In addition to these eight members of the Central Committee, the Tribunal sentenced to death Agapov, Al'tovskii, Ivanova and Morozov (the latter was also a member of the Central Committee, but only since 1919). Article 60 was applied to all four; to Agapov also Article 65; to Morozov Article 68; and to Ivanova Articles 64 and 76.

The Tribunal passed prison sentences of varying lengths on the other ten accused of the first group. With regard to Central Committee members Fedorovich, Rakov and Vedeniapin the Tribunal applied — similar to those of their colleagues who were sentenced to death — Articles 57 to 60, 65 and 76-2; moreover, Article 68 was applied to Vedeniapin. 'In view of the contents of their closing addresses to the court' (to which we shall return), however, they were given ten-year prison sentences.

Liberov and Artem'ev were also given ten-year sentences, both on the basis of Article 60, and Artem'ev also on the basis of Article 68. Article 60 was also applied to Utgof, Berg and L'vov, but 'in view of the small extent of the counter-revolutionary activities perpetrated by them', they were sentenced to five years imprisonment. Zlobin and Gor'kov were also found by the Tribunal to be punishable on the basis of Article 60. For both, however, the 'small extent of the counter-revolutionary activities perpetrated by them' was taken into account; for Zlobin, moreover, 'his conscientious work in Soviet institutions' and for Gor'kov his principled rejection of armed conflict were allowed for. They were given sentences of two and three years imprisonment, respectively.

The twelve accused of the second group were not charged under Article 60; this was due to the February 1919 amnesty which was said to apply to them because they had left the PSR. Article 60 did not apply to Ignat'ev, even without the 1919 amnesty, because he had not been a member of the PSR. Terrorist activities, however, were not considered to be covered by the amnesty.

Three of the twelve were sentenced to death by the court: Semenov and Konopleva on the basis of Articles 64 and 76; Ignat'ev on Articles 58, 59, 65, 66, 69 and 70. Efimov was given a ten-year prison sentence on the basis of Articles 64, 68 and 76. Fedorov-Kozlov, Usov and Zubkov were sentenced by the Tribunal, on the basis of the same Articles, to five years imprisonment, allowance being made for 'their non-leading role' in the crimes and 'their proletarian origins'. Pelevin was sentenced to three years on the basis of Articles 68 and 76. Dashevskii was given the same punishment on the basis of Articles 64, 68 and 76-2, the 'small extent' of the crimes perpetrated by him being taken into account. Stavskaia was given two years imprisonment on the basis of Article 68. Finally, Grigorii Ratner and Morachevskii were released by the Tribunal, although it considered Article 68 to be applicable to Ratner.

The Tribunal asked the Presidium of the VTsIK to pardon all accused of the second group because they had seen and acknowledged the iniquity of their crimes and had broken with their past.[30]

After the reading of the verdict — according to *Golos Rossii* — a secretary of the Tribunal visited the accused of the first group with the proposal that they submit a request to the VTsIK to change their death sentences into terms of imprisonment. Their spokesmen, Gots and Timofeev, however, answered that under no circumstances would the accused submit such a request for a pardon or for reduction of the sentence. The condemned Socialist Revolutionaries were then taken away in a prison van, accompanied by an exceptionally strong guard of mounted and motorized soldiers who held their weapons at the ready. Instead of the prison where they had been kept for the duration of the trial, they were taken to the prison on the Lubianka, which created the impression that they were to be executed immediately after pronouncement of the sentence.[31]

The next day, 8 August, the Presidium of the VTsIK published its findings. In its opinion, the trial had proven once again that, in the conflict between capitalism and the proletariat, the PSR had taken the side of capitalism and, in doing so, had committed the most terrible crimes against the revolution and the workers. The PSR still represented 'an embittered enemy which, notwithstanding the insignificance of its political influence in the country, can imply a great danger even in future, as a tool in the hands of the still powerful world capitalism.' The trial itself had given rise to 'a new crusade by imperialism with its social-democratic support against the Soviet Republic and its friends all over the world'. 'In the name of "justice", "humanity" and "mercy", the bourgeoisie of the Churchills, the Noulens's, the Giolittis, and the lackeys of this bourgeoisie, want to defend the right of its agents to organize revolts, to murder the leaders of the Soviet Republic, to blow up bridges and warehouses, to poison and to disorganize the Red Army and the Red Fleet, and to carry out military espionage on the instructions of the staffs of imperialism.'

During the trial, according to the Presidium, the imperialist bourgeoisie, by means of its servants the social democrats, had managed to persuade a considerable part of the working class to take up the defence of the Socialist Revolutionaries. Although, on the one hand, the Presidium completely endorsed 'the legitimacy and the revolutionary appropriateness' of the Tribunal's judgement, on the other hand it made allowances for 'the presence of these underdeveloped strata of the international working class, who are intimidated by the bourgeoisie and misled by social democracy'. In this case, the Presidium found that its task was 'to give the workers a clear lesson of revolutionary action'. It had decided, therefore, to confirm the verdict against the twelve members of the first group who had been condemned to death, but 'to suspend its enforcement'. This entailed the following:

If the PSR will effectively cease its underground, conspiratorial, terrorist activities against the regime of workers and peasants, oriented towards military espionage and revolt, it will thereby safeguard its leading members who have guided those activities in the past and who, during the actual trial, have reserved to themselves the right to continue those activities, from [the enforcement of] the highest penalty.
On the other hand, if the PSR pursues methods of armed conflict against the workers' and peasants' regime, this will lead unavoidably to the execution of the condemned inspirers and organizers of counter-revolutionary terror and rebellion.

The Tribunal's recommendation that the members of the second group should be pardoned was agreed to by the Presidium of the VTsIK.[32]

The Tribunal sentenced the accused on the basis of the Penal Code which had come into force in 1922, thus ignoring the principle of *nulla poena sine lege*: the accused were condemned on the basis of Articles which only became law shortly before the trial and long after the perpetration of the incriminating activities.

Secondly, the Tribunal condemned the accused for activities for which they had been given amnesty in 1919, taking as its point of departure that that February 1919 amnesty applied only to those who had broken their links with the PSR. This interpretation was not in agreement with the terms of the amnesty, however vaguely these may have been formulated.

Even apart from these two rudimentary defects, however, various criticisms can be made from the legal viewpoint. This has already been noted in the chapter on the judicial investigation with regard to the assessment of guilt. The most obvious defect was that the court condemned a number of the accused of the first group (in particular Donskoi, Gershtein, Gots and Ivanova) partly on the basis of Articles that referred to the perpetration of terror, although the judicial investigation had shown no evidence whatsoever of participation or complicity by these accused in acts of terror. The Tribunal thus did not seek the truth but rather to feed the propaganda machine, which the sentences enabled to depict the Socialist Revolutionaries as murderers.

In effect, the Tribunal condemned the accused on the basis of Article 60, which penalized the membership of any organization that carried arms against the Soviet regime with the intention of bringing about its overthrow. In 1918, i.e. four years prior to the trial, the PSR had indeed fought the Soviet regime with the use of arms. That was a generally known fact and had never been denied. But it should be noted that when the Socialist Revolutionaries had fought the Bolsheviks in 1918 it was not a case of resistance by a rebellious opposition to an established government, but a fight between two parties in a civil war. From the constitutional point of view, the Bolsheviks were then the rebels. After all, in October 1917 they had overthrown the sitting government and in January 1918 had dissolved the Constituent Assembly; the Socialist Revolutionaries, on the other hand, had supported the legal government and the Constituent Assembly.

Whatever the case, a trial of such magnitude was not needed in order to prove that the PSR had fought the Soviet regime in 1918 with the use of arms. In this respect, the Tribunal's conclusion was quite out of proportion to the scale of the trial, and a lot of fuss had been made unnecessarily.

That was not the point, however. The intention of the Bolsheviks in holding the trial was to show that, even after 1918, the Socialist Revolutionaries had continued to aim at the overthrow of the Soviet regime with the use of arms. The verdict pronounced at the trial against the principal leaders of the Socialist Revolutionaries could be used by the propaganda as proof that this had indeed been the case. That the Tribunal in no way furnished legal and convincing evidence to that effect was of minor importance. It was the sentence that counted.

Entirely in accordance with the wishes of Lenin, the trial had a propagandist objective. It had to bring home to the public how criminal was any political opposition to the Soviet regime and how dangerous it was for all who sinned in such a way. For that reason, and in contradiction to the facts, political opposition was represented during the trial as violent resistance and was punished as such.

The importance to the Bolsheviks of the preventive effect of the trial is illustrated by the pressure which the Tribunal exercised on the accused of the first group to force them to repent. The fact that they refused to do so was almost their greatest crime. The accused of the second group had also committed serious crimes, of course, but they had chosen the side of 'the proletariat' and had manifested their repentance. That was how it came about that Semenov and his group who *nota bene* had admitted their guilt for the terrorist attempts tried before the court, were pardoned, while the members of the first group, who denied having had anything to do with those attempts, were condemned to death.

'We should find it very strange if Gots, a man who in the depths of his soul is linked with the mentality of the tea trade, if lawyers, doctors and engineers suddenly were imbued with the proletarian ideology', wrote *Pravda* on 8 June (Gots's father was the son-in-law of Vul'f Vysotskii and had been a partner in the well-known firm of tea-merchants Vysotskii and Co.).[33] In explaining the social nature of the PSR, Bukharin said in his address, with Gots *et al.* in mind: 'In no other pseudo-revolutionary or revolutionary grouping will you find so many millionaires among the cadre leaders as in the cadre of the PSR.'[34] The Tribunal made similar classifying remarks. It was also for propagandist reasons that the verdict laid so much stress on the well-to-do origins of the accused of the first group, and on the 'proletarian origins' of such people as Fedorov-Kozlov, Usov and Zubkov among the second group. For the sake of convenience, no mention was made of the fact that Grigorii Ratner of the second group was of equally well-to-do family as his sister Evgeniia of the first group, or that Berg of the first group was just as much a worker as an Usov or a Zubkov. But quite apart from that, it is wellknown that the Bolshevik leaders originated in the same circles as the leaders of the PSR.

Although, as we shall see, the 'conditional death penalty' inflicted on twelve of the accused of the first group was a political compromise, it was also of propagandist significance. On the one hand, it stressed the tolerance of the Soviet government in that it did not put the death penalty into effect. On the other hand, it had the effect of a threat in that, whenever it considered it necessary, the Soviet government could execute those Socialist Revolutionaries who were now condemned to spend the rest of their lifes as hostages.

Finally, one suspects that the fact that some accused of the first group were condemned to death and others not was intended to give the impression that there was no unanimity among the group and that some of its members were prepared to bow the head to the Soviet regime. In actual fact, there was no reason at all to give a lighter punishment to Fedorovich, Rakov and Vedeniapin on the basis of the content of their closing addresses to the court, since the position they then took did not differ in essentials from that of their fellow accused. The proposal made by a secretary of the Tribunal to the effect that the accused should ask to be pardoned was apparently also intended to tempt them to different reactions.

HOW THE VERDICT WAS BROUGHT ABOUT

It is beyond doubt that the verdict did not result from independent deliberations by the Tribunal but from a decision taken by the leadership of the Communist Party. Unfortunately, very little is known about the consultations in the highest regions of that party. Quite a few reports about them appeared in the Russian emigré papers, but the accuracy of those reports cannot be checked. Nevertheless, they should be given some attention here because their purport at least seems to be largely correct.

Trotskii in particular was mentioned regularly among the advocates of a hard line with regard to the trial, together with Stalin and (although perhaps incorrectly, as we shall see) Bukharin (Lenin was ill). Moderation was apparently urged by those Bolsheviks whose duties entailed some degree of readiness to compromise (or perhaps who simply had rather more decency): Karl Radek and other representatives of the Comintern who considered themselves to be responsible for the Berlin Agreement; diplomats such as Lev Karakhan and Nikolai Krestinskii, who felt that too much intolerance would hamper the consultations with European governments; and people with a more specific government task such as Aleksei Rykov. The differences of opinion apparently came to a head with regard to the application of the death penalty.[35]

The final phase of the trial coincided with the Twelfth Conference of the Communist Party which was held in Moscow between 4 and 7 August. According to *Golos Rossii*, on the evening of 7 August when the Tribunal had already pronounced the death sentence against the principal accused, a closed session of the conference discussed whether or not that sentence should be enforced. Those who advocated moderation were in favour of changing the death penalty into one of exile abroad. Trotskii and the other hard liners, however, proposed that the accused should be given 24 hours in which to make a statement to the effect that they would relinquish all activities against the Soviet regime and that they had broken with the PSR. If the accused would meet this demand, it was suggested, the death penalty might be converted into five years forced labour in Northern Russia. If not, then the sentence must be put into effect immediately.

It was not until the next day, at a meeting of the Central Committee and after fierce discussion, that agreement was reached on a compromise solution suggested by Kamenev. This provided that the death sentence should be changed into a conditional one, which would not be put into effect if the members of the PSR would desist from any activities against the Soviet regime, whether at home or abroad. On the other hand, if the PSR should again have recourse to methods of armed conflict, then the verdict would immediately be enforced.[36]

That communist circles did in fact debate the application of the death penalty is confirmed by later writings and comments by western communists who at that time held positions in the Comintern. Some of these opposed the idea of executing the accused Socialist Revolutionaries, anticipating that this would make a bad impression abroad.

Victor Serge, then correspondent for the international communist journal *Inprekorr*, wrote in his memoirs that while in Berlin he had followed the course of the trial with great anxiety because some members of the Politbureau were in favour of applying the death penalty. 'Together with a few friends', he had 'conspired to prevent this catastrophe'. Among the people who exercised pressure in this way, Serge mentioned Zetkin, Sadoul and Souvarine.[37]

As we have seen, Jacques Sadoul argued in the courtroom against unnecessary bloodshed. Something of the position taken by Clara Zetkin and her party associate Ernst Meyer appears from the letters exchanged between the latter and his wife, Rosa Leviné-Meyer. According to this source, the question of the death penalty for the Socialist Revolutionaries was discussed at a meeting of the Executive Committee of the Comintern, when it met in Moscow on 6 August. Zetkin and Meyer then apparently declared themselves to be against the death penalty, and they also opposed the passing of a conditional death sentence which was proposed, according to this source, by Trotskii and not by Kamenev. Meyer wanted a complete pardon, and discussed this at a private meeting with Trotskii. On 7 August he wrote to his wife that to his great satisfaction, the Central Committee of the Russian Communist Party had that evening dropped 'that superfluous fuss about hostages'.[38] As we have seen, however, he rejoiced too early; the next day it appeared that the Presidium of the VTsIK had indeed converted the death sentence passed by the Tribunal into a conditional one.

The role played by the western communists was not very clear to outsiders. In their public appearances they conformed almost completely with the official position. In a letter to the author, Boris Souvarine, a Frenchman of Russian origin, explains his attitude in the affair as being due to the fact that, as a young communist, he was influenced strongly by leading Comintern figures such as Bukharin, Radek and Zetkin. These took an active part in the campaign against the Socialist Revolutionaries, and as a good communist he, Souvarine, therefore defended to the French public the policy followed by the Soviet regime in the affair. 'But in Moscow I have protested against certain (visible) irregularities of the trial and against the death sentence', writes Souvarine. 'De sorte que j'ai reçu des coups des deux côtés.'[39]

Another French communist of Russian origin, Charles Rappoport, was also in Russia during the trial. In his memoirs Rappoport has explained that, at a meeting of the Executive Committee of the Comintern, he voted together with Zetkin against the death penalty, which had been proposed by 'certain very highly placed' communists, but that they were given no support by the others. The official French representative, Louis-Olivier Frossard (described by Rappoport as an arrant opportunist), voted with the majority, and after the meeting even reproached Rappoport for his 'clumsiness'. Trotskii is said to have attacked Rappoport at that meeting and to have described him as 'a Pontius Pilate'. While Rappoport defended his position, Bukharin (with whom he had a close relationship) sketched him as an Orthodox priest with a long beard, reading from the Bible the commandment 'Thou shalt not kill'.[40] Both Rappoport and Meyer thus mention opposition on the part of Clara Zetkin (although not of each other).

Bukharin's role in all this remains obscure. Outsiders saw him as a proponent of the hard line. He derided Rappoport's opposition to the death penalty. In his letter to the author, Souvarine makes particular mention of Bukharin as a man who incited people such as he, Souvarine, to support the official policy as regards the trial. But in 1936, Bukharin told Boris Nikolaevskii that behind the scenes he had advocated that the death sentence not be enforced since he, together with his fellow delegates, had personally guaranteed this in Berlin. The Central Committee had not wanted to fulfil this guarantee, however, and, forced by party discipline, he had fiercely harangued against the Socialist Revolutionaries in public.[41] Unless Bukharin has given a different picture of his role than it was in reality, it seems that he had to cope with the same dilemma that faced Souvarine (and so many others). His position was even more complicated, however; standing higher on the hierarchical ladder as he did, he had not only to conceal his objections to the death sentence from the outside world, but also from his fellow communists on the lower rungs of that ladder.

The communists preserved a semblance of unity to the outside world. Only by exception was it possible to find a trace of disagreement (e.g. Sadoul's plea). The differences of opinion voiced behind the scenes were concerned not with the trial and its conduct as such (although some of its sharper aspects may have given rise to objections here and there), but only with the ultimate fate of the accused. It seems that opposition to the death penalty was voiced chiefly among Comintern circles, and was probably supported by the more moderate Bolsheviks.

Trotskii appears to have been the principal spokesman for the defenders of the hard line. He has described his position in his memoirs, giving as his opinion that the Socialist Revolutionaries were dangerous, so that half measures against them were not sufficient. But, ac-

cording to Trotskii, Clara Zetkin and other European communists —
'our humanitarian friends of the sort that is neither hot nor cold' —
urged that the lives of the accused should be spared. They did not
deny the necessity of repression, but considered that the execution
of 'an *imprisoned* enemy' was 'exceeding the limits of necessary self-
defence'. They found anything more than a prison sentence to be unnecessary. Trotskii did not agree. In his opinion, the Socialist Revolutionaries were terrorists who were apt to shoot at Bolshevik leaders.
Could the Bolsheviks restrict themselves to putting in prison people
who hoped to conquer power in the short term, and who sought to
eliminate or destroy those who were in power? He admitted, however, that execution of the Socialist Revolutionaries would also have
its disadvantages:

It was unavoidable that the Tribunal should pronounce the death sentence. But
its enforcement would inevitably be answered by a wave of terrorism. A prison
sentence, even a lengthy one, would only encourage the terrorists because they
had little belief in the durability of the Soviet regime. There was thus no other
solution than to make enforcement of the verdict dependent on the question of
whether the PSR would continue its terrorist activities, yes or no. In other
words: to declare the party leaders hostages.

Trotskii discussed this at his first meeting with Lenin after the
latter had recovered somewhat at his country home at Gorki. According to Trotskii, Lenin agreed 'immediately and with relief' to the
decision which he had proposed, and thought that no other solution
was in fact feasible.[42]

In her memoirs published in 1967, Lenin's secretary, Lidiia Fotieva, ascribed the idea of a conditional death penalty to Lenin himself. When, late in June, he was recovered sufficiently to turn his
attention to politics once again, he discovered that the trial of the
Socialist Revolutionaries was still in progress. He considered that
'this was not correct' because it 'kept so many people occupied who
were necessary elsewhere: Lunacharskii, Pokrovskii, Krylenko,
etc.'[43] On 11 July Lenin again started to discuss important affairs
with political leaders. On that day he received Party Secretary Stalin.
'I'm not allowed to read the papers; I'm not allowed to talk about
politics; I have to be careful not to touch any piece of paper that
might be left on the table in case it turns out to be a newspaper and I
should violate discipline', he said ironically, according to Stalin. But,
Stalin continues, Lenin once again radiated zest for his work and together they went over the most important matters.[44]

The trial of the Socialist Revolutionaries was one of those matters. According to Fotieva, Lenin gave as his opinion that the Socialist Revolutionaries should be given a 'conditional pardon' (Fotieva uses the word 'amnesty'). They had, according to what he had heard, declared that 'they would continue the armed fight against the Soviet regime'. He found that 'tactless and even foolish' of them and considered that 'a different verdict was indeed impossible.' In this way, and in accordance with the promise made in Berlin, the death penalty would not be put into effect. But the pardon should be conditional and annulled if 'the fight would be resumed'.[45]

According to Fotieva, the meeting with Trotskii did not take place until later. In the course of July, Lenin took up his work in full, and received various political leaders. On 5 August, before the above-mentioned party conference had discussed the fate of the accused, Lenin had another talk with Stalin, about which the latter reported to the conference (it is not known what Stalin said at that time).

Lack of proper source material has made it impossible to reconstruct the decision-making process regarding the trial with any accuracy, or the roles played therein by individual people. In his book on the origins and consequences of Stalinism, Roi Medvedev gives us to understand that Lenin had nothing to do with the trial of the Socialist Revolutionaries: he was seriously ill during the entire summer of 1922. According to Medvedev, the trial was organized by Stalin.[46]

Lenin was indeed ill at the time of the trial. Nevertheless, he concerned himself actively with its preparations up to a far advanced stage since his stroke did not put him out of action until the end of May. He was not available again for consultations until the final stage of the trial, when the nature of the sentence was under discussion. If we can believe Fotieva, Lenin considered that the trial had lasted too long. But he can have had no objection to its character. He himself had urged that demonstrative trials of the political opponents should be staged, and in that respect the organizers had adhered strictly to his instructions. The death sentences, too, were in agreement with what Lenin had said during the preparations for the trial. Medvedev's suggestion that Lenin had nothing to do with the trial is thus in undeniable contradiction with the facts. His assumption that Stalin had organized the trial is nothing more than an assumption. The names of Trotskii, Bukharin and Zinov'ev appeared far more frequently in reports regarding the trial than that of Stalin. Trotskii, in particular, was repeatedly in the foreground. Like Lenin, he thought highly of the propagandist value of political trials. Earlier, he had had plans for a large-scale show trial of Nicholas II,[47] and had also appeared as witness in the trial of captain Shchastnyi (1918) as well as in that of the 'Tactical Centre' (1920). It is possible, of course, that Stalin played an important role in secret, but Medvedev provides no such evidence. But whatever roles various people may have played, Charles Rappoport quite rightly says in his memoirs that 'the intervention by the government was beyond any doubt.'[48] Further particulars about that intervention will not be known until the archives in the Soviet Union are opened.

CHAPTER 8

THE PROPAGANDA CAMPAIGN

THE ORGANIZATION

'The trial of the Socialist Revolutionaries has pushed aside all other life in Russia', wrote a Socialist Revolutionary in Moscow to his party associates abroad on 12 June.

Apart from this trial, the Bolsheviks appear to have no needs, no cares at all. Such matters as the famine, industry, transport, the sowing of the fields, etc., etc., have all been relegated to the background or are given no attention at all. Tens of thousands of newspapers in the centre and in the provinces carry out the orders of the Bolshevik provincial committees, executive committees and all the other party branches, and from the first to the last page are filled with 'facts' about the traitorous and villainous activities of the Socialist Revolutionary 'bandits'.... In short, the Leviathan has thrown itself into the fight against 'the handful of Socialist Revolutionary bandits' with all its impressive penal and coercive apparatus, with technical means such as the post, the telegraph, the telephone, the railways, the aeroplane, the printing press, the newspapers, the journals, etc.[1]

In February 1922 Lenin had pronounced in favour of the organization of 'noisy, educative model trials', accompanied by plenty of 'tumult'. The trial of the Socialist Revolutionaries more than satisfied the demand for noise. As early as February and March, the Soviet press had publicized Semenov's and Konopleva's 'revelations' with suitable clamour. Afterwards it was comparatively quiet until — as we have seen — the Bolshevik leaders decided, after the conference of the three Internationals in Berlin, to intensify the propaganda against the socialists at home and abroad. The propaganda campaign around the trial then really started to be organized.

According to the plan drawn by the agitation and propaganda section of the Bolshevik Central Committee for the summer months of 1922, the trial should be surrounded by an extra vehement campaign against the Socialist Revolutionaries. A special 'agitation committee' was set up to take care of its organization. In April, this committee held a meeting at which approximately forty wellknown journalists were linked to certain newspapers for the duration of the propaganda campaign concerning the trial.[2] The agitation and propaganda section also set up a special press office to provide newspapers and journals with material that could be used during the campaign.[3]

According to *Golos Rossii*, a meeting of party agitators from all parts of the country was held in Moscow on 11 May. Public Prosecutor Krylenko and the leading propagandist Illarion Vardin instructed these people about the way in which they should handle the forthcoming trial.[4] On the same day, the Petrograd Provincial Committee of the Communist Party instructed the local press to intensify its propaganda against the Socialist Revolutionaries and also against the Mensheviks.[5] And on 19 May the Bolshevik Central Committee instructed the local party organizations to start immediately with the most energetic possible campaign, both written and spoken, about the trial, and within that framework to organize party meetings, large-scale workers demonstrations, etc.[6] These instructions were regularly repeated and further expanded during the following period, particularly at the lower levels of the party hierarchy.[7]

THE INSTRUMENTS

Written propaganda. Guidelines for agitators were made public while the trial was still in the preparatory phase. The 'Theses for agitators with respect to the trial of the Right Socialist Revolutionaries', edited by Lunacharskii, Bukharin and Krylenko on the orders of the agitation and propaganda section, formed a focal point in the campaign, being sent to the provincial committees of the Communist Party.[8] Special 'Theses for a report on the trial of the Socialist Revolutionaries' were published in Petrograd, while the Moscow Committee of the Communist Party produced 'The Socialist Revolutionaries "at work" against the Soviets'. Other publications included 'The Socialist Revolutionary murderers and the Social Democratic lawyers. (Facts and documents)' written by Vardin; a collection of propagandist articles about the Socialist Revolutionaries by the editor of *Izvestiia*, Iurii Steklov; two pamphlets about 'the victims of the Socialist Revolutionary terror' Volodarskii and Uritskii; and, of course, the actual Indictment, of which substantial numbers were printed, Semenov's pamphlet which had been reprinted by the State Publishing Office,[9] and that by Ignat'ev.[10]

During and after the trial were also published *Byvshie liudi*, i.e. something like the *ci-devants*, by Lunacharskii; 'What has the trial of the so-called "Socialist Revolutionaries" ascertained?' by Pokrovskii; 'What every worker should know about the trial of the Socialist Revolutionaries' by the former Menshevik, Nikolai Popov, who had gone over to the Bolsheviks; 'The Czechoslovaks and the Socialist Revolutionaries' by the Czechoslovak Bohumír Šmeral (in Russian); a pamphlet about the Socialist Revolutionaries and the Tambov uprising; a pamphlet about the Socialist Revolutionary activities in the Ukraine by Ivan Alekseev, who was a witness at the trial; 'The truth about the Socialist Revolutionaries' by G. Lelevich, published in Gomel' in Belorussia; a history of the PSR in two volumes covering the period up to 1907 by V.N. Meshcheriakov; 'The work of the Socialist Revolutionaries abroad', about the activities of the 'Administrative Centre'. During the campaign use was also made of 'The Mensheviks and the Socialist Revolutionaries in the Russian Revolution', written by Vadim Bystrianskii in 1921. Finally, the speeches for the prosecution, the pleas by the defenders of the second group, the closing addresses to the court by the accused of the second group, and the verdict reached by the Tribunal, including the decision taken in its regard by the VTsIK Presidium and a statement by the Executive Committee of the Comintern, were also published.

While these publications were intended chiefly for the agitators who could make use of them in their oral and written agitation, the press propaganda, especially that in the newspapers, was oriented more towards mass consumption. During the propaganda campaign around the trial, the press was filled with 'revelations', trial reports, comments, articles, workers' resolutions, letters, cartoons and poems, all referring to the trial. This has been established by the author with regard to such papers as *Pravda, Izvestiia, Trud, Rabochaia Moskva, Rabochaia gazeta, Krasnaia gazeta* (Petrograd) and *Bednota*; and to such journals as *Kommunisticheskaia revoliutsiia, Molodaia gvardiia, Vestnik agitatsii i propagandy,* and *Krasnaia nov'*. It may safely be assumed that newspapers and journals published in the provinces gave similar treatment to the trial. Furthermore, a bulletin called 'The trial of the Socialist Revolutionaries' was published each day during the trial.[11] Leaflets were also published, such as 'Into the streets! To the graves of the murdered leaders!' by the Petrograd Provincial Committee of the Communist Party on the eve of the 20 June demonstration.[12]

Meetings and demonstrations. The masses were brought into the campaign by means of a long series of meetings and demonstrations. For example, 'Meetings, assemblies and discussion groups should be organized in the large industrial enterprises', stated the plan of the agitation and propaganda section of the Moscow Committee of the Communist Party.[13] In some industries more than one meeting was held, e.g. in the *Trekhgornaia manufaktura* in Moscow, where the Communist Party cell listed three meetings as having been held.[14] The audience was addressed by an agitator who subsequently put a resolution to the vote. This resolution was accepted and sent to the newspapers. Many such resolutions were published by the papers, often in the most bloodthirsty wording.

The 20 June demonstration in Moscow has been discussed in a previous chapter. On the same day similar demonstrations were held in Petrograd,[15] Khar'kov,[16] Tula, Saratov, and other cities.[17] Although exact data about the provinces are lacking, it is known that demonstrations were held in various places on 20 June.[18] They were also held on other days. In an earlier chapter, for example, we have discussed the demonstrations against the western defenders of the Socialist Revolutionaries when they arrived in Russia on 25 May; there was another demonstration in Moscow on 15 June;[19] one by 'the working youth of Moscow' in front of the court building on the evening of 16 June;[20] and yet another on 2 June in Samara which, like Saratov, in the past was an important Socialist Revolutionary centre.[21]

Other means. The propaganda campaign also made use of films and exhibitions. The trial and the highlights of the campaign were filmed by the 'All-Russian Photo and Film Section' of the People's Commissariat for Education (*Vserossiiskii fotokinootdel*, or in short, VFKO), and some of this material was already being shown in the cinemas of Moscow when the trial came to its end.[22] It is not known whether this material is the same as that of the newsreel 'The trial of the Right Socialist Revolutionaries', made by the wellknown film director, Dziga Vertov.[23]

The most striking exhibition was set up in a room next to the courtroom in the House of the Trade Unions: 'The crimes of the Right Socialist Revolutionaries against the workers of Soviet Russia, in photos and documents'. The crimes of which the Socialist Revolutionaries were accused were illustrated with the aid of photos of blown-up bridges, of mangled corpses and of mass graves, with the portraits of the murdered Bolsheviks Volodarskii and Uritskii, with the revolver with which Fania Kaplan had tried to kill Lenin, with anti-semitic proclamations, etc.[24] In *Pravda* on 6 August an agitator suggested that when the trial had ended, this exhibition and copies of it should be taken to the villages.

We have seen that cardboard images of Vandervelde and Chernov 'icons' (Chernov as the Virgin Mother, with Kolchak as the Child Jesus and Denikin and Iudenich as angels, and drawn by Viktor Deni)[25] were carried during the 20 June demonstration in Moscow. In the street demonstration in Samara on 2 June, one van in the procession carried an image of Vandervelde sitting arm-in-arm with images of King Albert of the Belgians and of Tsar Nicholas II. These were accompanied by the slogan: 'Down with royalist socialism!'[26] Voitinskii writes that in the streets of Moscow travelling clowns staged performances in which they enacted the misdeeds of the Socialist Revolutionaries and their supporters: the buffoon Petrushka cudgelled the traitor Martov to death, emerged victorious from a hectic fight with the bandit Chernov, and beheaded Vandervelde and his fellows.[27] Finally, two posters about the trial were brought out by the Press Agency *Rosta*.[28]

THE SCOPE OF THE CAMPAIGN

It is clear that the propaganda campaign was broad in scope, but exactly how wide-ranging it was is difficult to ascertain. The print runs of various pamphlets used in the campaign are known: 10,000 copies of the 'Theses' were printed, and 20,000 and 25,000 copies respectively of Vardin's and Steklov's pamphlets; as many as 40,000 copies were made of the pamphlets about Volodarskii and Uritskii;[29] and 20,000 of the leaflet 'Into the streets!'. The newspapers, particularly the nationals, obviously had even larger editions (*Pravda*'s rapidly rising circulation, for example, had already reached almost 250,000 in 1921).[30]

There is no way by which we can even estimate the number of meetings that were held in connection with the trial, or the numbers of people who attended them. We know only that resolutions passed by such meetings were printed for many days in succession, sometimes dozens at a time. *Rabochaia Moskva*, for example, received more than 300 resolutions, all passed at various meetings in Moscow.[31]

Data are available, however, regarding the size of some of the demonstrations. According to reports in the Soviet press, 300,000 people took part in the 20 June demonstration in Moscow; 200,000 in that in Petrograd, and 120,000 in Khar'kov. These figures may be exaggerations,[32] but that the demonstrations were on a massive scale is beyond any doubt. Figures published with regard to other demonstrations include Samara, 15,000; the 15 June demonstration in Moscow, 15,000; the demonstration on the arrival of the western defenders in Moscow, 5,000; while 3,000 gathered in front of the court building on the evening of 16 June.

The propaganda campaign seems to have been at its most vehement in Moscow and Petrograd. It was also fairly large-scale in the provinces, however, as is shown by data at our disposal with regard to Khar'kov, Samara, Tula, Saratov, Ekaterinburg, Ivanovo-Voznesensk, Krasnodar, Sovetsk, the Urals, and the stations along the route taken by the western defenders, to mention only a few. In Donbass, for example, Izvestiia of 11 June reported that a meeting attended by 55,000 workers had demanded that the Socialist Revolutionaries be given a 'merciless trial'.[33] In a report on the campaign by the party committee of the Donets okrug (district), it was said that the demonstration held in the town with regard to the trial had been of 'impressive size' and had included 'the entire population of the town'.[34] In Rybinks 38 meetings about the trial were held in May and June.[35] Campaign reports from Vladimir province and from the Votskaia oblast' (now Udmurtskaia ASSR) mentioned volost' meetings and village gatherings on account of the trial,[36] and this seems also to have been the case in other rural areas. On the other hand, the piece by the agitator published in Pravda on 6 August, already referred to above, stated that the propaganda campaign had been much less effective in the rural areas where newspapers were far less common, than among the urban workers.

Finally, the propaganda campaign had a foreign element. The Internationale Presse Korrespondenz (Inprekorr), Die Rote Fahne, l'Humanité and other western communist newspapers devoted a good deal of attention to the trial. On 17 May, for instance, the Comintern, through the Presidium of its Executive Committee, appealed to the workers of all nations to follow the trial with great care,[37] an appeal that was published by the international communist press.

These newspapers treated the trial in the same spirit as the Soviet press. In addition, western communists took part in the propaganda campaign in Russia itself.

As regards the course of the campaign, after its initiation with the publication of Semenov's 'revelations', it was at its most heated from mid-May until a few days after the 20 June demonstration. It then continued at a somewhat lower level until some time after the end of the trial.

COERCION AND INTIMIDATION

There are indications that, notwithstanding the semblance of spontaneity upheld by the propaganda, the masses who took part in the demonstrations and meetings were not activated without some use of coercion. Mikhail Gendel'man asserted during the trial that the demonstrators in Moscow on 20 June had gathered not of their own will but because they were threatened by the GPU. According to Gendel'man, the demonstration that day had been preceded by large-scale arrests. Workers at the Prokhorov factory, for example, had been told that if they did not demonstrate this would signify that they favoured the Socialist Revolutionaries, and this in turn would mean that they could lose their jobs. Members of the public accused Gendel'man of slander, and he was interrupted repeatedly by Piatakov, who said that he could not allow Gendel'man to insult the workers of Moscow with his 'baseless and improbable allegation'.[38]

To what degree can force be said to have been used on 20 June? There are very few data in this respect, but apart from Gendel'man's statement, there are other signs that participation in this and similar expressions of popular indignation was not entirely voluntary.

In September 1922, in an item taken over from a Socialist Revolutionary underground paper, *Golos Rossii* reported that on 19 June prosecutor Lunacharskii had attended a meeting at the Prokhorov factory mentioned by Gendel'man in order to summon the workers to take part in the demonstration to be held the next day. But in addition to Lunacharskii the workers had also listened, and with a great deal of sympathy, to a Socialist Revolutionary who had spoken after Lunacharskii had guaranteed the workers that he would not be arrested. The Socialist Revolutionary's talk had made such an impression that a resolution proposed by Lunacharskii had failed to gain a majority. After the meeting the Socialist Revolutionary was arrested in spite of Lunacharskii's promise and, as a result, rioting broke out in the factory.[39]

Sotsialisticheskii vestnik also reported considerable resistance shown by the workers with regard to the anti-Socialist Revolutionary demonstrations and meetings, resistance which, according to that journal, was suppressed with the aid of threats of dismissal or of wage cuts. One of the examples cited by the journal in substantiation occurred at a state printing office in Moscow, where an anti-Socialist Revolutionary resolution failed to gain a single vote. Thereupon, a new manager was appointed who, although there was a glut of work, sent 200 of the 300 workers home until the autumn. A new meeting subsequently accepted a resolution according to which 'the highest penalty' should be applied to the Socialist Revolutionaries. *Sotsialisticheskii vestnik* reported 19 such instances.[40]

According to the Menshevik Boris Dvinov, the massive attendance of the 20 June demonstration was due to the workers' fear of starvation,[41] which was understandable after the famine winter of 1921-1922. An appeal by the Menshevik Central Committee not to take part in the demonstration therefore had little effect. Nevertheless, *Sotsialisticheskii vestnik* reported that three banners were carried in the procession with the slogan 'Down with the death penalty!'. The carriers of those banners are said to have been arrested the following night.[42]

As we have seen, a mass demonstration against the Socialist Revolutionaries was also organized in Petrograd on 20 June. In his diary published some years later, Pitirim Sorokin describes how he watched a procession of roughly 50,000 demonstrators, marching with banners which demanded the death penalty for the Socialist Revolutionaries. Among the crowds he saw many familiar faces, many students and workers whom he knew did not agree at all with the demand. They marched because otherwise they would lose their jobs. A few days prior to the demonstration, namely, the authorities had announced that anyone who did not take part would be sacked as a 'counter-revolutionary'.[43]

Soviet sources naturally make no mention of pressure on the people in connection with the action against the Socialist Revolutionaries. Now and again, however, we come across indications in that direction. In a letter published in *Pravda* on 30 June, for instance, 'an engine driver' denounced a certain Zagorskii, a non-party member of the Moscow Soviet, whose only mistake was that he had called upon the workers not to attend the 20th June demonstration.

Another example of intimidation, which had nothing to do with the 20 June demonstration but which took place in the same period, occurred at a conference of textile workers. According to the report on the conference published in *Trud* on 22 June, the delegates had included a certain Pegov who belonged to the group of non-party members. Pegov was 'unmasked' as a Socialist Revolutionary (it should be borne in mind that the propaganda readily branded sympathizers as Socialist Revolutionaries), and sent packing together with his 'supporters'.

THE SUBSTANCE OF THE PROPAGANDA CAMPAIGN

The objective of the entire propaganda campaign was to indoctrinate the population against the party of the Socialist Revolutionaries, and to justify that party's persecution in the eyes of the world as being an expression of the will of the people.[44] All the propaganda techniques which socialists had used on behalf of the accused in political trials before the revolution were now used by the communist authorities against the accused in a political trial. This was a new procedure at that time, but it has been much copied since.

Examination of the substance of the propaganda which was poured forth over Russia throws some further light on the intentions of the Bolsheviks in trying the Socialist Revolutionaries and on the atmosphere that they tried to create around the trial.

The trial should be seen against the backdrop of the situation in which Soviet Russia found itself in the early 1920s. In 1921 the Bolshevik leaders had decided to make a series of economic concessions, known as the New Economic Policy (NEP). With the help of these concessions they hoped to appease the discontent that had overtaken the mass of the population at the end of the civil war and which was an outcome of the general confusion in which the nation had then been left. During the winter preceding the trial, Russia had been ravaged by a dreadful famine. The Bolshevik leaders, however, were not prepared to complement their economic concessions with political concessions and to allow the Socialist Revolutionaries and the Mensheviks to act as a political opposition. Apparently, and probably not without justification, they feared that this would endanger their regime, the regime which they considered, probably with a considerable degree of sincerity, to be the only bulwark against a victory by the counter-revolution in Russia.[45] That was why the introduction of NEP was followed, not by political concessions, but by a campaign directed towards the final elimination of all political opposition. This campaign had to frighten off the population from alternative parties such as the Socialist Revolutionaries and the Mensheviks, and to instil in them the idea that good could only be expected from the Bolsheviks and only misery from their opponents. The trial of the leaders of the PSR was a focal element in this campaign.

That the Bolsheviks regarded the trial as an instrument of political indoctrination is shown by Lenin's instructions issued prior to the trial and by pronouncements by some of their spokesmen during the trial. This view was confirmed repeatedly during the propaganda campaign. Zinov'ev, for example, called the trial 'a great step forward' in 'the cause of the political education of the very broadest masses of town and country', whom it must teach to distinguish who were their friends and who their enemies.[46] Grigorii Evdokimov called the trial 'a school'.[47] Trotskii spoke of its 'great educational significance' and repeatedly of 'the lessons' of the trial.[48] A regional party conference in Ekaterinburg said that the trial should be used for 'the political education of the working class'.[49]

The lessons, it was said, were intended for 'the Russian workers and peasants' and for 'the international proletariat'. Those who primarily had to be indoctrinated (and intimidated) were the adherents and potential adherents of the Socialist Revolutionary leaders. That was why the propaganda distinguished between the verkhi and the nizy in the PSR: the party top (intellectuals) and the ordinary members and supporters (workers). The nizy, according to the propaganda, were genuinely disposed towards the revolution. They had realized that they had been cheated and betrayed by the 'depraved clique' at the top of the party, or, if they had not yet done so, would be brought to do so by the trial.[50]

In order to impress this representation of the facts on the population, the organizers of the trial and of the propaganda campaign made a number of such nizy declare in public that they had broken with the PSR: the members of the second group at the trial; people who, at meetings, testified to their repentance and remorse; and writers of letters that were published in the press.[51]

The trial and the propaganda campaign were intended to convince the Socialist Revolutionary *nizy* and all those who sympathized in any way with the PSR of two things: on the one hand that the leaders of the PSR were guilty of crimes against the revolution, against socialism, and against Russia and its population, and that their party therefore had no right to a political existence; on the other hand, that only the Communist Party could be allowed and was able to lead Russia, and that it was therefore obligatory to give it wholesale support. In Zinov'ev's formula, referred to earlier, the Socialist Revolutionaries were 'enemies', the communists 'friends'.

The former Socialist Revolutionary, V.A. Pupyshev, for example, in a letter published in *Pravda* on 12 July, declared that 'the only regime that in these times is able to maintain the achievements of the revolution, which is taking the only correct road towards creating a socialist state, and which is fulfilling the hopeful expectations of workers in all parts of the world, not with words but with deeds, is the Soviet regime.' And a workers' resolution ran: 'We declare with determination that no earthly or heavenly powers exist which can deflect us from the road shown to us by the Comintern. The road which leads towards a radiant future and towards the liberation of workers in the whole world.'[52]

In our discussion of the trial we have been able to ascertain the immensity of the charges brought against the Socialist Revolutionary leaders, charges which were expatiated upon and exaggerated by the propaganda. The Socialist Revolutionaries were represented not only as 'instigators' of attacks on Bolshevik leaders, but as people who committed murder with their bare hands, as it were. They were responsible not only for the attacks on Volodarskii and on Lenin, but also for that on Uritskii. Not only the Tambov uprising but also that of Kronstadt was 'the work of the Socialist Revolutionaries'.[53] They were even held to blame for the famine that had broken out in 1921. 'The hunger is also the fault of the Socialist Revolutionaries', according to a workers' resolution.[54] Another resolution ran: 'Our chaotic conditions and hunger are the results of the criminal adventurism of the Socialist Revolutionaries. They have set fire to the foodstuffs and grain in the Russian storage depots.'[55]

The Socialist Revolutionaries were described not only as opponents with wrong political beliefs. They were 'enemies of the people' (*vragi naroda*) as the Tribunal called them, 'bandits'.[56] The propaganda spoke of 'those vermin' (e.g. Bukharin),[57] of the Socialist

Revolutionary 'poison'.[58] In his *Byvshie liudi* Lunacharskii compared the Socialist Revolutionaries with 'microbes' which 'develop their obnoxious activities deep inside every abcess'. According to Lunacharskii the Soviet regime should arrange for 'an asepsis', 'a complete cauterization of all these bacteria through rigorous disinfection.'[59] During the 20 June demonstration, Bukharin compared the trial with the spike of aspen wood with which, according to popular tradition, the heart of a vampire has to be transfixed in order to put an end to its evil influence.[60]

The most horrifying aspect of the propaganda campaign around the trial and one that does not seem to have been justified by any political motive whatsoever, was that the population was incited to a bloodthirsty hate of these opponents who had already been eliminated — because in fact the Socialist Revolutionaries had been eliminated. We have already seen how bloodthirsty was the 20 June demonstration in Moscow. Other demonstrations and meetings were its equal in that respect. Resolutions that were accepted at meetings and sent to the press demanded severe punishment for the Socialist Revolutionaries, often death, and then frequently in such terms as: 'The mad dogs must be shot down';[61] 'Repay blood with blood'; 'There is only one punishment for such offal of the revolution: against the wall'; 'They should be doused with petrol and set on fire'; 'They ought to be torn to pieces, just as they tore us to pieces'.[62] 'No mercy. They are not even worth a bullet. The death of these brigands must be ignominious as brigands deserve.'[63]

The campaign against the Socialist Revolutionaries evinced some degree of contradiction. On the one hand it was asserted that they formed a pitiful little group without any adherents; on the other hand it was contended that the Socialist Revolutionaries formed a major risk.[64] The propaganda removed this contradiction by lumping the Socialist Revolutionaries together with all other adversaries of the Soviet regime: the Church, the anti-Bolshevik or at any rate not pro-Bolshevik intelligentsia, the monarchists, the Kadets, Boris Savinkov, the Mensheviks, the European socialists, the western powers, the international bourgeoisie, international capitalism; in short, the Russian and international 'counter-revolution' and its 'helpers'. Although the Socialist Revolutionaries in themselves were completely powerless, as part of this 'front' directed against the Soviet regime they were dangerous.

The PSR was 'a paid military espionage agency of the Entente'.[65] It was 'in fact an agency of the foreign governments' (according to Trotskii);[66] 'a division of the French-Czechoslovakian intelligence service'.[67] 'The French general staff' was 'the real leader of the politics of the Socialist Revolutionaries and the source of their finance.'[68] 'The financing of the Socialist Revolutionary adventures' was the work of 'the international bourgeoisie'.[69]

In addition to the imperialist powers, the Russian Orthodox Church also formed part of this counter-revolutionary 'front'. The Socialist Revolutionaries were therefore also depicted as helpers of the Church. 'The citizens of Sovetsk declare to all those enemies of the revolution who hinder the aid to the hungry, headed by Patriarch Tikhon and with the Socialist Revolutionaries as his principal helpers, that the proletariat will not forgive their base villainy and will relentlessly sweep them away', was the wording of one resolution.[70]

Those of the Russian intelligentsia who had not unequivocally chosen the side of the Soviet regime were also represented by the propaganda as being allies of the Socialist Revolutionaries.[71] 'Gots, Izgoev, Zinaida Gippius, Miliukov, Martov, Chernov: there are naturally gradations, but in principle they form one whole.' In this way, in *Krasnaia gazeta* of 20 June, Zinov'ev lumped together the Socialist Revolutionaries, the Mensheviks, the Kadets, and the non-party intellectuals personified by Aleksandr Izgoev and Zinaida Gippius.

Together with the Socialist Revolutionaries, the Mensheviks were the principal political adversaries of the Bolsheviks, and the propaganda campaign was also directed against them. Regular mention was made of the fact that the trial was not only of the Socialist Revolutionaries but also of the Mensheviks.[72] 'The party of the Mensheviks has associated itself with a united front from Miliukov to Chernov, a front that is oriented towards quashing the revolution,' according to Karl Radek.[73] And Nikolai Popov said about his former party comrades: 'When the Socialist Revolutionaries drown they will take the Mensheviks down with them in the maelstrom of scandal, treason and complete political ruination.'[74]

Finally, the European socialists who had taken up the cudgels on behalf of the Socialist Revolutionaries and who had even sent defenders to their trial, were also called their confederates. The propaganda reiterated repeatedly that 'Vandervelde and Co.', the 'yellow'

Internationals, 'international opportunism [*soglashatel'stvo*]', 'social traitorism', 'petty bourgeois "socialism" ', were also on trial.[75]

'Down with the murderers of the leaders of the working class, the Socialist Revolutionaries and their brothers-in-arms, the Mensheviks. Put that lot of opportunists of the Second and Second-and-a-half International, saboteurs of the proletariat's united front, into the pillory', ran one resolution.[76] Another, directed in particular against Vandervelde and his colleagues, ran: 'The Soviet government must keep a watchful eye on the foreign envoys of the defenders of the Socialist Revolutionaries, so that they do not get the chance for terrorist activities, such as an attack on the life of comrade Lenin.'[77]

The various opponents of the Bolsheviks were lumped together and were then required to dissociate from one another. The fact that they did not do so was supposed to prove that a correct portrayal of the situation was given in the propaganda.[78]

The propaganda campaign did not stop when the trial came to an end although it gradually became less violent. The sentence pronounced against the accused became a new factor, attention being drawn to the righteousness of the death sentence. 'The "party" of the Socialist Revolutionaries reserves to itself the "right", in addition to all its other activities, to perpetrate attacks on members of the Soviet government, when the politics of the latter do not please the Central Committee of the PSR, which has been ousted and condemned by the working people,' said Trotskii in an interview published in *Izvestiia* on 30 August. 'Permit us then to reserve to ourselves the right to shoot the leaders of the "party" of the Socialist Revolutionaries if it proves unable to appreciate the realities and to reconcile itself to the existing regime in Russia.'

On the one hand the propaganda emphasized the leniency that had been shown towards the accused. On the other hand it threatened that the sentence would be put into effect by the very first terrorist deed. It was Stalin who, a year later, according to the emigré paper *Dni*, once again repeated that threat in connection with the murder of the Soviet diplomat Vatslav Vorovskii in May 1923 by a rightist Russian emigrant. The actual murderers, according to Stalin, were 'the social traitors'. He reminded them that the conditional death sentence against the Socialist Revolutionaries was still in force and that the Russian communists, in retaliation for the death of Vorovskii, could now 'demand their friends.' By that he meant: could execute the condemned Socialist Revolutionaries.[79]

VERSES AND CARTOONS

Poets and cartoonists also played a part in the campaign against the Socialist Revolutionaries. No-one less than Vladimir Maiakovskii published in *Izvestiia* on 28 May a 'ballad of heroic Emile', i.e. Vandervelde. ' "Try them?! Because they shot at Il'ich?!/Why?! They've murdered two or three?!/I can't allow that! I am flying!"/And Emile pulled his trousers on.'

The regime's official poet, Dem'ian Bednyi, contributed a number of verses to the campaign. One of them, published on 20 July in *Pravda*, had the following lines: 'Timofeev is talking through his hat there,/And Gendel'man is gendel'manning on and on,/And Gots — whom will deceive/That bandit with his false pathos?/Words, words, words, words .../While everything is so clear as two times two.'

Pravda and *Izvestiia* published the following cartoons in consequence of the trial:

Pravda, 4 March: 'An illustration in a crime novel'. Viktor Chernov, with a distorted face, holds the 'revelations' by Semenov and Konopleva in his hand. The text runs: 'Caught' (cartoonist: Viktor Deni).

Pravda, 28 April: 'Types of Georgian women'. Martov, Vandervelde and Chernov sit, dozing, next to one another, dressed in Georgian women's clothing (cartoonist: Deni).

Pravda, 30 May: A seated Vandervelde, in a morning coat as always, holds his head — wrapped in a scarf and leaning on his right hand — dispiritedly turned away from a copy of *Pravda*, held in his hanging left hand and apparently filled with 'revelations'; his bespectacled eyes closed in misery; on his coat lapel is a '2' (cartoonist: Deni).

Izvestiia, 14 June: Vandervelde, in morning coat and wearing a monocle, declares as 'defender of the oppressed' to Patriarch Tikhon: 'Certainly Your Holiness, the Second International will also send me to your respected trial' (cartoonist illegible). (NB: a number of trials of Church officials were also held in this same period.)

Pravda, 4 July: 'Home again'. Vandervelde bows deeply before King Albert of the Belgians, holds the top hat that goes with his morning coat in his left hand, while he holds two of the King's fingers in his right hand. He says: 'I have been welcomed in a way befitting to Your Majesty's minister. Your portrait was even held up at the station' (cartoonist: Boris Efimov).

Pravda, 12 July: Chernov as coachman for 'the couple Foch — the Russian emigration' (cartoonist almost illegible: Deni?).

CHAPTER 9

THE REACTIONS

The trial of the Socialist Revolutionaries evoked numerous reactions, particularly outside Russia, not all of which were concerned with direct criticisms of the politics of the Bolshevik leaders. The Comintern declared itself to be in solidarity with Moscow, and those West European communists who had any objections kept them, with few exceptions, to themselves. Public criticism was uttered chiefly by international socialism and by what might be called progressive western public opinion. The protests were sometimes extremely severe and had significant consequences. The trial, for example, clearly contributed to the final failure of the attempts by the international socialist movement to achieve a united front. There were also reactions, however, which were little more than friendly warnings to the Soviet leaders that they should show due regard to humanity, while leaving out of consideration the policies followed by those leaders, or even emphatically supporting them. Finally, a number of positive reactions were voiced by non-communists.

The Bolshevik leaders could not completely ignore the criticisms from the West, and there are signs that those reactions had a certain influence on the course of events.

REACTIONS WITHIN RUSSIA

Criticisms voiced within Russia came primarily from the socialist parties. The Socialist Revolutionaries stood by their prosecuted leaders, as shown during the trial by the attitudes of some of the witnesses for the defence, but there was no scope for spectacular activities on their part. Party organizations protested, the underground press provided information and commentary. Party colleagues abroad were kept informed, for as far as possible in view of the defective communications. Finally, the prosecuted Socialist Revolutionaries had the support of their fellow prisoners, expressed in declarations of solidarity and in hunger strikes.[1]

In effect, the action against the Socialist Revolutionaries was also directed against the other socialist groupings in Russia, primarily the Mensheviks, but also against the Left Socialist Revolutionaries and the *Narod* group. The Menshevik Central Committee voiced its criticisms in various ways, including a proclamation in which it called upon the workers not to join in the demonstration on 20 June (a suggestion by Boris Dvinov that a counter-demonstration should be organized on that day was rejected) and a pamphlet protesting against the verdict.[2] The Left Socialist Revolutionaries in Russia also expressed their criticisms.[3] Isaak Shteinberg even voiced them in the Moscow Soviet, of which he was still a member.[4]

We have discussed the attitudes towards the trial taken by those who remained faithful to the PSR and by those who had broken with the PSR and chosen the side of the Communist Party. There were others, however, who, although they had left the PSR, had no wish to play a role such as that of members of the second group. Their attitude towards the trial was an ambivalent one, as was shown when some of them took the stand as witnesses. This applied in particular to Konstantin Burevoi who had stronger ties with the PSR than with the Communist Party. At the same time, however, he was extremely critical of the policies of his former party, particularly as regards the armed struggle against the Soviet regime and the relationship with the right wing of the PSR. On the one hand, this ambivalence caused him, as witness at the trial, to take his former colleagues in his protection to some extent; on the other hand, he condemned their attitude at that same trial in his book, 'Disintegration' (*Raspad*), published in Moscow in 1923. In Burevoi's opinion, the leaders of the PSR continued to cling to their old errors and had misrepresented the past. In his book he called the trial 'a major demonstration of the failures of the policies of the PSR.' The party had not taken up the challenge and had not presented a new policy at the trial. On the contrary, its old policies had suffered 'one more defeat'.[5]

If we leave out of consideration the few underground leaflets which were circulated from time to time by the opponents of the Bolsheviks, there was no longer an independent press in Russia in the early 1920s. The accused and their defenders consequently hadn't a chance that anything that they said during the trial would be reported with any degree of reliability. As a result, only a fraction of the charges that the accused had intended to hurl at their prosecutors, in accordance with tradition, filtered through to the public. Opinion shaping was completely in the hands of the Bolsheviks. It was therefore something of a miracle that at meetings of factory workers or of villagers they sometimes refused to vote in favour of sentencing the accused. The Soviet historians Gusev and Eritsian, in their history of the Socialist Revolutionaries, mention a few cases of such recalcitrant behaviour and of meetings 'at which members of the intellectual professions were in the majority', and at which attitudes towards the trial were 'cold and insincere' (quoted from a report by the agitation and propaganda section of a regional party committee).[6]

The intelligentsia, however, had very little chance of expressing any protest in public, added to which there were signs that they had become weary of politics, after the initial enthusiasm they had shown in 1917. The memoirs of the philosopher, Fedor Stepun, are characteristic in this respect. At the time of the trial, Stepun was living in the country where he worked in a sort of commune together with other people of like mind. Although some members of the commune, including Stepun himself, had been closely linked with the PSR in the past, they showed little interest in the trial. 'This apparently queer, almost traitorous attitude with respect of our political past', wrote Stepun, 'was due to the fact that none of us were really born for the political struggle but had become involved more or less incidentally, influenced by the spirit of the times and of the world around us.'[7]

But in Russia, in the year 1922, even an a-political attitude was not tolerated if it was accompanied by independent thought. 'The Bolsheviks are apparently not content with loyalty alone, i.e. with recognition of the Soviet regime as reality', wrote Stepun in 1923 after having been exiled abroad. 'They also require inward acceptance, i.e. recognition that their regime is right and good.'[8] In 1922 the Bolsheviks not only attacked their political adversaries, but also the 'counter-revolutionary' elements among the intelligentsia. Already in May of that year, Lenin had written to the chief of the GPU, Feliks Dzerzhinskii, that university professors and authors who — as he called it — helped the counter-revolution, were to be arrested as 'military spies' and sent into exile abroad.[9] The academic interest shown by the 'pseudo-non-party intelligentsia', according to the Communist Party conference of August 1922, was nothing other than a 'political cover-up'.[10] Immediately after the trial, the GPU arrested many wellknown intellectuals, who were interrogated about their political views, including their position with regard to the trial. Aleksei Peshekhonov writes that, in reply to this question, he said that he considered the trial to be the 'grossest mistake' made by the Soviet regime.[11] The majority of these intellectuals were then given one week in which to leave the country, an exodus which included many wellknown names.[12] According to Trotskii, they were exiled because they were 'potential tools in the hands of our possible enemies.'[13]

THE RUSSIAN EMIGRANTS

The initiative for a protest movement of any scope could only be taken outside the country. It was taken by Russian emigrants, and primarily by party associates of the accused, focused around the Foreign Delegation of the PSR in Berlin. In their daily paper *Golos Rossii*, the official party organ *Revoliutsionnaia Rossiia*, and in special bulletins in various languages, they published information about the trial, accompanied by their own comment. Their most important objective was to influence the international socialist movement and western public opinion. A number of appeals were made with the same purpose. On 12 June, for example, the Foreign Delegation of the PSR together with the Foreign Delegations of three other Russian socialist parties, i.e. the Mensheviks, the Left Socialist Revolutionaries and the *Bund*, appealed to all socialist parties in the world to support the defence of the accused.[14] On 11 August the Foreign Delegation of the PSR issued a statement in which it protested against the verdict.[15] After the close of the trial, the Socialist Revolutionaries continued to demand attention in the West for the fate of their party associates who were imprisoned in Russia. Their activities were not without result. 'In my opinion, the campaign that we unleashed in Europe at the time saved the lives of our comrades', Vladimir Zenzinov was able to write some time later, probably not without justification.[16]

One venture undertaken by the Socialist Revolutionaries abroad, which was not settled until after the trial, deserves particular attention. As we have seen, the Russian language paper *Novyi mir* was published in Berlin early in 1922 (until April) as a mouthpiece of the Bolsheviks. *Novyi mir* repeated the accusations against the Socialist

Revolutionaries published in the Soviet Russian propaganda. As a result, Viktor Chernov, member of the Foreign Delegation of the PSR, sued the editor of the paper, the German Kurt Kersten, for libel. His complaint was concerned in particular with two articles in which the Socialist Revolutionaries were accused of having perpetrated attacks on Bolsheviks leaders, and of having received funds from the German General Staff, the Russian bishops, and the French mission. The case was heard before a Berlin court on 30 October, and Kurt Rosenfeld appeared as one of Chernov's lawyers. The Socialist Revolutionaries had intended to make use of this opportunity to organize a sort of counter-trial before this independent court, at which they would be able to refute the charges made against the accused in Moscow. The Berlin court did not fall in with this idea, however, but did fine Kersten for contempt.[17]

As we have already seen on various occasions, the foreign representatives of the other Russian socialist parties also did their best for the prosecuted Socialist Revolutionaries. The Mensheviks around Martov and *Sotsialisticheskii vestnik* were particularly active. The Menshevik, Vladimir Voitinskii, edited the pamphlet 'The Twelve Condemned to Death', published by the Foreign Delegation of the PSR in October 1922 in Russian, German, English, French and Czech. The preface to the pamphlet was written by Karl Kautsky.[18]

In contrast to the socialists, the emigrated Russian Kadets showed little interest in the trial. One emigrant group which adopted a distinctive position was the *Smena vekh* (A Changing of Landmarks) movement, around the paper *Nakanune*, published in Berlin. The adherents of this movement were among those Russian emigrants (in particular liberals) who, after the introduction of the NEP, had changed their attitude towards the new regime in Russia and had accepted it as the lawful government. In the eyes of the *smenovekhovtsy*, the Bolsheviks had tamed the revolution and had saved Russia from chaos and destruction. Their anticipation was that the Bolshevik regime would now gradually adopt a national and bourgeois orientation, and they considered that Russian intellectuals could best stimulate this evolution by cooperating with the Bolsheviks.[19]

Nakanune followed the trial fairly closely, even sending its editor Iurii Kliuchnikov to Moscow for the purpose. Kliuchnikov was also summonsed as witness, but was not called upon to give evidence. His presence in Moscow, however, did not alter the fact that the trial reports in *Nakanune* were almost word for word replicas of those in the Soviet press.

According to *Nakanune*, the Socialist Revolutionaries abroad were making 'insincere noises' about the trial. After all, the accused were in danger 'neither of execution nor of forced labour'. The intention of the trial was not 'to punish' (*pokarat'*) but 'to show' (*pokazat'*).[20] The paper was very susceptible to Bolshevik reasoning and, about a week-and-a-half after the start of the trial, was thus able to write that 'the majority' of the accused had 'acknowledged the factual part of the Indictment'.[21]

The *Smena vekh* movement had little sympathy for revolutionary groupings such as the PSR. What it particularly valued in the Soviet regime was that the latter had been able to re-create considerable order out of revolutionary chaos. The only criticism which *Nakanune* allowed itself concerned the all-too-evident violations of orderly trial procedure. In particular, the paper seemed to disapprove of the events of 20 June, as a result of which it gave as its opinion that, irrespective of the political significance of the trial, the Tribunal should be guided 'by the law and not by passions'. As a 'state institution', the Tribunal should not be subjected to external pressures. In the paper's opinion, deviations from this principle undermined the prestige of the Soviet regime and put a weapon in the hands of its adversaries. The paper noted with satisfaction, however, that the Tribunal itself had realized that the courtroom incidents of 20 June had been a mistake. *Nakanune*'s reproaches, in fact, were directed primarily towards the accused and their defenders: the incidents had been caused by the behaviour of the accused, and the defenders' reaction to the incidents had been unwise and intended merely to add fuel to the flames.[22]

Nakanune did not lose faith in the Tribunal. In the paper's opinion, the Tribunal carried out 'the tedious and necessary work' that had to be expected of it: taking evidence, and verifying the charges. It anticipated that the verdict would depend solely upon this unsensational investigatory work.[23]

THE WESTERN SOCIALISTS AND COMMUNISTS

The socialist Internationals and their associated parties maintained their critical attitude towards the trial, prompted in particular by the emigrated Russian socialists and by the defenders of the Socialist Revolutionaries who returned to Berlin on 23 June. The latter now continued the defence in other ways from outside Russia.[24]

The severe criticisms uttered by the western socialists with regard to the events in Moscow[25] were not without result. 'Yes, it must be admitted', declared Bukharin to Nikolaevskii in 1936, 'you Socialists were able in the early twenties to put all of Europe on its feet and to make execution of the sentence against the Socialist Revolutionaries impossible.'[26]

The (conditional) death sentence contravened the Berlin Agreement and even the Vienna Union was ultimately convinced that, for the time being at least, a united front of socialists and communists was not feasible.[27] On the other hand, the rapprochement that took place between the Second International and the Vienna Union in May 1923 led to the setting-up of a united Labour and Socialist International in Hamburg (with which the PSR now associated itself).

The 1922 trial confronted the western socialists with the real situation in Soviet Russia. Nevertheless, the influence of this and similar experiences should not be over-estimated. For some years after the trial the Labour and Socialist International and its associated parties still occasionally spoke up for the persecuted socialists in Russia. Many western socialists, however, proved reluctant to make a continual stand against the less sympathetic practices of the Soviet regime. Those who had hoped that the socialists would adopt a principled position against the violence and terror practiced in the name of socialism in Soviet Russia, were thus disappointed.

Although some of its representatives fought behind the scenes on certain matters, in public the Comintern declared itself to be entirely in solidarity with Moscow. On 9 August the Executive Committee of the Comintern issued a statement in which it pointed out the justice of the sentence and appealed to the international proletariat to unite around Soviet Russia.[28] The national communist parties also expressed solidarity with Moscow, but this gave rise to certain problems. We shall examine their behaviour on the basis of three examples.

The greatest solidarity was shown by the German Communist Party whose paper, *Die Rote Fahne*, was almost a match for the Soviet press in its attacks on the Socialist Revolutionaries and their 'allies'. Other German-language propaganda literature was also published in connection with the trial, including translations of the pamphlets by Semenov, Vardin and Bystrianskii; also, Zetkin's pamphlet 'We Accuse!',[29] and the collection of articles 'To the Pillory'. We have already seen that the German-language organ of the Comintern, *Inprekorr*, which was published in Berlin, devoted considerable attention to the trial.

On 14 August, after the verdict had been made known, the German Communist Party organized in Berlin a demonstration against the Socialist Revolutionaries in which, according to reports in the communist press, eight thousand people took part.[30] The crowds were addressed by the communists Fritz Heckert of Germany, Alois Muna of Czechoslovakia, and Albert Treint of France. When the two German socialist parties, SPD and USPD, organized a demonstration in Berlin on 22 August in which they called for the release of the condemned Socialist Revolutionaries and for putting an end to the persecution of the socialists in Russia, the communists tried to create a disturbance.

That the trial caused some friction in the ranks of the French Communist Party has already been shown on the basis of the recollections of Souvarine and Rappoport, both of whom outwardly showed complete support for the Bolshevik position.[31] Souvarine also took part in the 20 June demonstration in Moscow, and Rappoport in that in Petrograd. Sadoul published a pamphlet entitled 'Les S.R. et Vandervelde'. The French party paper, *l'Humanité*, also took the part of Moscow and refused, for example, to publish a protest by Romain Rolland. Nevertheless, the tone of *l'Humanité* was milder than that of *Die Rote Fahne*, a fact to which some people took umbrage. At the Fourth Congress of the Comintern held later in 1922, the French representative Lauridan attacked the director of *l'Humanité*, Marcel Cachin, on this matter. In Lauridan's opinion, which was applauded by the congressionists, the French Communist Party and *l'Humanité* had not shown sufficient opposition to the 'campaign of lies and demagoguery' against the Moscow judges.[32]

The Dutch Communist Party expressed its solidarity with Moscow in an article by Jansen (pseudonym for Jan Proost) in *De Communistische Gids*[33] and in the pamphlet 'Murdered Innocence.....?!!!', written by Alex Wins. The party paper *De Tribune* also backed the

Russian communists but allowed some critics to voice their opinions. It printed the text of a protest telegram sent by Gerrit Mannoury, professor of mathematics and party member, to the Supreme Tribunal in Moscow; the paper added the comment, however, that in the editors' opinion there was no reason for protest. In his telegram Mannoury refuted the conception that revolutionary jurisdiction had to be class jurisdiction, and considered a death sentence to be 'in conflict with the communist ideals of intellectual power and humanity'.[34] Apart from one letter of approval to the editor,[35] he received only criticisms. Jacques de Kadt replied to the plea against a death sentence with a typical example of revolutionary rhetoric: 'If you want to intimate that for communists not "Life" but communism is supreme, then you must also have the courage to say that whoever fights against communism has in our eyes forfeited the right to "Life".' De Kadt considered a death sentence to be necessary and legitimate, although he added that the communists had no desire at all to shed blood.[36] Less than a year later, during a journey to Moscow, that same De Kadt heard from his escort, a supporter of the 'Workers Opposition' in the Russian Communist Party, that the trial of the Socialist Revolutionaries had been nothing but 'a show'.[37]

THE LEFT INTELLECTUALS IN THE WEST

The trial also caused repercussions in leftist intellectual circles in the West, *communisants* and others. In the first place, mention must be made of Maksim Gor'kii and Anatole France, two authors whose moral authority was taken into account by the leaders in Moscow. Before the start of the trial, Anatole France had appealed to the Soviet government not to commit any acts against its political adversaries which might be interpreted as revenge.[38] The Russian communists, who attached great value to Anatole France's usually fairly favourable opinion about their policies, then invited the author, by means of an appeal signed by Zinov'ev and Frossard, to attend the trial and so to convince himself that he had been talked into taking a biased view.[39] Anatole France did not take up this invitation.

Although after issuing his exhortation, Anatole France continued to hold a very favourable opinion of the Soviet experiment,[40] he once again stood up for the accused during the trial. On 30 June, disturbed at the way in which the trial was progressing, and on

Martov's initiative, the Mensheviks in Berlin approached Maksim Gor'kii who was then living in that city. They entreated him with some urgency that he and Anatole France should together intervene with an appeal to the Soviet government, in order to prevent a bloody conclusion to the trial.[41]

The next day, 1 July, Gor'kii immediately addressed himself to the Soviet government with the warning that if the trial should result in 'murder' of the Socialist Revolutionaries, this 'crime' would lead to a 'moral blockade' of Russia by 'socialist Europe'.[42] On 3 July, in a letter to Anatole France, he wrote that the trial had acquired 'the cynical character' of 'a public preparation for the murder of people who have with sincerity served the cause of the liberation of the Russian people.' He urged upon Anatole France that he should again approach the Soviet government, pointing out to it 'the inadmissibility of this crime'.[43]

A week later, on 10 July, Anatole France replied that, although he had not studied the trial sufficiently to be able to form a definitive opinion about it, he wholeheartedly backed Gor'kii's appeal to the Soviet government.[44] This exchange of letters was reproduced in the western press.

The Bolsheviks, however, refused to accept any criticisms and much resented Gor'kii's 'tactless and unwise' behaviour.[45] In *Izvestiia*, on 16 July, Karl Radek wrote that Gor'kii should not 'misuse' his privilege as belletrist 'to write all sorts of nonsense'. In *Pravda*, on 18 July, the propagandist Sergei Zorin considered that even a good writer could not be allowed to soil the face of the Russian worker 'with bourgeois shit'. Dem'ian Bednyi asked, in a verse printed in *Pravda* on 20 July, what was wrong with Gor'kii, who had so suddenly become 'the weeper of the Socialist Revolutionaries'. Evgenii Zamiatin writes that, somewhere in the Russian countryside, he had come across a newspaper with the headline 'Gor'kii dead', referring to 'the political death' of Gor'kii.[46] And when Lenin read the 'sordid letter' written by Gor'kii to Anatole France, his first impulse was to 'abuse' Gor'kii in the press.[47]

Anatole France was also criticized in the communist press. Nevertheless, the communists were inclined to treat the two 'fellow travellers' — 'a petty bourgeois fellow traveller of the Russian revolution', thus Gor'kii was called by Radek in *Izvestiia* on 20 July — as friends who had strayed from the path rather than as enemies. In *Izvestiia* on 23 July, Charles Rappoport defended Anatole France, though perhaps rather dubiously, by assuming that the latter had allowed himself to be misled. An article in the German paper, *Die Rote Fahne*, published on 15 July, considered that in the treatment of its enemies the Soviet government should not allow itself to be guided by 'artistic sentimentality', but at the same time accused the social-democratic press of 'defiling the sincere revolutionary sentiments' of Gor'kii and Anatole France in that it tried to exploit the 'purely human documents' of these two artists in its 'offensive baiting of the revolution'. *Pravda* and *Izvestiia* reprinted this article on 21 July. And Lenin, in a letter to Bukharin dated 7 September, wrote that instead of pitching into Gor'kii too strongly, it might be better to talk to him.[48]

Apart from Gor'kii and Anatole France, many other leftist intellectuals made themselves heard. One of those who helped to get the campaign into motion was the 78-years old Socialist Revolutionary Ekaterina Breshkovskaia. On 6 July Breshkovskaia addressed an open letter to all progressive-thinking people in the world, and in particular to Romain Rolland, Gerhart Hauptmann, H.G. Wells and G.B. Shaw, appealing to them all to devote their energies to saving the lives of the accused.[49] In his reply on 14 July Rolland wrote that he concurred 'with every protest against every judicial murder'. He adjured the Russian communist leaders in their turn not to make themselves guilty of oppression but to save the lives of their former comrades-in-arms and fellow revolutionaries.[50] *l'Humanité* refused to publish the letters by Breshkovskaia and Rolland, much to the fury of the latter.[51] Rolland then managed to get both letters published in *Le Journal du Peuple*, the paper of Henri Fabre who had been expelled from the French Communist Party in 1922 because of his attitude of excessive independence.

In addition to Gor'kii, France, Rolland, Hauptmann, Wells and Shaw, the protest was supported by Alphonse Aulard, Henri Barbusse, Georg Brandes, Marie Curie, Eugene Debs, Albert Einstein, Charles Gide, George Lansbury, Fridtjof Nansen, Paul Painlevé, Bertrand Russell, Charles Seignobos, Georges Sorel, John Turner, Sidney Webb and many others. These protests did not entail absolute condemnation of Bolshevik policies, nor did they lead to the 'moral blockade' of the Soviet regime with which Gor'kii had threatened. Some made it quite clear that they felt no sympathy at all towards the accused and that, fundamentally, they agreed with the Bolsheviks. Henri Barbusse, in a piece in *l'Humanité* on 2 August, made it known that the aim was to save the lives of the accused but that 'this mercy' must not signify acquittal. 'We do not have the right to demand for counter-revolutionaries anything other than a simple act of leniency', wrote Barbusse. 'It is not our intention to associate ourselves with the libel campaign that has been instigated against Russian jurisdiction in general and against the hearing of this case in particular, nor publicly to cry for an apology for the crimes of counter-revolutionaries.' It was hardly surprising that on 15 August, after the decision regarding the punishment of the Socialist Revolutionaries had been made known, *Pravda* reproduced Barbusse's article.

After the trial, the journal *Clarté*, of which Barbusse was editor, turned upon those who described the sentence as 'a deed of scandalous barbarity'. To allow 'another voice' to be heard, the journal published Sadoul's speech to the court and an impassioned description of the 20 June demonstration in Moscow by Magdeleine Marx (known after her marriage as Magdeleine Paz). 'In this way our readers will be able to form an idea of the behaviour of the Socialist Revolutionaries and of their crimes against the proletarian revolution, as well as of the true extent of their popularity among the working class of Soviet Russia', wrote the editor.[52]

Another wellknown journal with Bolshevik sympathies was the American *The Nation*, in which Abraham Epstein wrote that one must not judge the Soviet Russian system of justice by a trial such as that of the Socialist Revolutionaries. 'Political expediency' might make a nation act 'in ways contrary to its own best convictions.' Russia's 'revolutionary system of justice' was, in Epstein's opinion, 'basically fair and equitable.'[53]

In the same issue of *The Nation*, the American journalist Paxton Hibben went much further in an eye-witness account of the trial. Although he wrote that only attendance at the trial could bring home its whole significance to the observer, his report was full of inaccuracies. The vociferous campaign, for instance, had apparently escaped his notice. According to Hibben, the trial took place in a calm, completely orderly atmosphere and roused not the slightest public excitement; the audience in the courtroom was unmoved, and Krylenko's speech for the prosecution 'unemotional'. Hibben accepted the charges against the accused without question. The fact that they had taken money from foreign governments he considered to be particularly serious. In his view, they had, 'as the hired tools' of these governments, which, as revolutionaries, they themselves despised, brought war and pillage to Russia, caused famine and epidemics, brought ruin and death to millions of Russians. In Hibben's opinion, however, apart from the verdict rendered by the court and by the audience, the severest verdict against the Socialist Revolutionaries had been rendered by time. 'The romantic day of the Byrons and the Shelleys and the Garibaldis' — whom he bracketed together with the accused — was after all gone for ever: 'What is strong, what is permanent is the steady, hard realism of Lenin and Trotzky and Kamenev and Chicherin and Krassin and the rest. It may be bad; it may be good. But it is so.'[54]

Not without reason, the writer of an open letter in *The Nation*, in referring to Hibben's article, found that 'getting hand-picked information' was evidently 'not conducive to accuracy'. She wondered whether the eyes and ears functioned differently in Russia to elsewhere.[55]

'BOURGEOIS' CIRCLES

Although communist propaganda asserted that international capitalism had started to harass Soviet Russia on account of the trial of the Socialist Revolutionaries, reactions to the trial were voiced principally by leftist circles and interest in 'bourgeois' circles appears to have been fairly meagre. For the purposes of the present study, therefore, there was no reason to sift through the liberal and conservative western press. The impression is unavoidable that 'the capitalists' saw the trial, if it drew their attention at all, as a senseless argument between two sects. If they could bring themselves to show understanding for one of the parties, then it was usually for the stronger of the two. This is illustrated by an interview printed in the Dutch *Algemeen Handelsblad* with the director of the Netherlands-Baltic Trade Association, O. Mielziner. According to that interview, when he had visited Russia Mielziner had become firmly convinced that the accused would not be put to death. But he wondered what people in Europe really wanted. The accused, after all, had 'themselves admitted that they had conspired against the government and against its leaders', and had 'refused to promise to abstain from doing so.' He also thought that the European socialists had shown 'an unbelievable lack of tact' by sending in a case such as this a Liebknecht to Moscow as a defender. 'The great agitation among the Bolshevik population' against the defenders could, in his opinion, be imputed to this fact. The name of Liebknecht was 'worshipped by these Russians as that of a saint', so that the sending of a Liebknecht had caused enormous indignation. 'Any other would have been understood, but not this one,' according to Mielziner.[56]

CHAPTER 10

THE END

REVISION OF THE SENTENCE

Immediately after the end of the trial, the 22 condemned Socialist Revolutionaries were taken to the prison on the Lubianka and there confined, in isolation from each other and from the outside world. According to information provided by their party comrades outside Russia, it seems that some months passed before they came to know that the death sentence pronounced against twelve of their number was of a conditional character.[1] They protested against the strict prison regime with occasional hunger strikes. Nevertheless, considerable time lapsed before the authorities did anything to ameliorate their conditions. For one of the prisoners, however, it was all too much: Sergei Morozov, approximately 35 years old, committed suicide on 21 December 1923 by slashing his wrists.[2]

Shortly after, the Soviet authorities revised the sentence, possibly prevailed upon to some extent by the intervention of western socialists.[3] On 14 January 1924, a year-and-a-half after pronouncement of the sentence, the Presidium of the Central Executive Committee (TsIK) announced that it had converted the sentences of those who had been condemned to death to five years imprisonment, and that it had halved the prison sentences of ten and five years. It was true, said the Presidium, that the adherents of the convicted Socialist Revolutionaries had not discontinued their counter-revolutionary activities against the Soviet Republic, but the overall strengthening of the Soviet regime meant that such activities on the part of 'a handful of embittered emigrants and the annihilated and routed groups of their adherents in the country, who have lost any link with the working masses of the USSR', no longer represented a real threat. According to the Presidium's decree, after serving their sentences, the convicted Socialist Revolutionaries would be exiled for a three-year term within the USSR, under supervision of the GPU.[4]

In view of the fact that their sentences had included the period during which they had been on remand, the moment for 'releasing' the convicted Socialist Revolutionaries was now not far distant. In the middle of 1924 they were moved from the Lubianka to Butyrki Prison, which brought an end to their complete segregation. They were now placed in a section of their own which had open cells and was separated from the rest of the prison,[5] and were allowed to be visited by their relatives. Some of the prisoners in turns even stayed for a week or two on a GPU *dacha* outside Moscow, where they could be together with their families and regain some of their strength in the country air.

While in Butyrki Prison the convicted Socialist Revolutionaries met members of the English trade union delegation which visited Russia in 1924. On 22 November 1924, prior to that visit, the Socialist Revolutionaries had written a letter to the delegation in which they discussed the approach sought by the socialist International Federation of Trade Unions, or Amsterdam International, to the communist Red International of Trade Unions, or Profintern. In the opinion of the Socialist Revolutionaries, an amalgamation of these two organizations could only be admissible if the Amsterdam International could persuade the Profintern to ensure that all socialist, anarchist and syndicalist groupings in Russia should receive the right of unrestrained propaganda and organization. If the Bolsheviks were to reject this demand on grounds of 'the difficult domestic situation', that would be a mendacity. 'We declare anew that among the Russian socialist parties there is not one which would advocate intervention or which, at the present time, would organize an armed revolt,' wrote the Socialist Revolutionaries.[6] It is not known whether or not the delegation received that letter.

On 27 November, members of the English delegation, including A.A. Purcell and John Turner, visited Butyrki Prison in the company of a few high-ranking GPU officials. In no way did the Englishmen take advantage of all possibilities open to them. With the exception of Turner, they remained in the corridor with their escorts and did not go into the cells.

The delegation's members described this visit in their official report on their journey. In their view, conditions in the prison were not bad. The prisoners, according to the delegates, had voiced more criticisms of the difficult lot of their comrades elsewhere in Russia than of their own situation. They had made no secret of their opposition to the Soviet regime. The delegates wrote further that they had asked the Soviet authorities whether an amnesty was feasible for the prisoners. The Soviet authorities had shown 'an appreciation of its [the delegation's] arguments', but had expressed the fear that 'such clemency might lead to further bloodshed.' The delegates had therefore restricted themselves to making suggestions as to how conditions in the prison might be improved in one or two respects. Under the given circumstances, they did not feel that they 'could take the serious responsibility of pressing for the release of such irreconcilables'. They thought that there were no obstacles, however, to the prisoners being sent into foreign exile.[7]

Turner, who had spoken with Evgenii Timofeev while visiting Butyrki Prison, reported on his talk elsewhere, saying that Timofeev was in good health and was still 'fiercely opposed to the present regime in Russia.' In Turner's opinion, it had done Timofeev good to realize that 'there are people abroad who are interested in the imprisoned Russian revolutionaries.' At the end, he had asked Turner to give his best wishes to the western defenders in the 1922 trial.[8]

Another visitor to the Soviet Union in 1924 was the Dutchman Edo Fimmen, representative of the Amsterdam International. A few months later, on 15 January 1925, *Izvestiia* printed an article by the Bolshevik Dmitrii Sverchkov in which he reported on a talk which he had had in October 1924 with Fimmen during the latter's journey home. According to Sverchkov, Fimmen had gained a very favourable impression of the situation in the Soviet Union and had ascertained that many lies were told about it in other countries. For example, he had personally been able to check the stories about what was said to be the wretched lot of those Socialist Revolutionaries who had been tried in 1922. When he had wanted to visit Gots, the latter proved not to be in prison at all, but to be staying with his family on a *dacha* in the neighbourhood of Moscow, where he was recuperating under very pleasant circumstances. 'Why do you keep quiet about it?', Fimmen had asked Sverchkov, according to the latter's article. 'Why don't you publish it and expose the lies that are told about you; why don't you refute the reports about the brutality with which you are said to treat the political prisoners?'

As a result, Abram Gots wrote an open letter to Fimmen, dated 1 February 1925, which he managed to smuggle out of prison. That letter made it clear that Gots knew nothing at all about any visit by Fimmen. Gots wrote that he realized that many foreigners adopted an attitude towards Russia 'as though it was a fairyland with un-

limited possibilities, where all sorts of miracles are conceivable.'
Reality, however, according to Gots, was not so beautiful. He described the hardships which he and his fellow prisoners had had to
undergo during their five-year imprisonment under the Soviet regime.
In the two-and-a-half years since the trial, according to Gots, they
had endured 18 communal and individual hunger strikes, lasting for a
total of 366 days. He observed that people such as Fimmen and
Purcell apparently thought that Bolshevism was something beautiful
and that Soviet prisons were palaces, but he wondered how they
would react if, in their own countries, the communists led by Wijn-
koop (incorrectly written as 'Wijntraub') and Pollitt were to grab
power. He thought that they would resist. And only then would they
understand why the Socialist Revolutionaries not only cherished 'a
bitter hatred' against the communist dictatorship, but also felt 'a dis-
dainful compassion' for the 'inwardly contradictory, hopelessly insincere' actions of those who, in their attempts to achieve reconcili-
ation with the communists, were tossed hither and thither between
two poles: who 'become enraptured with Muscovian practice and at
the same time reject for their own country that practice which they
so extol.' Gots pointed out to Fimmen that his name was being used
'as a screen behind which to disguise the worse form of arbitrariness
and despotism,' and asked why he had so willingly clothed himself
'in the Kremlin's livery.'[9]

Fimmen then made it known in the Belgian paper *Le Peuple* that
Sverchkov had invented the entire story. He declared that he had
never met Gots and had never said the things of which Gots accused
him in his letter. Nevertheless, he ended with the remark that the
Flemish activists in Belgian prisons 'would willingly exchange their
lot for that of the socialists in the Russian prisons.'[10]

The sentences of most of the Socialist Revolutionaries who were convicted in the 1922 trial expired in the course of 1925, and they were
each allocated a place of exile by the GPU. Dmitrii Donskoi, the first
to be released at the end of 1924, was initially to be sent by the GPU
to Turukhansk in Northern Siberia. Only after many protests was
this changed to Narym, further south. The GPU then wanted to send
Evgeniia Ratner and Arkadii Al'tovskii to places that were equally far
from the civilized world: Ratner with her three young children (varying from 6 to 13 years of age) and her fairly old and sick mother,
were to be sent to Ust'-Tsil'ma on the Pechora in the far north; and

Al'tovskii to Cherdyn', situated a little more favourably in the north of the province of Perm'. In protest, the convicted Socialist Revolutionaries started a hunger strike on 28 January 1925, demanding that they should be exiled to places with reasonable chances of existence. Not until the condition of the prisoners became critical after nine days did the authorities promise to meet this demand.[11]

Gots and Timofeev were released in May 1925, Gots to be exiled to Ul'ianovsk (formerly Simbirsk) on the Volga, and Timofeev to Kokand in Central Asia. In July, however, they were back in prison again: Gots due to his letter to Fimmen. Notwithstanding a hunger strike, they were condemned in an administrative procedure to two years imprisonment. In protest, the remainder of their comrades who were still in Butyrki Prison also started a hunger strike on 9 October. That same evening they were forcibly removed from their cells and transported to various places throughout Russia. When their condition became critical, however, the authorities knuckled under. After a hunger strike that had lasted for a good three weeks, the prisoners were returned to Moscow, where they brought their strike to an end on 1 November. Gots was sent to continue his exile in Ul'ianovsk. Timofeev, who had finally landed up in the Lubianka in Moscow, was assigned to Ural'sk as his place of exile, after yet one more hunger strike.[12]

The banishment of the convicted Socialist Revolutionaries brought an end to their activities as a group.

THE FURTHER SUPPRESSION OF THE PSR

The 1922 trial was not considered by the Bolsheviks to be the end to their action against the PSR and other oppositional parties.[13] During and after the trial, in fact, the repression of their political adversaries was intensified. Legal prosecution of the Socialist Revolutionaries and of members of other 'anti-Soviet groupings' was the exception rather than the rule. In general they were sentenced by the GPU in an administrative procedure, usually to exile to far distant parts of the country (exile of Socialist Revolutionaries to other countries was a fairly rare occurrence).

At first, this state of affairs was in fact illegal because, when the GPU was established in February 1922, it had been ordained that political crimes should in future be handled 'solely through the courts.'[14] The legislation, however, was modified later that same year.[15]

The active Socialist Revolutionaries and members of other opposition parties disappeared into prisons or into exile, or into the concentration camps which began to come into fashion in the early 1920s.[16] Particularly famous from those days is the concentration camp on the Solovetskii islands (Solovki) in the White Sea where, starting in 1923, many Socialist Revolutionaries, Mensheviks, Left Socialist Revolutionaries, and anarchists were sent.[17] Tragic things happened on Solovki, such as the massacre by the guards on 19 December 1923 when six people (including five Socialist Revolutionaries) were shot dead,[18] but on the whole the regime was not bad. It soon appeared that it could be very much worse. In 1925 the special treatment which the socialists had enjoyed as political prisoners was brought to an end, and those who had been on Solovki were divided among various prisons and places of exile.

During the propaganda campaign that accompanied the trial of the Socialist Revolutionaries the impression had been created that more important political trials were on the way, both against Socialist Revolutionaries and against members of other groups. Nothing much came of these plans,[19] however, only a few minor political trials being held in the period after the major trial.[20] The most important of these was the trial of the leaders of the PSR's Transcaucasian organization in Baku on 1-10 December 1922. Amongst other charges, these leaders were accused of having given orders for incendiarism in the Baku oilfields. The structure of this trial showed considerable similarity with that of Moscow. There were two groups of accused: the real accused, and those who in effect were witnesses for the prosecution. Surprisingly enough, however, the accused of the second group were handed-out the severest sentences. An explanation of this amazing verdict is not to be found in the news about the trial published in the Soviet press. According to *Revoliutsionnaia Rossiia*, however, the trial in fact miscarried because some accused of the second group admitted in the courtroom that they had made false statements under pressure (in which none other than Lavrentii Beriia is said to have played a role). This presumably explains the sentence. If so, then the partial failure of the Baku trial perhaps contributed to the abandonment of further major public trials.[21]

The assault on the PSR, however, was continued through other means. We have seen that in the political campaign around the Moscow trial efforts were continually made to play off the ordinary PSR members, the *nizy*, against the leaders, the *verkhi*. At a Communist Party conference in August 1922, Zinov'ev described these tactics as follows: the 'organized anti-Soviet parties' were not only to be suppressed by repressive means, but also by depriving them of 'all that is of value of their human material, all that is capable of supporting the Soviet regime.'[22] These tactics were continued after the Moscow trial. A movement was set up of *byvshie*, i.e. former Socialist Revolutionaries who publicly declared that they had broken with the PSR and had chosen the side of the Soviet regime.

After some preparations,[23] an 'All-Russian Congress of Ordinary [*riadovye*] Socialist Revolutionaries' met in the House of the Trade Unions in Moscow from 18-20 March 1923, surrounded by quite a lot of publicity.[24] Forty-five delegates were present, representing, it was said, more than 850 former Socialist Revolutionaries. The congress sharply criticized the PSR and its leaders. It declared the party to be dead, and called for firm cooperation with the Communist Party as being the only representative of 'genuine Socialist Revolutionary principles and traditions'.[25] The former member of the Central Committee of the PSR, Prilezhaev, who was not a delegate but a guest, called the '*eserovshchina*' (a pejorative term for the PSR, its concepts and its politics) 'an ulcer' which required 'a lengthy cure'.[26] Apart from Prilezhaev, who had left the Party five years earlier, there was no-one present at the congress who had previously held a prominent position in the PSR. The propaganda explained this circumstance as evidence that 'the proletarian elements' in the PSR 'have completely renounced their former ideology and leaders.'[27]

The congress appointed an Executive Committee which occupied itself with the organization of further activities, the principal of which was to persuade other (former) Socialist Revolutionaries to sign the congress's resolution. It seems that imprisoned Socialist Revolutionaries were also approached in this way. A month after the congress, one thousand former party members were said to have declared themselves in sympathy with the decisions of the congress; by October 1923 this total was said to be three thousand.[28] The Executive Committee terminated its activities in February 1924, after reporting that two thousand Socialist Revolutionaries had joined the *byvshie* movement, and that many others had declared their support for the decisions taken by the congress.[29] The results of the movement thus do not seem very impressive if we bear in mind that at its peak the PSR had some hundreds of thousands of members.

THE END OF THE SOCIALIST REVOLUTIONARIES

Bolshevik propaganda declared the PSR to be dead. And in a certain sense it was right. A more neutral observer such as Konstantin Burevoi, in his book published in 1923, also considered the role of the PSR in the Russian revolution to have come to an end.[30] And in the PSR itself, reality had ultimately to be acknowledged. In 1929, for example, the Socialist Revolutionary emigrant Mark Slonim posited that the party's role in the Russian revolution had been brought to an end with the 1922 trial.[31]

The PSR indeed showed only few signs of life in Russia, certainly after 1925. Up to that year, the party had still evinced some activity, had still issued a few illegal publications, and still had a rather shaky party organization. In 1925, however, reportedly as a result of treachery, the members of the still surviving, and apparently the last, Central Bureau of the PSR were arrested.[32]

In the Soviet Union there was no longer any political opposition of any significance outside the Communist Party after 1925. Repressive measures were henceforth directed mainly towards the opposition within that party.[33] 'We do have room for other parties as well,' declared Bukharin to a 'Congress of Friends of the Soviet Union' in 1927. 'But the fundamental difference between the existence of parties in the West and here is that the only conceivable situation here is the following: one party is in power and all the others are in prison.'[34] At that moment the situation outlined by Bukharin largely conformed with reality. Inside that one ruling party, however, the process was being repeated which had earlier occurred between the Bolsheviks and the other parties.

The post-1925 history of the PSR in Russia is nothing more than the history of the vicissitudes of the Socialist Revolutionaries in their prisons and places of exile. 'The vicious circle closed around use,' wrote one of them in her memoirs. 'Three years in prison were followed by three years in exile, then three years "minus" [a prohibition on living in the larger towns] and another arrest.'[35] They were no longer active in politics, and they had lost faith in the chances of successful resistance.[36] Nevertheless, in the early 1930s the measures against supporters of other parties were sharpened once again. Even those who had long ago given up any political activity were now arrested. In the course of the 1930s and the very early 1940s, practically all the Socialist Revolutionaries still in Russia perished, a fate which they shared with their former party comrades who had turned their backs on the PSR, and with many of their former rivals, the Bolsheviks.

In 1957, more than 35 years after she had left Russia with her family, Ol'ga Chernova, stepdaughter of Viktor Chernov, visited Ekaterina Peshkova in Moscow. Peshkova, the widow of Maksim Gor'kii, had since 1918 directed the work of the 'Political Red Cross' in Russia, sometimes called the 'Association for Help to Political Prisoners'. Within the ever-decreasing possibilities available to her, she had always been particularly active on behalf of the imprisoned Socialist Revolutionaries (in the past she had herself been a member of the PSR). The organization was finally abolished in 1937.[37] Peshkova told Chernova that 'all the Socialist Revolutionaries have perished', considering it improbable that more than two or three of them had outlived the terror.[38]

Only two Socialist Revolutionaries are known with certainty to have survived the Stalinist terror: Ekaterina Olitskaia and Mina Svirskaia. Olitskaia was arrested in 1924 and was not released until after the death of Stalin. Her memoirs were published abroad in 1971. She died in 1974.[39] Svirskaia was arrested in 1921. She was summonsed as witness for the defence in the 1922 trial, but was not called upon to give evidence.[40] She was released in 1956 and emigrated in about 1976 to Israel, where she died late in 1978.

The accused in the 1922 trial also perished, as did almost all those who had been involved in the trial. Sergei Morozov's suicidal end in 1923 has already been noted. About the further fate of the others the following is known.

After serving his prison sentence, Abram Gots was banished to Ul'ianovsk (Simbirsk) where he worked for the planning office of the local industry. ('Fonctionnaire des finances, il jouissait d'une réelle autorité', writes Victor Serge in his memoirs about Gots in exile.)[41] As an exile, Gots was obliged to report daily to the GPU.[42] The new wave of repression at the beginning of the 1930s seems to have moved him to Semipalatinsk.[43] Subsequently he was moved to Alma

Ata in Central Asia, where he again worked for the planning office in the years that remained until his final arrest. The archives of the Hoover Institution in Stanford, California, include some photos of Gots, visibly aged, together with his family in Alma Ata.[44]

There are two versions of how Gots met his end. The first originated with an anonymous western socialist who was released from Soviet imprisonment in 1945. In addition to Gots, this account also refers to one of the Mensheviks who had made unavailing efforts in 1922 to defend the accused Socialist Revolutionaries, Mark Liber, who had also spent the intervening years in prison and in exile. According to this report, after being arrested once again in July 1937, Gots and Liber were put into Alma Ata prison where, in October, they shared a cell with the informant. They were subjected to inhuman torture and ultimately 'confessed' to being counter-revolutionaries who aimed at the overthrow of the Soviet regime, doing so in the vain hope of thus being able to save at least the members of their families. Subsequently they were condemned to death, without any form of trial, by the 'Special Board' of the NKVD (*Osoboe Soveshchanie NKVD*) which was seated in Moscow, and were executed in November 1937. In the opinion of this unknown western socialist, their 'confessions' did not detract from their greatness: they had kept their faith in a better future and had remained faithful to their ideals until the last moment. In taking their leave, Gots and Liber had impressed upon the western socialist that, if he should ever regain his freedom, he should let their party comrades know that they had never capitulated to their victors, nor abandoned their ideals. 'Greet our friends for us and tell them that we have born the name of revolutionary with pride. However difficult it is for us to be accused of being counter-revolutionaries, we know that history will pass a different judgement.... Better times will come for Russia and for the whole world. And then history will judge our actions.'[45]

The wife of Abram Gots, the children's specialist Sara Nikolaevna Gots, née Rabinovich, made great efforts to save her husband but achieved nothing more than one last meeting. Gots had changed so much that at first his wife did not recognize him. Sara Gots was also arrested in the autumn of 1937 and was sent to a prison camp near Karaganda. Their son, a student, was also arrested and, according to our information, was ultimately sent to Kolyma.[46]

There is also another story. If this one is true, then the account given above is incorrect at least insofar as the date of execution of

Gots is concerned, in that he was still alive in 1939. In that year, namely, the second informant was in Butyrki Prison together with Mikhail Gendel'man. The latter told his fellow prisoner that, in the previous April, their captors had confronted him with Gots, intending to stage a show trial of the Socialist Revolutionaries on the basis of their statements. According to Gendel'man, however, they had not allowed themselves to be misused. Gots is said to have then been sent into exile.[47]

Finally, according to official Soviet sources, Gots worked as an economist until 1937, and died in 1940,[48] from which we may probably conclude that he was indeed arrested in 1937. Both stories may thus be correct, with the proviso that the execution of Gots did not take place in 1937 but was postponed until 1940. Officially, the 'Special Board' was not allowed to impose a death sentence, only prison sentences to a maximum of ten years. It is questionable, however, whether such a formality had any effect on the fate of Gots and Liber. According to the Great Soviet Encyclopedia, Liber did indeed die in 1937, namely on 4 October, which approximates the information given by the anonymous western socialist.

As regards Gots's family, according to Svirskaia (with whom I have corresponded), his daughter, who was also a doctor, went to Peshkova at the end of World War II to ask advice about where she would be allowed to settle down after demobilization, so that she could live together with her mother. Peshkova told Svirskaia that after 1956 she had received a New Year's card from Sara Gots, but she knew nothing about the fate of Gots's son.[49]

After serving his prison sentence, Evgenii Timofeev was ultimately exiled to Ural'sk where he stayed during the second half of the 1920s. He also worked for the planning office. The archives of the Hoover Institution contain three letters which Timofeev managed to send abroad to Vladimir and Emma Voitinskii during those years. Among other things, he discussed how many years he and Gots had already 'done': Gots 15 years all told (including ten before the revolution); Timofeev more than 17. His comrades were 'faring well' he wrote with a certain irony, 'because they keep silent [Ukrainian: *bo movchat*], as Shevchenko said.' They did not occupy themselves with politics but only with planning, and also with such innocent matters as archeology.[50]

Early in the 1930s, Timofeev was sent to a more distant place of exile, Samarkand,[51] where the cotton industry employed him as an economist. Svirskaia mentions a special favour enjoyed by Timofeev: now and again he was taken to Moscow where he was shown about. In 1936 he was once again brought to Moscow, but this time to Butyrki Prison. In 1936 and 1937 one of his cell-mates was a former chairman or vice-chairman of the Moscow Soviet who survived the terror and, after 1956, told his story to Svirskaia.[52] Timofeev is said to have been executed in 1941.[53]

Dmitrii Donskoi was exiled first to Narym and then apparently to Tiumen', slightly to the east of the Urals. He died in 1936.[54]

Mikhail Gendel'man also spent the rest of his life in exile (part of the time in Tobol'sk) and in prison. Early in the 1930s he is said to have been arrested once again and, after four months imprisonment in Nizhnii-Novgorod, to have been exiled to Surgut in Northern Siberia.[55] If we can accept the story related above about Gots, then Gendel'man was still alive in 1939.

After the expiration of her prison sentence, Evgeniia Ratner was ultimately exiled to Samarkand, where she worked as an economist. She suffered from cancer, but in Samarkand it was not possible to operate on her properly. Only after considerable discussion and after intervention by the 'Political Red Cross' would the authorities finally give her permission, in the spring of 1931, to go to Leningrad. The operation had been left too long, however, and she died in that same year.[56]

Mikhail Likhach was also sent into exile after his prison sentence, to be arrested again in Voronezh in the early 1930s. He was sent to Cheliabinsk prison where in that same year, 1931, he died of pneumonia in the prison hospital.[57]

Lev Gershtein had been exiled since the early 1930s in Orenburg, where he worked for a bank. Victor Serge — now himself an exile — witnessed the end of Gershtein. He had been seriously ill (he suffered from a heart complaint) and was unable to get the necessary medical care in Orenburg. He asked permission to go to the hospital in Kazan'. That permission was eventually granted but too late, no earlier than the day of his death in 1935. According to Serge, Gershtein died in terrible poverty but retained his idealism and his belief in democracy until the last.[58]

The two Ivanovs were kept in Butyrki Prison until 1926. Elena Ivanova tried to commit suicide in July 1926, but failed due to the accidental intervention of the guard. She and her brother were sent into exile that same year.[59] Early in the 1930s, Nikolai Ivanov was in exile in Samarkand, together with Svirskaia.[60] Nothing further is known about the fate of his sister.

Vladimir Agapov was transferred temporarily to Riazan' during the hunger strike of the convicted Socialist Revolutionaries in October 1925.[61] Later that year he was exiled to Orenburg where he remained until the new wave of arrests in 1931. It is not known where he then went.[62]

In the second half of the 1920s Mikhail Vedeniapin was in exile in Penza where he worked as an economist.[63]

Florian Fedorovich had been banished since the mid-1920s to Orenburg, where he also was an economist. According to Svirskaia, who was also in Orenburg, Fedorovich had to report to the GPU each day. He died of blood poisoning on 28 November 1928, after a fall in the public baths.[64] An interesting detail is that *Izvestiia* published an obituary of Fedorovich in its issue of 6 December 1928.

In 1933 Aleksandr Liberov and Efrem Berg were in Suzdal' prison, together with Olitskaia. Berg had been given a three-year sentence after which, it is said, he was exiled to Merv (now Mary) in Central Asia, where he died in 1935.[65]

After serving his prison sentence, Mikhail L'vov was exiled to Cherdyn'. His wife Nadezhda died there in 1926 in childbirth, due to lack of medical care. L'vov was refused permission to go to a more suitable place of exile with the child. He left nevertheless, was caught, and sentenced to three years to be served in Suzdal' prison.[66]

Vladimir Utgof, after serving his sentence, was banished in the second half of the 1920s to Samarovo in the province of Tobol'sk.[67]

After serving the three-year sentence imposed on him at the trial, Grigorii Gor'kov was exiled to Tsaritsyn (now Volgograd). He was arrested when trying to escape from his place of exile, to be sent in 1924 to Suzdal' concentration camp and later, after a hunger strike, to Cheliabinsk concentration camp. Later still he was exiled to Turtkul' in Uzbekistan. The latest news that we have been able to find about Gor'kov was that he was arrested once again in Voronezh in the early 1930s.[68]

Nothing at all is known about the further fate of Dmitrii Rakov, Nikolai Artem'ev and Pavel Zlobin. Finally, with regard to Arkadii Al'tovskii, Svirskaia heard that he 'has returned' (*vernulsia*), apparently meaning that he has survived 'the *Gulag*', the only one of the 22 accused in 1922 to do so.[69] Further details are not known.

For as far as is known, the ultimate fate of the accused of the second group was no better than that of the first group. No details are available about the lot of Iosif Dashevskii, Fedor Efimov, Filipp Fedorov-Kozlov, Iurii Morachevskii, Pavel Pelevin, Konstantin Usov and Fedor Zubkov. About Grigorii Ratner is known solely that in the 1920s he published a number of books about agriculture and collectivization.

After the trial, Vladimir Ignat'ev worked for the government, and is perhaps the same V.I. Ignat'ev who published several books on public law during the 1920s. He was later arrested, but no details are known about his end.[70]

After carrying out her assignment at the trial, Faina Stavskaia was admitted to the Communist Party and was later given the management of a historical library. In 1937, however, she was arrested and executed.[71]

Lidiia Konopleva was later also arrested, to die in imprisonment in 1940.[72]

Grigorii Semenov is said to have spent some time after the trial in a sanatorium in the Crimea, together with Stavskaia. According to *Golos Rossii*, Semenov was boycotted by the other patients, even though they were all communists.[73] In 1923 he published his memories of the October days of 1917 in the journal *Prozhektor*. His name was in the news again in 1938 in connection with the trial of Bukharin, who was said to have been in touch with Semenov in the early 1930s. The latter had proposed to Bukharin that he, Semenov, should organize a terrorist group with the aim of perpetrating attacks on Stalin and Kaganovich, and Bukharin had agreed, so was contended at the trial. Through Semenov and Semen Chlenov — also known from the 1922 trial as defender of the second group — Bukharin was further said to have been in touch with the leaders of the PSR in Russia and abroad, who had agreed to cooperate in terrorist activities.[74] According to the documents of the trial, Semenov's case as well as that of Chlenov, had been handled separately.[75] The biographical lexicon, *Who Was Who*, states that Semenov had been arrested and had died in prison in the preceding year, 1937.[76] Chlenov also was a victim of the Great Purge.[77]

Most of the other people who had been involved in the trial also met a bad end. The witnesses for the defence were kept in prison after the trial. In 1923 Vasilii Filippovskii was on Solovki, and he died in Kolyma in the 1940s after a lifetime of imprisonment and exile.[78]

Also on Solovki were Aleksandr Gel'fgot, Boris Ivanov and Vsevolod Shestakov, and also Mikhail Tseitlin, Iurii Podbel'skii and Vladimir Merkhalev. Tseitlin's wife was killed in the December 1923 shootings mentioned earlier. In 1924 Fedor Sorokin was in Suzdal' concentration camp. Their lot was the same as that of the other Socialist Revolutionaries. Merkhalev died in exile at the end of the 1920s.[79] Shestakov died in 1938.[80] It is not known when the others died. Vladimir Rikhter, who had gone underground during the trial, was arrested shortly after, was then sent to Suzdal' concentration camp and died in exile in 1932, suffering from 'hunger typhoid'.[81] Vladimir Vol'skii was sent to Solovki, then into exile, and died in 1937.[82]

As we have seen in an earlier chapter, the more neutral witnesses were also subjected to repressive measures after the trial. Their further fate has been traced as follows. Konstantin Burevoi, a disillusioned man, turned his back on politics and concentrated on Ukrainian literature. Nevertheless, he was arrested in 1934 and put to death.[83] According to *Izvestiia* of 18 December 1934, Burevoi and a group of others had been tried before the Supreme Tribunal in Kiev on 13-15 December on charges of terrorism, sentenced to death, and immediately executed. All that is known about Nikolai Rakitnikov is that he was later exiled to Central Asia,[84] as was Iakov Dedusenko.[85] Nikolai Sviatitskii, who had worked as an economist in government service after 1922, was arrested early in the 1930s and died in 1937.[86]

Despite his courageous behaviour during the trial, Andrei Feit was left unmolested. He was medical director of the sanatorium *Vorob'evye Gory* in Moscow, and was the author of a number of medical works. He died a natural death betimes in 1926.[87]

Nikolai Kondrat'ev was director of the Moscow Institute for Conjunctural Research in the 1920s. He was arrested in 1930 because he was said to have been involved in the organization of a peasants' party. He gave evidence at the trials of the Mensheviks and of the Industrial Party and then perished. According to some sources he had become insane while in prison.[88]

Aleksandr Verkhovskii held important military posts until he was arrested in 1937. He died in prison in 1941.[89]

Little is known about what further befell the witnesses who had supported the Indictment. Moisei Rafes worked for the Comintern as propagandist. He was arrested during the Great Purge and died in 1942.[90] Ivan Maiskii became a career diplomat and survived the

Great Terror. He seems to have been arrested shortly before Stalin's death. According to one source he was imprisoned for two-and-a-half years; according to another he was in prison for a shorter term and was released immediately after the death of Stalin.[91] In February 1966 he supported an appeal to the party leadership, warning against rehabilitation of Stalin. He died at a mature age in 1975.

We have already noted that the Russian defenders of the first group were subjected to repressive measures after having laid down their task. Since the mid-1920s Nikolai Murav'ev had been a member of the Moscow College of Advocates. He died in 1936.[92]

Aleksandr Tager published in the years after the trial, including a book which came out in 1933 about the notorious Beilis trial of 1913. He was killed during the 1930s.[93] Vladimir Zhdanov also published after the trial and in 1932 was still registered as member of the College of Advocates.[94] Otsep, who had not come much into the limelight in the 1922 trial, acted as defending counsel at the trial of the Industrial Party in 1930.

Finally, as regards the Bolshevik judges, prosecutors and defenders: Pokrovskii and Lunacharskii died timely natural deaths, but Piatakov, Krylenko, Bukharin and most of the others perished during the Great Terror.

CONCLUSION

'Ce sont les despotes maladroits qui se servent des baïonettes:
l'art de la tyrannie est de faire les mêmes choses avec des juges.'

(Camille Desmoulins)

The trial of the Socialist Revolutionaries had a political objective. Shortly before the announcement of the trial, Lenin had issued instructions to the People's Commissar for Justice in which he insisted that 'noisy, *educative* model trials' of political opponents should be organized. Lenin was not concerned that these trials should exercise justice or establish the truth; this was made all too clear by his opinion that the judges should accommodate themselves to the will of those in power. The trials in question, he considered, should serve the repression and the propaganda.

As we have seen, Lenin's conception of a trial as an instrument of political indoctrination was shared by the other Bolshevik leaders. In 1923 Krylenko said, very expressively: 'A club is a primitive weapon, a rifle is a more efficient one, the most efficient is the court.'[1]

The idea of utilizing political trials for demonstrative purposes was not completely new. Prior to the revolution, a tradition had grown up in Russia which required the accused in political trials to hurl their own accusations in the faces of those in power, an exercise that was intended to indoctrinate the masses and to intimidate the authorities. The new element was that the Bolsheviks, as *government*, now used the political trial to hurl 'the truth' in the faces of the *accused*, and to indoctrinate and intimidate the people. It goes without saying that this was not conducive to correct legal procedures.

Notwithstanding this, the trial of the Socialist Revolutionaries was less a legal farce than the political trials that were later to take place under Stalin, and in which accused, prosecutors and court followed a script that had been previously agreed upon. In the most literal sense, the performers in those trials acted a legal *farce*, a stage play, although it was far from being comic. The 1922 trial was not completely a farce. Only some of the accused, defenders and witnesses acted conform to the wishes of the prosecutors and judges. The first group of accused handled independently and made genuine attempts to defend themselves. Intimidation could not prevent the defenders of this group from laying down their task in protest against the fact that it was made impossible for them to fulfil that task properly, or that some witnesses retained their independence to a greater or lesser degree. This caused the 1922 trial to run far less smoothly than the later trials, and also enabled it to show many characteristics of a genuine trial.

The legal shortcomings were many. The trial was intended not so much to examine the deeds of individual accused on the basis of the law, as to bring discredit to the accused of the first group and to the political orientation that they represented. It was not restricted to punishable offences, but was directed in particular against the political tactics and the ideology of the PSR. Matters were raised with which the accused had had nothing whatsoever to do ('guilt by association'). The Tribunal was unfair towards the accused and their defenders. It rejected their political arguments, saying that this was a legal trial; their legal arguments, however, were either made out to be political or were rejected because the trial was a political affair. The accused and their defenders were subjected to all sorts of restrictions and were strongly handicapped as against the prosecutors and their helpers, who were able to have their own way almost without restraint. The public in the courtroom had plenty of opportunity to show its partiality. The Tribunal rejected in so many words all legal norms that apply in a constitutional state, notwithstanding the fact that in the eyes of the world it wanted to be seen to use them to some extent. It violated the law. The Chairman of the Tribunal gave a speech to a street demonstration at which the death sentence was demanded for the accused. The Tribunal also permitted a demonstration to take place inside the courtroom, at which the death sentence was also demanded.

The judicial investigation was defective. The testimony of the witnesses and the other evidence was of very little conclusive value. The Tribunal did not concentrate on that which could be proven, but then, its case was not intended to bring the truth to light, but to make propaganda against the Socialist Revolutionaries. Although the Tribunal insisted that it was impartial in its search for the facts, its judgement was not objective and was insufficiently substantiated by the evidence. The Tribunal ignored the *nulla poena sine lege* principle, and sentenced the accused on the basis of Articles of Law that had been enacted only a short time before the trial and long after the incriminating acts had been perpetrated. The principal items in the Indictment, on the basis of which the accused were sentenced, concerned events for which they had been granted amnesty in 1919. The fate of the accused was determined not by an independent judicial body, but by the political authorities.

The judicial shortcomings were inherent in the trial which, after all, was not a legal case but a political demonstration which had to evince the outward characteristics of legality. This caused a certain ambivalence in the behaviour of those who were entrusted with the conduct of the trial, but did not change its actual character.

Moreover, the events in the courtroom were not of sole, or even of primary significance. The trial was intended to serve as the impulse for a major propaganda campaign. The propaganda did not take the findings of the Tribunal as its point of departure, and in fact ignored all niceties of distinction in the Tribunal's judgement. To all intents and purposes, the guilt of the accused was a foregone conclusion in the campaign, even before the opening of the trial. The propaganda made use of a few stereotyped, simplified accusations, which were implanted in the minds of the masses by constant repetition, and particularly by reiteration at demonstrations and meetings, and in resolutions. The propaganda incited the people to bloodthirsty hatred of the Socialist Revolutionaries, not only of the accused but of the political orientation that they represented.[2]

It is quite obvious, both from the trial itself and from the propaganda campaign with which it was surrounded, that the Bolsheviks saw it as an instrument with which to achieve their own political ends. No records are available of the consultations about the trial held in camera by the highest realms of the party. The answer to the question of which goals the Bolshevik leaders wanted to achieve with the aid of the trial must therefore remain hypothetical, incurring some risk of attributing, after the event, greater rationality to the methods of the Bolsheviks than they actually deserve.

The trial might have been intended to justify the repressive measures against the Russian socialists. If that was the case, however, it was probably only a secondary objective. In addition, there are clear signs that an attempt was made to have the Socialist Revolutionaries serve as scapegoat for the enormous economic difficulties in which the country found itself after the civil war.[3] But this does not adequately explain the motivations of the Bolsheviks.

The principal objective of the Bolsheviks in holding the trial of the Socialist Revolutionaries was probably to break the opposition of the socialist parties to their regime. It might be thought that the result of the civil war had shown that the Socialist Revolutionaries and the Mensheviks were not at all powerful. The Bolsheviks themselves proclaimed continually that the Socialist Revolutionaries and the Mensheviks signified nothing at all, and only formed a risk in that they were tools of international capitalism which made them carry out espionage, sabotage and terror, and organize an armed struggle against the Soviet regime. By painting this danger in glaring colours, the Bolshevik propaganda depicted a contradictory image of the Socialist Revolutionaries as both insignificant individuals and as dangerous enemies.

In reality, the Bolsheviks were undoubtedly very apprehensive of the Socialist Revolutionaries and the Mensheviks, and not without reason. After the civil war great dissatisfaction manifested itself among the masses, not only among the peasants but also among the workers, a dissatisfaction that took the form of revolts and strikes. If free elections had then been held, the Socialist Revolutionaries and the Mensheviks would undoubtedly have been dangerous opponents. The Bolsheviks reacted to this explosion of discontent by introducing their New Economic Policy, but they were determined not to give the socialist opposition any chance of acquiring a firm basis. And it was then that they launched a campaign aimed at the ultimate destruction of the socialist opposition; the trial of the Socialist Revolutionaries formed an important element of that campaign, if not the most important.

The trial and the propaganda campaign that accompanied it were thus intended to break the active nucleus of the socialist opposition. By threatening the active members of the opposition at one moment with the possibility of execution, and at the next tempting them with the chance of being released, the Bolsheviks tried to force them to their knees: to show repentance, to relinquish all political activity and to subjugate themselves to the Soviet regime. They were required to repudiate their ideals and to dissociate themselves from their party associates abroad; in this way attempts were also made to sow discord among them. In comparison with all this, the trial's repressive function was of less significance: the Bolshevik leaders had other means of repression at their disposal.

Above all, however, the trial was intended to rob the opposition of its influence, or potential influence over the people. It had to make it quite clear to the masses that the socialists in Russia had no right to a political existence; that only the communists had the right and the ability to govern the country; and that it was dangerous to associate in any way with these political adversaries. The trial was thus intended to simultaneously indoctrinate and intimidate broad layers of the population.

Finally, the Bolsheviks wanted to justify the suppression of the socialist opposition in the eyes of the world as an expression of the will of the people. To this end, use was made of a new technique of mass mobilization. This had earlier been used by revolutionary movements against the ruling powers, with the purpose both of indoctrinating the adherents and of intimidating the authorities. This time, however, the government itself adopted this technique, with the purpose both of indoctrinating the mobilized masses, of intimidating the domestic opposition, and also of legitimizing its own policies.

It is possible that the intervention by western socialists contributed to the fact that the Bolshevik leaders, who now had to demonstrate that the government had the support of the people, decided on such a large-scale application of this technique.

That the PSR was chosen as first target in the campaign against the socialist opposition was not without reason. Only a few years earlier, as shown by the results of the elections for the Constituent Assembly, the Socialist Revolutionaries had enjoyed a very substantial support among the Russian people. Although the many millions who had voted for the PSR in 1917 were probably no longer all on the side of the Socialist Revolutionaries, certainly not in an active sense, the PSR continued to represent at least a potential danger in the eyes of the Bolsheviks. Added to this was the fact that the Socialist Revolutionaries had been more energetic in their resistance to the Bolshevik dictatorship in the past than had the Mensheviks. On the one hand that made them more dangerous, and on the other hand it made it easier for the Bolsheviks to raise accusations against them around which a propaganda campaign could be constructed. In fact, however, that campaign was directed also against the rest of the opposition, in particular the Mensheviks.

There was also a distinct connection between the suppression of the socialist opposition and that of the opposition inside the Communist Party, with which a begin was made in the same period. Early in the 1920s, for instance, the Bolshevik Gavrila Miasnikov, a supporter of the 'workers' oppositon' within the Communist Party, championed freedom of expression and of the press, and the right of the workers and peasants to independent organization. When Miasnikov advocated these ideas at a party meeting in 1921, Zinov'ev declared that he must be either 'a Socialist Revolutionary or sick'. Zinov'ev threatened Miasnikov that if he did not shut up, he would be expelled from the party. 'Any attempt to utter a word of criticism results in the bold one being put on the list of the Mensheviks and the Socialist Revolutionaries, with all the resultant consequences,' declared Miasnikov later (mid-1921) in this regard. In August 1921 the Central Committee prohibited him from speaking in public; in February 1922 he was expelled from the party.[4] Shortly after, he was arrested, put into prison for three-and-a-half years, and subsequently sent to a place of exile within the Soviet Union.[5]

At the party conference in August 1922 Zinov'ev also criticized what, in his view, was the misplaced opposition within the Communist Party, which played into the hands of the Mensheviks and the Socialist Revolutionaries. And at the 13th Party Congress in May 1924, Stalin described the members of the opposition in the Communist Party as helpers and mouthpiece of the opposition outside the party, i.e. the Mensheviks and the Socialist Revolutionaries.[6]

If the trial of the Socialist Revolutionaries is compared with subsequent political trials in the Soviet Union, the independent attitude taken by the real accused — those of the first group — immediately attracts attention. Like the Bolsheviks, these accused intended to use the trial for political purposes, wanting to turn it into a political demonstration against the Bolshevik regime. They were hopelessly disadvantaged, however, as compared to their accusers who had assured themselves of an almost complete monopoly of the communications media.

Notwithstanding this, the 1922 trial also showed some similarity with the later trials in as far as the behaviour of the accused was concerned. The accused of the second group endorsed the Indictment in full and indulged themselves in self-accusations. Their motives were various. Fedorov-Kozlov, for instance, had obviously succumbed to the pressure that had been brought to bear on him; Semenov and Konopleva were immoral adventurers and opportunists; Grigorii Ratner gave the impression of having acted from conviction, however depraved a conviction may seem which made him say that, on behalf of the revolution, a man could send not only his former party comrades, but also 'his own sister [Evgeniia Ratner] to the scaffold.'

The accused Socialist Revolutionaries displayed great courage during the 1922 trial, and this was recognized by the Bolsheviks. 'Brave people beyond all question', said Mikhail Pokrovskii early in 1924 with regard to the Socialist Revolutionaries. 'They were tried by us. I served as a prosecutor, and I might say with complete objectivity that they conducted themselves splendidly at the trial, even though they were threatened with a 90 percent chance of execution.... Personal courage? The Socialist Revolutionaries had that to a sufficient degree.'[7]

At later trials there was no question of any defence such as that shown by the Socialist Revolutionaries. A number of the accused at the so-called Shakhty trial in 1928 did not endorse the Indictment completely, but that was the last time — if we do not consider behaviour such as that shown by Bukharin in 1938. Only people 'of the second group' were admitted to later trials. Such people can always be found. But the remarkable thing is that people were found to play this role who were of far greater political calibre than a Semenov. Should this be imputed to lack of courage on their part?

This seems to be contradicted, for instance, by the case of Isaak Rubin. As a Menshevik in 1922, Rubin had resisted the will of those in power and had offered his services to the Socialist Revolutionaries as defending counsel. As a result, he was put in prison. In 1924 he withdrew from all political activity. In 1931, 14 'Mensheviks' were put on trial, all of whom, with one exception, had long given up their membership of the Menshevik Party, or had not belonged to it at all. As one of the accused, Rubin now endorsed the Indictment, although it was even more improbable than the 1922 Indictment.[8]

What caused a man such as Rubin to show such different behaviour in 1931 to that in 1922? In a number of respects, the accused in the later trials were in a different position to the Socialist Revolutionaries in the 1922 trial. The latter could still have illusions about the character and the permanence of the regime, could still have illusions that they would be able to achieve something, or would at least leave a memory behind them that would serve as an example to others. In the 1930s, however, the accused could have had very few illusions left about the existence of a public opinion or about any moral support among the masses. Such illusions, in their case, could only have given way to feelings of desolation, of hopelessness.

Secondly, the regime in 1922 had not yet developed its full faculty for coercion and terror, and moderating forces were still active within the government. Notwithstanding the lack of compromise shown by the Bolsheviks and their socialist opponents, the one to the other, the mutual feelings of comradeship which dated back to the times of their joint struggle against the Tsarist regime had not completely disappeared. Mina Svirskaia shows in her memoirs, for instance, that a man such as the former Menshevik Ivan Maiskii, who had joined the Communist Party in 1921, had maintained friendly relations with unconverted Socialist Revolutionaries such as Svirskaia herself, or the Central Committee member, Florian Fedorovich, until shortly before the 1922 trial at which Maiskii appeared as witness for the prosecution.[9] According to Svirskaia, Mikhail Frunze, a prominent Bolshevik who held a high position in the Red Army, even tried during the trial to arrange a meeting with that same Fedorovich, a good friend of Frunze since their mutual exile before 1917 and now one of the accused.[10]

Lastly, the Socialist Revolutionary accused in 1922 received considerable support from their socialist colleagues and from other leftist circles in the West. In the 1930s, however, these circles left the accused largely to their lot, which could only increase their feelings of isolation.

In this connection, it might be asked whether the trial of the Socialist Revolutionaries was indeed a 'show trial'. A characteristic of the classical show trial, after all, is that the accused 'confess'. 'The crux of the show trial is the confession', says the American expert on Stalinism, R.C. Tucker.[11] Seen in this way, the 1922 trial was far from perfect as a show trial. But Tucker's definition to some extent disregards another characteristic of the show trial: the large-scale use that is made of it for propaganda purposes. The trial of the Socialist Revolutionaries was no less an instrument of political indoctrination than the latter, classical show trials.

In its basic essentials, and leaving out of consideration that which

Soviet historians contend on this point, historiography shows two contrasting positions regarding the question of the evolution of the communist regime in Russia from its 'Leninist' to its 'Stalinist' stage. According to one position, Stalinism started under Lenin; according to the other, Stalinism cannot be seen as anything other than a degeneration of Leninism. When we speak of Stalinism we think not in the last place of the trials that were held in the 1930s, the classical show trials of Stalin's former rivals in the Bolshevik Party leadership. What can we say when we compare these 'Stalinist' trials with a 'Leninist' trial such as that of the Socialist Revolutionaries in 1922? We have been able to ascertain that on some points the latter deviated considerably from the Stalinist trials. But on the other hand, a number of elements which determined the character of the Stalinist trials were already clearly evident in the 1922 trial; the conclusion is then unavoidable that, if there was any question of a degeneration of the Bolshevik regime, this was already fairly far advanced in 1922. In other words, it started under Lenin and not, as suggested by Medvedev, through no fault of his.

We have no knowledge about what the Bolshevik leaders thought about the results of the 1922 trial. We do know, however, that there was no follow-up for a long time. Why? It is possible, of course, that the Bolshevik leaders considered that the desired results had been achieved to a sufficient degree and that further major political trials were not necessary. It might also be, however, that the idea of further trials was abandoned because the results of the 1922 trial were deemed to be not completely satisfactory.

When, at the end of June or early in July, Lenin learned that the trial still continued, his reaction was somewhat censorious. He considered that it was occupying the time of many people who had urgent work to do elsewhere. Indeed, a number of Bolshevik leaders took a very intensive part in the lengthy trial. The more matter-of-fact among the Bolshevik leaders perhaps considered that too much time and energy had been devoted to the trial, and their reservations were perhaps strengthened by its negative side effects. The trial had become an embarrassing factor in diplomatic consultations with European governments. It disturbed relationships with the western socialists, even with those of the centre in the Vienna Union on whom the Comintern had fastened its hopes in the question of achieving greater unity in the international socialist movement. It was causing the Second International and the Vienna Union to drift closer together. It gave rise to public criticism of the policies of the Soviet government among the *communisants*. It even caused some degree of friction within the Comintern. And the trial met objections among the Russian intelligentsia.

The trial certainly had intimidation as one of its objectives, but in the eyes of the more practical and more moderate among the Bolshevik leaders, the scales had perhaps tipped too far towards hostility and intimidation. It is possible that in their view this hostility, not only towards the immediate political opponents in Russia but also towards the latter's 'allies' in Russia and abroad, made more propaganda against the Soviet regime than in its favour. The trial also directed attention, probably more than was considered desirable, to phenomena which the Bolshevik leaders would have preferred to keep concealed from the outside world: the existence in Russia of a political opposition and of political prisoners. The leaders wanted only favourable attention from the outside world, and they preferred repression to be kept behind the scenes.

Many elements in the 1922 trial were detrimental to the propagandist effect that it was meant to have. The 'show' element was present in full force; as far as that was concerned, the 1922 trial was not outdone by the later trials. On the other hand, instead of acknowledging guilt, the accused at the 1922 trial dared to defend themselves, and were able to do so — at least within certain limits. To some extent they had the chance to defend their own policies and to attack those of the Bolsheviks. It is true that the charges against them were highly biased and to a considerable extent untrue, but in comparison with the charges made at the later trials, they seem almost models of objectivity. All these elements had a significantly disadvantageous effect on the propagandist value of the trial (although in some respects they were advantageous because they gave the trial some semblance of being the genuine article).

Perhaps these negative experiences, supplemented by those of the Baku trial, contributed to the fact that no follow-up to the 1922 trial occurred for some years. Not until the end of the 1920s, when the period of the New Economic Policy was coming to its end, did the Bolshevik leaders once again take up the instrument which they had tested in 1922 — but by then it was obvious that they had learned their lesson.

ABBREVIATIONS USED IN THE NOTES

GR	*Golos Rossii*
Izv	*Izvestiia VTsIK*
NC	Nicolaevsky Collection (Hoover Institution, Stanford)
OZ	*Obvinitel'noe zakliuchenie* (see *Bibliography*)
Pr	*Pravda*
Protsess I	*Protsess P.S.R. Rechi gosudarstvennykh obvinitelei* (see *Bibliography*)
Protsess II	*Protsess eserov. Rechi zashchitnikov i obviniaemykh* (see *Bibliography*)
RR	*Revoliutsionnaia Rossiia*
SV	*Sotsialisticheskii vestnik*
Wauters	*Compte-rendu des cinq premières journées du procès des Socialistes Révolutionnaires à Moscou*, by A.J. Wauters (LSI archives, No. 96, IISH)

NOTES

Preface
pages vii-xii

1   See p. 179.
2   On the history of the Socialist Revolutionaries prior to the October Revolution of 1917, see the works listed in the *Bibliography* by Radkey, Perrie and Hildermeier.
3   Radkey, *The Election*, pp. 16-17.
4   *Rapport*, p. 8. The Bolshevik Bystrianskii, in a work dated 1921, calls the PSR in 1917 'a party of almost a million members' (Bystranski, p. 35). See also Radkey, *The Agrarian Foes*, pp. 236-237. The present Soviet historiography gives various estimates of the number of members of the PSR in 1917, running from 400,000 to 700,000: Spirin, *Klassy*, p. 49; Idem, *Krushenie*, pp. 301-302; Astrakhan, pp. 232-233. The criteria for membership were not entirely clear, and the registration was defective.
5   Sukhomlin, *Sotsialist-Revoliutsioner*, No. 2 (October 1929), p. 16.
6   Krylenko, *Za piat' let*, p. 325.
7   See e.g. the works listed in the *Bibliography* by Golinkov, Gusev and Eritsian, Soboleva, Podbolotov, Zlobina, Etenko, Barikhnovskii; see also *Neotvratimoe vozmezdie*. Krylenko's speech was re-published in 1964 (Krylenko, *Sudebnye rechi*, pp. 82-298), shortened versions of the speeches of the other principal prosecutors followed in 1965 (*Sudebnye rechi*, pp. 5-43).
8   *Belaia kniga*, p. 406.
9   Solzhenitsyn, Vol. I-II, pp. 358-371.
10 Medvedev, pp. 743-746.
11 See the works listed in the *Bibliography* by Schapiro, Shub, Ziehr, Baynac (*La terreur*), Orlov. See also note 11 to the *Conclusion*.
12 See e.g. *Proletarskaia revoliutsiia*, 1924, No. 8-9, p. 369.

Chapter 1
pp. 1-21

1   *Dekrety*, Vol. 2, pp. 430-431.
2   He did not reach his destination, however, because he was shot by soldiers of the Red Army when passing the front line. *Kogan-Bernshtein*, pp. 38-52; Burevoi, pp. 42-50; *Proletarskaia revoliutsiia*, No. 20, pp. 267-270; Zand, p. 77; Popov, *1918 god*, pp. 204-205.
3   *Byloe*, No. 16 (1921), p. 32.
4   Burevoi, p. 27.
5   NC 7, No. 55: Chernov, '*Chernovskaia gramota*', pp. 3-15, Hoover Institution, Stanford.
6   *Sovremennye zapiski*, No. 45 (1931), pp. 348-352.
7   Lenin, Vol. 50, p. 239.
8   Spirin, *Klassy*, p. 300.
9   Sviatitskii, pp. 134-152; Burevoi, pp. 59-61; *K prekrashcheniiu*, pp. 38-51; Sverdlov, Vol. 3, pp. 114, 227-228; Gusev/Eritsian, p. 350.
10 *Narodovlastie* I, pp. 57-58; *K prekrashcheniiu*, p. 111.
11 *Sovremennyi moment*, pp. 15-23; NC 7, No. 9, Hoover Institution, Stanford. On the

attitude of the Central Committee's Moscow Bureau: *Izvestiia* (Moscow Bureau), January 1919, NC, not catalogued, Hoover Institution, Stanford.

12 NC 7, No. 26, Hoover Institution, Stanford.
13 *Izv*, 5 February 1919; *K prekrashcheniiu*, p. 66; Vishniak, *Vserossiiskoe uchreditel'noe sobranie*, p. 214; Sverdlov, Vol. 3, pp. 129, 227-228.
14 *Dekrety*, Vol. 4, pp. 436-437.
15 Vardin, p. 10.
16 *Narodovlastie* I, pp. 61-62.
17 *Delo naroda*, 21 March 1919, Melgunov Collection 1-7, Hoover Institution, Stanford.
18 *Krasnyi arkhiv*, No. 20 (1927), pp. 156-165; *Protsess* II, pp. 54, 79, 189; *RR*, No. 21-22, p. 20.
19 *Izv*, 3 July 1919.
20 Chernov, *Pered burei*, p. 406; *Narodovlastie* I, pp. 62-63.
21 Resolution of the Central Committee of 5 April 1919, NC 7, No. 14, Hoover Institution, Stanford.
22 *K prekrashcheniiu*, pp. 52-86.
23 *Izveshchenie o IX Sovete P.S.R.*, Arkhiv PSR, No. 223, IISH, Amsterdam, and NC 7, No. 7, Hoover Institution, Stanford.
24 Burevoi, pp. 74-82.
25 Shestak, p. 99; Chemerisskii, p. 82; Petrov, p. 54.
26 *Listok Dela naroda*, No. 4, Arkhiv PSR, No. 622/4, IISH, Amsterdam.
27 Gusev/Eritsian, p. 356.
28 Idem.
29 *Listok Dela naroda*, No. 6, Prilozhenie, Arkhiv PSR, No. 622/4, IISH, Amsterdam; Burevoi, p. 87.
30 *Listok Dela naroda*, No. 6, Prilozhenie, Arkhiv PSR, No. 622/4, IISH, Amsterdam; Burevoi, p. 88-89.
31 Burevoi, p. 91.
32 *Pr*, 6 December 1919; Gusev/Eritsian, pp. 358-359; *Voprosy istorii*, 1965, No. 11, p. 27; Zand, p. 115; Burevoi, p. 96.
33 *RR*, No. 7, p. 89; *SV*, 1921, No. 5, p. 12.
34 *Lenin i VChK*, pp. 415-416.
35 Burevoi, p. 97; *Lenin i VChK*, pp. 349-350, 406.
36 *RR*, No. 7, p. 89; *SV*, 1921, No. 5, p. 12.
37 *RR*, No. 11, pp. 31-32.
38 Burevoi, p. 117.
39 Siberia: appeal of the 'Siberian Union of Socialist Revolutionaries' of August 1919, NC, not catalogued, Hoover Institution, Stanford; Rakov, *Pr*, 11 July 1922 ('Political Centre'). Ekaterinoslav: Spirin, *Klassy*, p. 303; Zand, p. 153. Khar'kov: Zand, p. 113. Nikolaev and Baku: Gusev, p. 359. Black Sea region: *RR*, No. 16-18, p. 48. Transcaucasia: NC 7, No. 32, Hoover Institution, Stanford. On the attitude of the PSR towards the Soviets, see also E. Ratner, *Izv*, 23 June 1922; Gots, *Izv*, 13 July 1922.
40 *The Mensheviks*, p. 186.
41 *OZ*, p. 40; *Proletarskaia revoliutsiia*, 1921, No. 1, pp. 114-121.
42 Paris: NC 7, No. 12, Hoover Institution, Stanford; Spirin, *Klassy*, p. 302; *OZ*, p. 40. Kiev: *Biulleten' TsK PSR*, No. 1, Arkhiv PSR, No. 622/7, IISH, Amsterdam; B. Ivanov, *Pr* and *Izv*, 6 July 1922; cf. also Radkey, *The Sickle*, p. 475. Ekaterinoslav: Spirin, *Klassy*, p. 303; Zand, p. 153. Ekaterinodar: Gusev, p. 302; Zand, p. 110.
43 Cf. *OZ*, p. 53.
44 Chaikin, p. 140.
45 Tschernow, *Meine Schicksale, passim*.
46 Steinberg, *Spiridonova*, p. 250.
47 *Iz istorii V.Ch.K.*, p. 354.
48 *Novyi zhurnal*, No. 121, p. 153; Chernov Andreyev, p. 18.
49 Arkhiv PSR, No. 622/10, IISH, Amsterdam; *Volia Rossii*, 6 September 1921.
50 NC 7, No. 12, Hoover Institution, Stanford; *RR*, No. 1, p. 32. For the consultations: Vardin, pp. 13-14.

51 NC 7, No. 12, Hoover Institution, Stanford; *RR*, No. 1, pp. 29-30. On the attitude of the PSR towards the war with Poland: Arkhiv PSR, No. 173, IISH, Amsterdam.
52 Lunacharskii, p. 70; *OZ*, p. 47; *Vestnik agitatsii i propagandy*, 1921, No. 11-12, p. 14. For a letter by Vedeniapin on support for the Red Army: *Protsess* II, pp. 78-79, 204-205.
53 *OZ*, p. 43; Lunacharskii, p. 72.
54 *Za narod*, No. 1, p. 23; *RR*, No. 11, p. 3.
55 NC 7, No. 17, Hoover Institution, Stanford; *GR*, 8 September 1922.
56 On his estrangement from the PSR, see also *Protsess* II, p. 234; Gusev/Eritsian, p. 373.
57 Sorokin, *Leaves*, p. 172.
58 Lenin, Vol. 37, pp. 188-197.
59 Gusev/Eritsian, p. 373.
60 Verkhovskii, *passim*.
61 *RR*, No. 31, p. 20.
62 See e.g. Bezpalov, *passim*; *RR*, No. 8, pp. 28-29.
63 Latsis, pp. 16-17.
64 Svirskaia, *Vospominaniia*, p. 10, archive of B. Sapir.
65 *SV*, 1921, No. 1, p. 14; letter to Chernov, NC 236, No. 66, Hoover Institution, Stanford; Vandervelde/Wauters, p. 174. On Savinkov's expulsion, see Radkey, *The Agrarian Foes*, pp. 315, 401-402.
66 *SV*, 1921, No. 14-15, p. 10.
67 *Vestnik agitatsii i propagandy*, 1921, No. 16-17, pp. 33-34.
68 Zorin, p. 8.

Chapter 2
pp. 22-46

1 See e.g. Dvinov, p. 61; *SV*, 1931, No. 21, p. 14, although this account by Nikolaevskii should be read with some scepticism (cf. *Leninskii sbornik*, Vol. 37, p. 289); Aronson, p. 89. See also Serge, *Mémoires*, pp. 180-181; Schapiro, pp. 207-208.
2 See e.g. Zinov'ev, *Vestnik agitatsii i propagandy*, 1921, No. 20-21, pp. 1-5; Lenin, Vol. 43, p. 242.
3 On the Socialist Revolutionaries' opinion of the NEP, see the letter signed by ten members of the Central Committee and sent from Butyrki Prison in September 1921: NC 7, No. 17, Hoover Institution, Stanford, and *GR*, 8 September 1922.
4 Golinkov, *Krakh*, p. 299; *Izv*, 8 February 1922.
5 *RR*, No. 1, p. 27.
6 *Lenin i VChK*, p. 546.
7 Voitinskii, p. 30; *GR*, 17 March 1922. On Semenov's role during the October Revolution: *Prozhektor*, 1923, Nos. 6, 9; Semenov, p. 8.
8 *Izv*, 28 June 1922; *Pr*, 30 June 1922; *Protsess* II, p. 169; Voitinskii, p. 32; Vandervelde/Wauters, p. 172; *GR*, 23 March 1922; Shklovskii, p. 216.
9 Semenov, p. 44.
10 *GR*, 18 March 1922.
11 *Pr* and *Izv*, 30 June 1922; see also Zenzinov, *Novaia Rossiia*, No. 42-43, p. 11.
12 Vandervelde/Wauters, p. 174; Bezpalov, p. 77.
13 *GR*, 23 March 1922.
14 Rakitnikov, *Izv*, 28 June 1922; Bezpalov, p. 77; see also Semenov, *Pr*, 30 June 1922.
15 *GR*, 23 March 1922.
16 *Izv* and *Pr*, 25 July 1922; Golinkov, *Krakh*, p. 307. On Konopleva, see also Shklovskii, pp. 208, 216.
17 *Dzerzhinskii*, p. 267.
18 Lenin, Vol. 44, pp. 396-400.
19 The article by Brandenburgskii had appeared before in *Ezhenedel'nik sovetskoi iustitsii*, 2 March 1922.
20 *SV*, 1922, No. 8, p. 10; Idem, No. 9, p. 10; Dvinov, p. 114.
21 *GR*, 11 March 1922.
22 NC 7, No. 19, Hoover Institution, Stanford.

23   *RR*, No. 1, pp. 30-31; *Za svobodu*, No. 18, p. 40.
24   *RR*, No. 8, pp. 29-30; Donneur, p. 114.
25   Letter from Butyrki Prison of October 1921, *RR*, No. 14-15, pp. 38-41.
26   NC 7, No. 17, Hoover Institution, Stanford; *GR*, 8 September 1922; Arkhiv PSR, No. 593/II/11, IISH, Amsterdam; see also E. Ratner, *RR*, No. 21-22, p. 31.
27   *Nachrichten*, 2. Jahrg., No. 3, pp. 6-7.
28   *RR*, No. 19, p. 16.
29   Idem, p. 19.
30   *SV*, 1922, No. 7, p. 14.
31   Letters to Rubanovich of 21 and 25 March 1922, NC 7, No. 49, Hoover Institution, Stanford.
32   On the origins of the term: Compère-Morel, pp. 926-929; *Internationales Handwörterbuch*, Vol. 2, pp. 2038-2039; *Sovetskaia istoricheskaia entsiklopediia*, Vol. 5, p. 536.
33   Lenin, Vol. 45, pp. 89-90.
34   Dvinov, pp. 114-115.
35   *SV*, 1922, No. 6, p. 14.
36   See e.g. *GR*, 2 April 1922.
37   On the expectations of the Socialist Revolutionaries in other directions, see NC 7, No. 39, Hoover Institution, Stanford.
38   Report of the meeting written by the Socialist Revolutionaries: NC 7, No. 42, Hoover Institution, Stanford.
39   See *RR*, No. 16-18, p. 48.
40   *RR*, No. 19, pp. 1-11.
41   Donneur, pp. 190-191; minutes of the Foreign Delegation of the PSR, 2 April 1922: NC 7, No. 39, Hoover Institution, Stanford.
42   Donneur, p. 187.
43   Kurskii, *Pr*, 21 March 1922; see also Lenin, Vol. 45, p. 48.
44   *Protokoll der internationalen Konferenz, passim.*
45   Idem, p. 47.
46   *Mezhdunarodnaia sotsialisticheskaia konferentsiia*, p. 60.
47   Rosmer, pp. 218-219.
48   Lenin, Vol. 45, pp. 140-144.
49   Idem, pp. 145, 531.
50   *Bericht*, p. 49.
51   See *Die Rote Fahne* and *Vorwärts*, 4 and 5 May 1922.
52   Donneur, p. 238.
53   Soboleva, *Oktiabr'skaia revoliutsiia*, p. 21.
54   Serge, *Mémoires*, p. 181.
55   Lenin, Vol. 45, p. 534.
56   Idem, pp. 149-151.
57   Dvinov, p. 116.
58   NC 7, No. 39, Hoover Institution, Stanford.
59   Donneur, pp. 225, 227; LSI Archives, No. 93, IISH, Amsterdam.
60   *GR*, 29 April 1922; Donneur, pp. 227-228, 232.
61   NC 7, No. 19, Hoover Institution, Stanford; Paul-Boncour, Vol. 2, p. 78.
62   Donneur, p. 233.
63   Morgan, p. 372.
64   NC 7, No. 19, Hoover Institution, Stanford.
65   Wheeler, pp. 173, 321, 354, etc.; Morgan, pp. 393, 410, 411, 465.
66   NC 7, No. 19, Hoover Institution, Stanford.
67   *Bericht*, p. 30.
68   *Inprekorr*, 1922, No. 63, p. 487.
69   *Bericht*, pp. 47-48.
70   *GR*, 8 June 1922; see also *Volia Rossii*, No. 26-27, p. 24.
71   Rappoport, *Ma vie*, Vol. 2, pp. 80, 82, Archives Rappoport, IISH, Amsterdam.

Chapter 3
pp. 47-61

1   *SV*, 1922, No. 8, p. 10; Idem, No. 12, p. 12; Golinkov, *Krakh*, p. 310; Wauters, p. 5.
2   Krylenko, *Za piat' let*, p. 238; Wauters, p. 5, see also pp. 3, 8, on particulars regarding the preliminary investigation. On Rozmirovich's activities during the preliminary investigation, see e.g. Lenin, Vol. 54, pp. 257-258.
3   Shklovskii, pp. 245, 341, 344, 384; on his return in 1923, see Shklovsky, p. XXIII.
4   *Znamia truda* (Odessa), No. 13 (March 1922), NC, Hoover Institution, Stanford; Krylenko, *Za piat' let*, p. 258.
5   Interview with B. Sapir, 3 September 1974, Amsterdam; S. Kuresha, 'Taganka-Solovki-Butyrki', *Slovo*, No. 356, 11 (12?) December 1926, Melgunov Collection 9-51, Hoover Institution, Stanford.
6   Interview with B. Sapir, 3 September 1974, Amsterdam.
7   *RR*, No. 21-22, p. 20.
8   Medvedev, p. 745.
9   *Pr*, 16 May, and *Izv*, 7 July 1922.
10 *Izv*, 19, 20, and 21 July, and *Pr*, 25 July 1922.
11 *Pr* and *Izv*, 23 June 1922. On Agranov's attitude in this connection, see also Mel'gunov, 'Sud...', pp. 50, 54.
12 *Izv*, 30 June, and *GR*, 13 July 1922. On the interrogation by Agranov of Burevoi: *Protsess* II, p. 28.
13 *GR*, 21 May 1922.
14 *Izv*, 30 May, 1 and 2 June 1922.
15 See also Kurskii, *Pr*, 19 April 1922.
16 *The Trotsky Papers*, Vol. 2, p. 708.
17 *OZ*, p. 108. See also Krylenko, *Za piat' let*, p. 317; *Izv*, 25 July 1922.
18 See e.g. *GR*, 9 June 1922; *Volia Rossii*, No. 23-24, p. 24.
19 On him, see *Izv*, 21 February, 10 March and 21 May, and *Pr*, 6 April and 21 May 1922.
20 Shvekov, pp. 139, 141; Kuritsyn, p. 96.
21 Kuritsyn, pp. 96-97.
22 Lenin, Vol. 45, pp. 189-191.
23 *Sbornik dokumentov*, pp. 123-124.
24 Kuritsyn, p. 100; *Istoriia zakonodatel'stva*, pp. 188, 232.
25 Donneur, pp. 245-248.
26 Idem, pp. 250-251; *Inprekorr*, 1922, No. 75, p. 573.
27 NC 7, No. 39, Hoover Institution, Stanford.
28 *GR*, 19 May, and *Izv*, 20 May 1922. Cf. Vandervelde/Wauters, pp. 101, 103.
29 On the last two, NC 7, No. 39, Hoover Institution, Stanford.
30 Paul-Boncour, Vol. 2, p. 80.
31 *GR*, 19 May, and *Izv*, 20 May 1922.
32 *Izv*, 27 May 1922.
33 *Trud*, 27 May 1922.
34 *Pr*, 27 May 1922.
35 *Berliner Tageblatt*, 24 June 1922; *GR*, 25 June 1922; De Kadt, pp. 301-302; interview with Mrs O. Lang, 14 March 1976, New York.
36 Vandervelde/Wauters, p. 36.
37 *Izv*, 28 May 1922.
38 Vandervelde/Wauters, pp. 158-160.
39 *GR*, 1 July 1922; Vandervelde/Wauters, p. 91.
40 It has not been possible to establish the initials for all these people.
41 *Izv*, 2 June 1922.
42 Pokrovskii, p. 5.
43 Dvinov, pp. 131-135; *The Mensheviks*, p. 257.
44 *Istoriia zakonodatel'stva*, p. 130.
45 *Pr*, 28 May, *Izv*, 1 June, and *GR*, 3 June 1922.
46 *Izv*, 9 June 1922.

47   *Pr*, 9 June 1922.
48   *GR*, 25 June 1922.
49   See e.g. *Pamiat'*, No. 3, p. 262.
50   *Bericht*, p. 74; *Izv*, 8 June 1922.
51   Idem. See also Bell, p. 254. With regard to the behaviour of the foreign witnesses during the trial: *Izv*, 16 and 27 June, and *Pr*, 20 June 1922.
52   *GR*, 20 and 30 June 1922.
53   *SV*, 1922, No. 13-14, p. 15; Mel'gunov, *Vospominaniia*, Vol. 2, pp. 76, 78. With regard to an action against one of the Russian lawyers: *GR*, 27 June 1922.
54   Arkhiv PSR, No. 212, IISH, Amsterdam.
55   Vandervelde/Wauters, p. 30.

Chapter 4
pp. 62-82

1   Vandervelde/Wauters, p. 114.
2   Mackenzie, p. 234; Popoff, *Unter dem Sowjetstern*, p. 99; *Inprekorr*, 1922, No. 91, p. 676.
3   See e.g. Bell, p. 254.
4   See e.g. Vandervelde/Wauters, p. 125; Popoff, *Unter dem Sowjetstern*, p. 99; Mackenzie, p. 238; *Trud*, 13 June 1922; *Trud* (Mosk. Org. P.S.R.), No. 5 (28 July 1922), NC, Hoover Institution, Stanford.
5   *SV*, 1922, No. 15, p. 7.
6   Vandervelde/Wauters, pp. 117, 129.
7   *Pr* and *Izv*, 9 June 1922.
8   *Pr*, 9 June 1922.
9   Wauters, p. 12.
10   Vandervelde/Wauters, p. 94; Wauters, pp. 48-49.
11   *Pr*, 14 and 16 June 1922; Golinkov, *Krakh*, pp. 313-314; Wauters, pp. 51-52; Vandervelde/Wauters, p. 96.
12   *Pr*, 14 June 1922. On 'Pinkerton's National Detective Agency', see Friedman, *passim*.
13   Wauters, p. 50.
14   Vandervelde/Wauters, p. 96.
15   Idem, pp. 97-98.
16   *Pr*, 16 June 1922.
17   Idem.
18   *Izv*, 16 June 1922.
19   Rosenfeld, *Die Freiheit*, 27 August 1922; Brandler, *Die Rote Fahne*, 29 August 1922.
20   Vandervelde/Wauters, pp. 98, 69-70.
21   See e.g. *Izv*, 15 June, and *Trud*, 16 June 1922.
22   Mackenzie, pp. 240-241; Marx, p. 35.
23   Cf. also Polonskii, pp. 87, 130; Losskii, p. 219.
24   *Trud*, 21 June, and *Pr*, 22 June 1922.
25   *GR*, 1 July 1922.
26   *Pr*, 22 June 1922.
27   Idem.
28   Mackenzie, pp. 240-241.
29   *Pr*, 22 June 1922; Mackenzie, pp. 240-241.
30   *Bednota*, 22 June 1922.
31   *Pr*, 22 June, and *Trud*, 22 and 23 June 1922.
32   Simonian, p. 162.
33   *Pr, Izv* and *Trud*, 22 June 1922.
34   *Pr*, 22 June 1922; Golinkov, *Krakh*, p. 315; Dvinov, *GR*, 4 August 1922.
35   *Pr* and *Izv*, 22 June 1922.
36   *Sbornik tsirkuliarov*, pp. 49-50.
37   *Trud*, 23 June, and *Pr*, 24 June 1922.
38   *Pr* and *Izv*, 24 June 1922.

39 *Pr*, 24 June 1922. For the reactions of the accused who had been deeply disappointed in Kon, see *Biulleten' Golosa Sotsialista-Revoliutsionera* (Khar'kov), No. 4 (20 July 1922), NC, Hoover Institution, Stanford.
40 *Pr*, 24 June 1922.
41 Idem.
42 *Izv*, 25 June, and *Nakanune*, 30 June 1922.
43 *Izv* and *Trud*, 25 June 1922.
44 *Pr* and *Izv*, 25 June 1922.
45 *Pr*, 25 June 1922.
46 *GR*, 30 June 1922.
47 *Izv*, 27 June 1922.
48 *Izv* and *Trud*, 27 June 1922.
49 Popoff, *Tscheka*, p. 59; *Nasha zhizn'*, November 1922, p. 86; *GR*, 26 August, 1 and 29 September, 14 October 1922.
50 Wauters, p. 14; Vandervelde/Wauters, p. 119.
51 Speech of Gendel'man, Arkhiv PSR, No. 212, IISH, Amsterdam.
52 *Trud*, 9 June 1922; Wauters, pp. 16-17.
53 Speech of Gendel'man, Arkhiv PSR, No. 212, IISH, Amsterdam. See also e.g. *Pr*, 2 July, and *Izv*, 4 July 1922.
54 *Izv*, 23 June and 6 July, and *Pr*, 6 July 1922.
55 *Izv*, 15 June, and *Pr*, 16 June 1922.
56 *RR*, No. 21-22, p. 20.
57 Wauters, pp. 45-46; *Izv* and *Trud*, 14 June 1922.
58 Mel'gunow, *Vospominaniia*, Vol. 2, p. 78; Melgunow, *Der rote Terror*, p. 227; *RR*, No. 21-22, p. 20.
59 *Izv*, 24 June 1922.
60 On Burevoi: *Pr*, 28 June and 16 July, *Izv*, 7 and 16 July, and *Trud*, 4 July 1922; *Protsess* II, p. 28.
61 Melgunow, *Der rote Terror*, p. 227; Mel'gunov, *Vospominaniia*, Vol. 2, p. 78.
62 A protest written by Burevoi to the Tribunal was shown to me by his daughter, Mrs O. Iatsenko, during an interview in New York on 6 May 1976.
63 Krylenko, *Za piat' let*, p. 161.
64 *Izv*, 16 July 1922.
65 *Izv*, 28 June 1922.
66 See e.g. *Bednota*, 21 June 1922.
67 *Pr*, 23 June 1922.
68 Letters written by Burevoi to his wife on 17 and 23 August 1922, shown to me by his daughter.
69 Sorokin, *Leaves*, p. 299; Idem, *A long journey*, p. 192.
70 Letter by 'Moskoventus' of 6 October 1922, NC 7, No. 37 (3), Hoover Institution, Stanford; *SV*, 1922, No. 21, p. 15.
71 *Izv*, 13, 19, 20 and 21 July, and *Pr*, 25 July 1922.
72 *Izv*, 31 August 1922.
73 *Pr* and *Izv*, 24 June 1922.
74 *Izv*, 24 June 1922.
75 Wauters, p. 3; Pokrovskii, p. 4.
76 See e.g. Wauters, pp. 4, 8, 14, 21-22.
77 See e.g. *Izv*, 22 June 1922; Wauters, p. 24; Arkhiv PSR, No. 212, IISH, Amsterdam.
78 *Krasnaia gazeta*, 18 June 1922.
79 *Izv*, 24 and 27 June 1922.
80 *Pr* and *Izv*, 24 June 1922.
81 Idem.
82 *Pr* and *Izv*, 23 June 1922. See also *Biulleten' Golosa Sotsialista-Revoliutsionera* (Khar'kov), No. 4 (20 July 1922), NC, Hoover Institution, Stanford.
83 *Protsess* II, p. 239.
84 *Pr*, 16 and 25 July, and *Izv*, 16 and 23 July 1922; *Protsess* II, p. 83; Arkhiv PSR, No. 212, IISH, Amsterdam.

85   *Izv*, 18 June 1922.
86   *SV*, 1922, No. 15, p. 7.
87   L'vov in his closing address to the court, *RR*, No. 21-22, p. 30.
88   *SV*, 1922, No. 15, p. 7.

Chapter 5
pp. 83-104

1   *OZ*, p. 80; *Izv*, 15 July 1922; *Kratkii otchet*, p. 11. For similar statements by other Socialist Revolutionary leaders: Idem; *Kratkii otchet*, pp. 35, 75-76, 124; *Delo naroda*, 17 November 1917.
2   *OZ*, pp. 79-83; *Izv*, 15 July 1922; Krylenko, *Za piat' let*, pp. 239-248.
3   *Izv*, 15 July, and *Pr*, 1 August 1922; *RR*, No. 21-22, p. 19.
4   *Izv*, 15 July 1922; Pokrovskii, pp. 45-47; Arkhiv PSR, No. 212, IISH, Amsterdam.
5   *Pr*, 16 July 1922; Pokrovskii, pp. 47-48.
6   Chernov, *Kommentarii*, pp. 79-81, 85, NC 7, No. 54, Hoover Institution, Stanford; minutes of the Central Committee of the PSR, 12 December 1917, NC 7, No. 10; proclamation of the Central Committee, 8 February 1918, NC 7, No. 52, and *OZ*, p. 17. Cf. Radkey, *The Sickle*, pp. 184, 329-335.
7   *Izv*, 18 and 19 July 1922; Golinkov, *Krakh*, pp. 319-320.
8   *Izv*, 20 July 1922; for the statement of the Central Committee: *Pr*, 6 September 1918.
9   *Pr*, 18 July 1922; Pokrovskii, pp. 54-58, 60-61; Arkhiv PSR, No. 212, IISH, Amsterdam.
10   *Izv*, 20 July 1922; Pokrovskii, pp. 59-61; Golinkov, 'Razgrom', p. 146; Idem, *Krakh*, p. 323; Arkhiv PSR, No. 212, IISH, Amsterdam.
11   *Pr*, 18, 21 and 22 July, and *Izv*, 21 July 1922; Arkhiv PSR, No. 212, IISH, Amsterdam.
12   *Izv*, 21 July, and *Pr*, 22 July 1922; *RR*, No. 21-22, p. 13; Arkhiv PSR, No. 212, IISH, Amsterdam.
13   *Proletarskaia revoliutsiia*, No. 18-19, pp. 282-285.
14   *Gosudarstvennyi perevorot*, pp. 152-153. See also *GR*, 25 February 1922.
15   *OZ*, p. 93.
16   *Protsess* II, p. 83.
17   *Pr*, *Izv*, and *Trud*, 16 July 1922.
18   *OZ*, p. 88; *Izv*, 18 July, and *Pr*, 4 August 1922.
19   Randall, p. 153. I have not been able to trace the original of this letter.
20   Olitskaia, Vol. 2, p. 143.
21   *Zakliuchenie, passim*.
22   *Protsess* II, pp. 25-28.
23   An edition published after the October Revolution was confiscated by the Bolsheviks. A complete text in a French translation ultimately appeared in Paris in 1930.
24   Spiridovitch, pp. 469-473. Cf. also Hildermeier, p. 376.
25   *Pr*, 18 and 22 July, and *Trud*, 22 July 1922.
26   Cf. Schapiro, p. 154.
27   Cf. Gots and Timofeev, Wauters, pp. 16-17; Gots, Arkhiv PSR, No. 212, IISH, Amsterdam.
28   *Pr*, 18 July 1922; see also, however, Chernov, *RR*, No. 16-18, pp. 11-12.
29   Krylenko, *Za piat' let*, pp. 285-299.
30   *Protsess* I, pp. 234-236.
31   *Izv* and *Pr*, 20 July 1922; *RR*, No. 21-22, pp. 17-18, 20. Cf. Savinkov, pp. 26-27, 32; *Le Matin*, 26 August 1919. See also: *Delo Borisa Savinkova*, p. 55.
32   *Pr* and *Trud*, 25 July 1922; *RR*, No. 21-22, pp. 21, 27; *Protsess* I, p. 235.
33   *OZ*, pp. 34-40; *Izv*, 8 July 1922; Krylenko, *Za piat' let*, pp. 184-190.
34   *Izv*, 30 June and 8 July, and *Pr*, 8 July 1922.
35   *Volia Rossii*, 1 January 1921.
36   *Izv*, 12 July 1922.
37   *OZ*, pp. 40-44; Krylenko, *Za piat' let*, pp. 193-196, 202-211.
38   Cf. Podbel'skii, NC 7, No. 35, Hoover Institution, Stanford.

39　Radkey, *The Unknown Civil War*, p. 119.
40　*Pr*, 25 July and 3 August 1922.
41　*Izv*, 12 July 1922.
42　*Kak tambovskie krest'iane, passim*. See also *Pr*, 25 July 1922.
43　*OZ*, p. 44.
44　*The Trotsky Papers*, Vol. 2, p. 484.
45　Archive of Russian and Eastern European History and Culture, Columbia University, New York, box 7522.
46　*Protsess* I, p. 228.
47　Radkey, *The Unknown Civil War*, pp. 119, 198-199.
48　Idem, p. 198.
49　*GR*, 15 July and 4 August 1922; *Deiatel'nost'*, pp. 12-13, NC 232, No. 4-A, Hoover Institution, Stanford; *Izv*, 8 July 1922.
50　*Izv*, 12 July 1922; Krylenko, *Za piat' let*, pp. 220-233. See also *Rabota eserov zagranitsei, passim*.
51　*Pr*, 9 July 1922; *RR*, No. 21-22, p. 12.
52　*Deiatel'nost', passim*, NC 232, No. 4-A, Hoover Institution, Stanford; *GR*, 15 July and 11 August 1922.
53　*Sotsialist-Revoliutsioner*, No. 2 (October 1929), p. 13.
54　Idem, pp. 16-17.
55　*Pr*, 9 July 1922; *RR*, No. 21-22, p. 12.
56　*Kommunisticheskaia revoliutsiia*, 1922, No. 9, p. 88.
57　*Izv*, 13 July 1922.
58　*Izv*, 2 June 1921.
59　Arkhiv PSR, No. 593/II/9, IISH, Amsterdam.
60　NC 7, No. 17, Hoover Institution, Stanford; *GR*, 8 September 1922; *RR*, No. 14-15, pp. 38-41.
61　NC 7, No. 40, Hoover Institution, Stanford. See also NC 7, No. 39 and 41.
62　*Izv*, 13 July 1922.
63　*Pr*, 5 August 1922.
64　*RR*, No. 9, pp. 3-6.
65　Krylenko, *Za piat' let*, pp. 233-234.
66　Idem, pp. 125-126. See also *Pr*, 18 June, and *Izv*, 16, 17 and 22 June 1922.
67　*Protsess* I, p. 222.
68　Pokrovskii, pp. 25-26; *Izv*, 22 June, and *Pr*, 27 June 1922.
69　Krylenko, *Za piat' let*, pp. 127-134, 144-145.
70　*Izv*, 28 June 1922.
71　Timofeev, *Izv*, 29 June and 2 August 1922.
72　Krylenko, *Za piat' let*, pp. 173, 151.
73　*Pr* and *Izv*, 27 June 1922; Vladimirova, pp. 212-214; Golinkov, *Krakh*, p. 117.
74　Timofeev, *Izv*, 2 August 1922.
75　Lunacharskii, p. 46. Cf. Radkey, *The Sickle*, pp. 366, 453, 492-493.
76　*Pr*, 4 and 5 July, and *Izv*, 4 and 5 July and 2 August 1922.
77　Krylenko, *Za piat' let*, pp. 159-164.
78　*Izv*, 28 June 1922.

Chapter 6
pp. 105-118

1　*Protsess* II, p. 97.
2　*RR*, No. 21-22, p. 9.
3　Lunacharskii: *Protsess* I, pp. 3-77; *Pr*, 4 August 1922. Pokrovskii: *Protsess* I, pp. 79-116. Zetkin, Muna and Bokányi: Idem, pp. 117-152. Krylenko, *Za piat' let*, pp. 140, 143, 176-184, 189, 191-193, 195, 239-240, 322-327. Bukharin: *Protsess* II, pp. 109-144; *Pr*, 5 August 1922.
4　Luxemburg, pp. 67-120; quotation: p. 109.
5　*RR*, No. 21-22, p. 9. For the background to Bukharin's incorrect statement, see Luxemburg, p. IV; Zetkin, *Ausgewählte Reden*, Vol. 2, pp. 386-388.

6   *Pr*, 25 June 1922.
7   Timofeev: Wauters, pp. 23-26; *Pr*, 11 June and 8 July 1922. Gots: *Trud* (Mosk. Org. P.S.R.), No. 5 (28 July 1922), NC, Hoover Institution, Stanford; *Pr* and *Izv*, 22 June 1922. E. Ratner: *Izv*, 23 June 1922; *RR*, No. 21-22, p. 6.
8   Gots, *Izv*, 8 July 1922.
9   Krylenko, *Za piat' let*, p. 189.
10   Gots: *Izv*, 8 July 1922; Krylenko, *Za piat' let*, pp. 188-189; *RR*, No. 21-22, pp. 10-11, 28. Timofeev: Wauters, pp. 28-29; *Pr*, 11 June and 8 July, and *Izv*, 8 July 1922. Also: *Pr*, 5 August 1922.
11   Gots: *RR*, No. 21-22, pp. 7-9; E. Ratner: Idem, p. 6; also: *Pr*, 5 August 1922.
12   Timofeev: *Pr*, 11 June 1922; Wauters, p. 29. E. Ratner: *Izv*, 15 July 1922. Berg: Krylenko, *Za piat' let*, p. 103; Pokrovskii, p. 4. Gots: *RR*, No. 21-22, p. 11. Al'tovskii: Idem, p. 22. Vedeniapin: Idem, p. 26. Also: *GR*, 1 July 1922.
13   Gots: *RR*, No. 21-22, p. 9; E. Ratner: Idem, pp. 32-33, 5-6.
14   *RR*, No. 21-22, pp. 31-33.
15   *Pr*, 5 August 1922.
16   *RR*, No. 21-22, pp. 32-33.
17   *Pr*, 5 August 1922.
18   *RR*, No. 21-22, p. 33.
19   Idem, p. 11; Vandervelde/Wauters, p. 124. See also: NC 7, No. 17, Hoover Institution, Stanford, and *GR*, 8 September 1922.
20   *RR*, No. 21-22, pp. 32-33.
21   Idem, pp. 27-28.
22   Timofeev: *GR*, 11 August 1922; Gots: *RR*, No. 21-22, pp. 11, 28.
23   *Protsess* II, p. 106.
24   Idem, p. 237.
25   Idem, p. 221.
26   *Pr*, 11 June 1922.
27   *Protsess* II, pp. 209-210.
28   Idem, pp. 227, 212, 193.
29   *Izv*, 22 June 1922.
30   Cf. Timofeev, *Pr*, 5 August 1922.
31   *Izv*, 24 June 1922.
32   *Pr*, 2 July 1922. See Timofeev, *Pr*, 8 July 1922; Rakov, *Pr*, 3 August 1922.
33   *Izv*, 28 June 1922.

Chapter 7
pp. 119-140

1   Zetkin, *Wir klagen an!*, p. 5; *Protsess* I, p. 136.
2   *Protsess* II, p. 141.
3   *RR*, No. 21-22, p. 21.
4   Krylenko, *Za piat' let*, p. 291.
5   Idem, pp. 138, 282, 296. Cf. also Lunacharskii: *Protsess* I, pp. 19-20.
6   Krylenko, *Za piat' let*, pp. 105, 138.
7   A fictitious humoristic author in the 19th century, a collective pseudonym for A.K. Tolstoi and the Zhemchuzhnikov brothers.
8   Krylenko, *Za piat' let*, pp. 321-327.
9   *Izv*, 1 August 1922.
10   Arkhiv PSR, No. 212, IISH, Amsterdam; *RR*, No. 21-22, p. 21.
11   *Izv*, 2 August 1922.
12   *RR*, No. 21-22, pp. 21, 12.
13   *Protsess* II, pp. 21-22.
14   Idem, p. 58.
15   Idem, p. 46.
16   Idem, p. 185.
17   *Pr*, 5 August 1922.
18   Idem.

19   See p. 15.
20   *RR*, No. 21-22, p. 26.
21   Idem, p. 33.
22   Idem, pp. 23.
23   Idem, pp. 28-29.
24   *Protsess* II, p. 205.
25   Idem, p. 223.
26   Idem, pp. 225, 228.
27   Idem, pp. 238, 241.
28   *GR*, 12 August 1922.
29   Mackenzie, p. 243; *GR*, 30 August 1922; *SV*, 1922, No. 17, p. 9.
30   *Protsess* I, pp. 217-239.
31   *SV*, 1922, No. 17, p. 9; *GR*, 30 August 1922; Mackenzie, p. 244.
32   *Protsess* I, pp. 241-244.
33   Cf. the rhyme 'Chai Vysotskogo, sakhar' Brodskogo, i Rossiia Trotskogo' ('Vysotskii's tea, Brodskii's sugar, and Trotskii's Russia'), which was intended to suggest that 'the Jews' controlled Russia in all spheres.
34   *Protsess* II, p. 130. Cf. also Radkey, *The Sickle*, pp. 478-479.
35   See e.g. *GR*, 21 June, 25 July, 5, 9 and 23 August, and 6 September 1922; *SV*, 1922, No. 15, p. 7; also: letter by Golder to Herter, 10 August 1922, Golder Collection, box 33, Hoover Institution, Stanford.
36   *GR*, 12 August 1922; *SV*, 1922, No. 17, p. 9.
37   Serge, *Mémoires*, pp. 181-182.
38   Leviné-Meyer, pp. 33-34; Meyer-Leviné, p. 56; Löwy, p. 186. According to Löwy these events occurred in June, but this is probably incorrect.
39   Letter by B. Souvarine, 22 December 1974.
40   Rappoport, *Ma vie*, Vol. 2, pp. 82-83, Archives Rappoport, IISH, Amsterdam; *Novaia Rossiia*, No. 45, p. 15.
41   Nicolaevsky, pp. 5, 10.
42   Trotskii, *Moia zhizn'*, Vol. 2, pp. 209-212.
43   Fotieva, p. 181.
44   Stalin, Vol. 5, p. 135. Cf. also Lenin, Vol. 54, p. 279.
45   Fotieva, p. 183.
46   Medvedev, p. 744.
47   *Trotsky's Diary*, p. 80.
48   Rappoport, *Ma vie*, Vol. 2, p. 82, Archives Rappoport, IISH, Amsterdam.

Chapter 8
pp. 141-155

1   NC 7, No. 37 (2), Hoover Institution, Stanford.
2   Soboleva, *Oktiabr'skaia revoliutsiia*, p. 21; according to Podbolotov, the meeting was held on 19 May: Podbolotov, p. 72.
3   Gusev, p. 364; Gusev/Eritsian, p. 408.
4   *GR*, 18 May and 3 June 1922.
5   Podbolotov, pp. 72-73, 107.
6   Soboleva, *Oktiabr'skaia revoliutsiia*, p. 22.
7   Cf. e.g. *Vestnik agitatsii i propagandy*, 1922, No. 7, pp. 109-110; Gusev/Eritsian, pp. 408-409.
8   Gusev/Eritsian, p. 406.
9   Podbolotov, pp. 75-76.
10   See also Gusev, p. 364; Gusev/Eritsian, p. 408.
11   Podbolotov, p. 75.
12   Idem, p. 74.
13   Zlobina, p. 101.
14   Gusev/Eritsian, p. 412.
15   *Krasnaia gazeta*, 21 June, and *Pr*, 25 June 1922.
16   Gusev/Eritsian, p. 409.

17   Zlobina, p. 101.
18   See e.g. *Kommunisticheskaia revoliutsiia*, 1922, No. 8 (32), p. 161.
19   Zlobina, p. 100.
20   *Izv*, 17 June 1922.
21   *Trud*, 4 June 1922.
22   *Rabochaia Moskva*, 9 August 1922.
23   *Istoriia sovetskogo kino*, Vol. 1, p. 312. I have seen a fragment of a film about the trial in a BBC television documentary about Stalin.
24   Kersten, p. 19; *Inprekorr*, 1922, No. 99, p. 710; Podbolotov, p. 75; Herriot, p. 26.
25   Polonskii, pp. 87, 130; for other posters with regard to the Socialist Revolutionaries: Idem, pp. 20-21, 86-87, 129.
26   *Trud*, 4 June 1922.
27   Voitinskii, p. 42.
28   Gusev, p. 364; Gusev/Eritsian, p. 408.
29   Idem.
30   Kuznetsov/Fingerit, Vol. 1, p. 21.
31   Gusev/Eritsian, p. 409.
32   The British journalist Frederick Mackenzie estimated the number of people who took part in the demonstration on 20th June in Moscow to be 150,000 (Mackenzie, p. 240), Magdeleine Marx estimated them to be 200,000-300,000 (*Clarté*, 1 September 1922, p. 477), or even 400,000-500,000 (Marx, pp. 35-39), while a third eye-witness, the Menshevik Boris Dvinov, talks of 'tens of thousands' (Dvinov, p. 137). Isaak Shteinberg also speaks of tens of thousands (I. Steinberg, *The Fate of Krylenko*, p. 1, Steinberg Papers, YIVO, New York). Pitirim Sorokin saw a demonstration against the Socialist Revolutionaries in Petrograd at which he estimated that 50,000 people took part (Sorokin, *Leaves*, pp. 296-297).
33   Ziehr, p. 48.
34   Etenko, p. 79.
35   Barikhnovskii, p. 132.
36   *Kommunisticheskaia revoliutsiia*, 1922, No. 8 (32), pp. 161, 162.
37   *Bericht*, pp. 52-57.
38   *Pr* and *Izv*, 24 June 1922.
39   *GR*, 22 September 1922.
40   *SV*, 1922, No. 15, pp. 7-8.
41   Dvinov, p. 137.
42   *SV*, 1922, No. 15, pp. 7-9.
43   Sorokin, *Leaves*, pp. 296-297.
44   Cf. Vardin, *Pr*, 23 June, and Trotskii, *Pr*, 24 June 1922.
45   See e.g. Radek: *Kommunisticheskaia revoliutsiia*, 1922, No. 9, pp. 74-78, *Izv*, 14 and 22 June 1922.
46   *Krasnaia gazeta*, 18, 20 and 21 June, and *Pr*, 20 and 25 June 1922.
47   *Krasnaia gazeta*, 21 June 1922.
48   *Krasnaia gazeta*, 25 May, and *Izv*, 30 August 1922.
49   Zlobina, p. 101.
50   E.g. Trotskii, *Pr*, 16 May and 8 June, and *Krasnaia gazeta*, 25 May 1922; *Protsess* II, pp. 3-6.
51   E.g. E. Trupp, *Krasnaia gazeta*, 21 April, and *Izv*, 7 May 1922; V.A. Pupyshev and N.V. Makarochkin, *Pr*, 12 July 1922.
52   *Trud*, 25 May 1922.
53   Neradov, *Izv*, 23 May 1922.
54   *Krasnaia gazeta*, 23 May 1922.
55   *Trud*, 25 May 1922.
56   *Pr*, 22 June 1922.
57   *Inprekorr*, 1922, No. 127, p. 830; *Krasnaia gazeta*, 10 June 1922.
58   *Krasnaia gazeta*, 17 June 1922.
59   Lunacharskii, pp. 80-81.
60   *Pr*, 22 June 1922. Cf. Flerovskii, *Vestnik agitatsii i propagandy*, 1922, No. 4-5, p. 55.
61   *Trud*, 25 May 1922.

62 *Krasnaia gazeta*, 28 May 1922.
63 Idem, 7 June 1922.
64 Cf. Radek, *Pr*, 19 July 1922.
65 Moscow Committee of the Communist Party, Gusev/Eritsian, pp. 414-415.
66 Trotskii, *Izv*, 30 August 1922.
67 *Pr*, 28 July 1922.
68 Chicherin, *Pr*, 15 August 1922.
69 *Trud*, 18 June 1922.
70 Idem, 13 June 1922.
71 See e.g. *Krasnaia nov'*, 1922, No. 4 (8), p. 280.
72 Vardin, p. 24; *Rabochaia Moskva*, 17 and 23 June 1922; Gurskii, *Izv*, 29 July 1922; Zetkin, *Wir klagen an!*, p. 21.
73 *Kommunisticheskaia revoliutsiia*, 1922, No. 9, p. 78; see also: Radek, *Pr*, 10 and 25 August 1922.
74 *Molodaia gvardiia*, 1922, No. 4-5, p. 270; see also: *Kommunisticheskaia revoliutsiia*, 1922, No. 11-12, p. 48.
75 Trotskii, *Izv*, 28 May, and *Krasnaia gazeta*, 30 May 1922; Steklov, *Izv*, 16 and 20 May 1922; Radek, *Izv* and *Trud*, 7 June 1922; Erde, *Izv*, 26 July 1922; *Bericht*, pp. 52-57.
76 *Krasnaia gazeta*, 7 June 1922.
77 *Pr*, 25 May 1922.
78 See e.g. *Pr*, 28 July 1922.
79 *Dni*, 29 November 1923.

Chapter 9
pp. 156-169

1 *GR*, 19 September 1922; *SV*, 1922, No. 18, p. 11; *RR*, No. 21-22, p. 37; NC 7, No. 19, Hoover Institution, Stanford.
2 Dvinov, pp. 136-145; *SV*, 1922, No. 15, pp. 8-9.
3 *Znamia*, 15 September 1922, pp. 51-53.
4 *Izv* and *Trud*, 7 June 1922.
5 Burevoi, pp. 120-124.
6 Gusev/Eritsian, pp. 409, 413. Cf. also *SV*, 1922, No. 16, p. 11.
7 Stepun, Vol. 3, p. 174.
8 *Sovremennye zapiski*, 1923, No. 17, p. 359.
9 Lenin, Vol. 54, pp. 265-266.
10 Zinov'ev, p. 55.
11 Peshekhonov, p. 72.
12 See e.g. *Pr*, 31 August 1922.
13 *Izv*, 30 August 1922.
14 *SV*, 1922, No. 12, p. 3.
15 *GR*, 13 August 1922.
16 Zenzinov, *Protsess S.R. v Moskve v 1922*, p. 2, Archive of Russian and Eastern European History and Culture, box 4221, No. 6, Columbia University, New York.
17 *Prozess Tschernoff gegen Kersten*, Arkhiv PSR, No. 771/I, IISH, Amsterdam; *Dva protsessa*, Idem, No. 771/II. This sentence did not prevent Kersten from publishing a book in 1925 about the trial of the Socialist Revolutionaries, in which he once again repeated the Soviet propaganda in full. In discussing the accused, for instance, Kersten considered that 'the petty bourgeois physiognomy' was generally 'a noticeable characteristic of all these types' (Kersten, p. 62).
18 For the correspondence with Kautsky about this: Kautsky Archives, D XIX 30 and 31, IISH, Amsterdam.
19 See Oberländer, *passim*; see also L. Schapiro, *The Slavonic and East European Review*, December 1955, p. 71. For a recent view: Agurskii, *passim*.
20 *Nakanune*, 4 June 1922.
21 Idem, 20 June 1922.
22 Idem, 29 June 1922.
23 Idem, 18 July 1922. I have not been able to consult a complete set of *Nakanune* and therefore cannot report on the paper's opinion of the sentence.

24 An open letter which Vandervelde wrote to Trotskii in this connection was not answered by the latter until ten years later: *Biulleten' oppozitsii*, No. 32, pp. 40-41; Vandervelde's reply to Trotskii: *Le Peuple* (Bruxelles), 13 January 1933.
25 See e.g. Donneur, pp. 275-276, 278.
26 Nicolaevsky, pp. 10-11.
27 *Nachrichten*, 2.Jahrg., No. 8, p. 2; *SV*, 1922, No. 17, pp. 13-14.
28 *Pr*, 9 August 1922.
29 Zetkin's attitude with regard to the trial was criticized by the Dutch socialist, Mathilde Wibaut, in an open letter published in *Het Volk* on 22 August 1922; for Zetkin's reply, see 'Kleine Korrespondenz', IISH, Amsterdam.
30 Podbolotov, p. 85.
31 See e.g. Souvarine, *Inprekorr*, 1922, No. 78, pp. 587-588, and *l'Humanité*, 10 August 1922.
32 *Protokoll des Vierten Kongresses*, pp. 498-499.
33 *De Communistische Gids*, 1922, No. 7-8, pp. 477-485.
34 *De Tribune*, 24 July 1922.
35 Idem, 8 August 1922.
36 Idem, 10 August 1922.
37 De Kadt, pp. 301-302.
38 *l'Humanité*, 20 March 1922.
39 *Izv*, 7 June 1922.
40 See e.g. the interview with Anatole France in *Berliner Tageblatt* of 23 June 1922.
41 Letter by Martov to Nikolaevskii, 30 June 1922, NC 137, No. 1, Hoover Institution, Stanford.
42 NC 137, No. 1, Hoover Institution, Stanford; Wolfe, plate XIX.
43 NC 137, No. 1, Hoover Institution, Stanford; Wolfe, plate XVIII.
44 *l'Humanité*, 11 July 1922.
45 *Krasnaia nov'*, 1922, No. 4 (8), p. 280.
46 Zamiatin, p. 93.
47 Lenin, Vol. 54, p. 279.
48 Idem.
49 *Le Journal du Peuple*, 16 July 1922.
50 Idem.
51 *Survey*, 1974, No. 2-3, p. 152.
52 *Clarté*, 1 September 1922, p. 475.
53 *The Nation*, 27 September 1922, p. 316.
54 Idem, pp. 299-300.
55 *The Nation*, 6 December 1922, p. 607.
56 Cited in: Wins, p. 36.

Chapter 10
pp. 170-185

1 *Dni*, 3 February 1923; *RR*, No. 41, p. 20.
2 *RR*, No. 33-34, p. 34; Idem, No. 37-38, p. 21; Abramovitch, pp. 31-32.
3 An exchange of letters between Adler and Abramovich in early 1924, SAI Archives No. 2623/30 and 31, IISH, Amsterdam.
4 *Izv*, 15 January 1924.
5 See e.g. *Arkhiv russkoi revoliutsii*, Vol. XIX, p. 102; Brunowski, pp. 132-133.
6 *RR*, No. 43, p. 18.
7 *Russia*, pp. XVI-XVII, 16.
8 *Bulletin des Vereinigten Komitees*, No. 10, pp. 3-4.
9 *RR*, No. 43, pp. 16-18.
10 *Dni*, 28 June 1925.
11 *RR*, No. 42, p. 23.
12 *Dni*, 29 January 1926; *RR*, No. 46, p. 28; Olitskaia, Vol. 2, p. 53.
13 See e.g. *Izvestiia Ts.K.R.K.P.(b.)*, 1922, No. 7, pp. 3-4.
14 See p. 22. For a protest: *Letters*, pp. 231-234; *SV*, 1922, No. 19, p. 13.

15 *Izv*, 18 August and 19 October 1922.
16 See *Politicheskii dnevnik*, pp. 60-61.
17 See e.g. Olitskaia, Vol. 1, pp. 190-290. For a report on the political prisoners in Russia: *Izv*, 21 September 1924.
18 *SV*, 1924, No. 4, p. 1.
19 See e.g. *Rabochaia Moskva*, 17 June, *Pr*, 26 July, and *Izv*, 29 July 1922; *SV*, 1922, No. 8, p. 10.
20 See e.g., for the Socialist Revolutionaries: *RR*, No. 23, pp. 19-21; Idem, No. 31, pp. 6-14, 22; *Izv*, 11 August and 29 November, and *Pr*, 29 November and 27 December 1922. For the Mensheviks: *Izv*, 18 and 21 August 1923; *Proletarskaia revoliutsiia*, No. 22, pp. 215-232. For the Left Socialist Revolutionaries: *Puti revoliutsii*, pp. 279-319. Further, mention can be made of the trial of Perkhurov in 1922 and that of Savinkov in 1924.
21 *Pr*, 1, 5, 10, 12, 14, and 15 December, and *Izv*, 1 and 13 December 1922; *RR*, No. 33-34, pp. 16-22; *SV*, 1922, No. 16, p. 12; Idem, No. 22, p. 13. See also: Krylenko, *Pr*, 11 July 1922.
22 Zinov'ev, p. 11.
23 *Trud*, 3 June, and *Izv*, 13 July 1922; *RR*, No. 31, p. 21; *Rapport*, p. 8. See also Bezpalov, p. 147.
24 *Izv*, 18, 20, 21, and 22 March 1923.
25 *Izv*, 21 March 1923.
26 Idem.
27 Central Committee of the Communist Party, Gusev/Eritsian, p. 415. See also: Bukharin and Steklov, *Izv*, 22 March 1923; *Dvenadtsatyi s"ezd*, p. 664. For other meetings of *byvshie*: *RR*, No. 44, p. 17; *Katorga i ssylka*, No. 71, pp. 197, 204-205; *Izv*, 28 December 1923; Podbolotov, p. 89. See also: Loiko, *passim*.
28 *Izv*, 15 and 17 April, and 12 October 1923.
29 Idem, 2 February 1924.
30 Burevoi, p. 131.
31 Arkhiv PSR, No. 772/1, IISH, Amsterdam.
32 Olitskaia, Vol. 2, p. 117.
33 Cf. Carr, *Socialism*, Vol. 2, p. 481.
34 *Trud*, 13 November 1927.
35 Olitskaia, Vol. 2, p. 79.
36 Idem, Vol. 1, p. 308; Vol. 2, pp. 19-20.
37 *Pamiat'*, No. 1, pp. 313-323; Idem, No. 3, pp. 523-538.
38 *Novyi zhurnal*, No. 124 (1976), p. 195; Chernov Andreyev, p. 210. Cf. Olitskaia, Vol. 2, p. 64.
39 On Olitskaia, see also: Plyushch, pp. 152-161, 247, 290.
40 *Izv*, 4 July 1922. On Svirskaia and her friendship with Esenin, see: *Ogonek*, 1980, No. 40 (October), p. 24.
41 Serge, *Mémoires* (revised edition, Paris 1978), p. 175.
42 Letter by Nikolaevskii to Chernov, 16 June 1928, Chernov Papers, No. 14, IISH, Amsterdam; letter by Timofeev to Voitinskii, 11 May 1929, NC 218, No. 4 (2), Hoover Institution, Stanford.
43 *RR*, No. 77-78, p. 30.
44 NC 7, No. 65, Hoover Institution, Stanford.
45 *Za svobodu*, No. 18, p. 122; *SV*, 1947, No. 10, p. 201; notes by Zenzinov, Archive of Russian and Eastern European History and Culture, box 4321-8-a and box 4421, Columbia University, New York.
46 Idem.
47 *SV*, 1950, No. 10, p. 199.
48 *Velikaia Oktiabr'skaia Sotsialisticheskaia Revoliutsiia*, p. 95.
49 Letters by M. Svirskaia of 26 April and 11 June 1978.
50 NC 218, No. 4 (2), Hoover Institution, Stanford.
51 *RR*, No. 77-78, p. 30.
52 Letter by M. Svirskaia of 26 April 1978.
53 *Who Was Who.*

54   Letter by Dan to Adler of 11 February 1925, SAI Archives, No. 2597/8, IISH, Amsterdam; *Who Was Who*.
55   *RR*, No. 77-78, p. 30.
56   *SV*, 1931, No. 21, p. 13; *Volia Rossii*, 1931, No. 7-9, p. 682.
57   *Sotsialist-Revoliutsioner*, No. 6 (April 1932), pp. 13-14; Svirskaia, *Vospominaniia*, p. 43, Archive of B. Sapir; letter by M. Svirskaia of 11 June 1978.
58   Serge, *Destin*, pp. 98-99; Idem, *Mémoires*, p. 182; letter by M. Svirskaia of 26 April 1978.
59   *Dni*, 3 October 1926.
60   Letter by M. Svirskaia of 26 April 1978.
61   Olitskaia, Vol. 2, p. 53.
62   Letter by M. Svirskaia of 26 April 1978.
63   Letter by Timofeev to Voitinskii of 2 April 1929, NC 218, No. 4 (2), Hoover Institution, Stanford; letter by M. Svirskaia of 26 April 1978.
64   *Biulleten' Amerikanskoi Federatsii*, No. 2-3, p. 12; letter by Timofeev to Voitinskii of 2 April 1929, NC 218, No. 4 (2), Hoover Institution, Stanford; letters by M. Svirskaia of 26 April and 11 June 1978; Svirskaia, *Vospominaniia*, p. 43, Archive of B. Sapir.
65   Olitskaia, Vol. 1, p. 268; Vol. 2, pp. 141-142.
66   *Dni*, 29 January 1926; Abramovitch, pp. 45-46; letter by M. Svirskaia of 11 June 1978.
67   *SV*, 1925, No. 23-24, p. 15; Idem, 1927, No. 7, p. 16; Idem, 1928, No. 19, p. 16.
68   *Dni*, 14 November 1925; *RR*, No. 42, p. 25; *SV*, 1925, No. 4, p. 12.
69   Letters by M. Svirskaia of 26 April and 11 June 1978.
70   *Who Was Who*; on Ignat'ev see also *Proletarskaia revoliutsiia*, 1926, No. 2, p. 89.
71   Medvedev, p. 746.
72   *Who Was Who*.
73   *GR*, 13 October 1922.
74   *The Great Purge Trial*, pp. 20, 171, 383-385, 566, 686-687. For a denial by the concerned Socialist Revolutionaries abroad that they had been in contact with Semenov or Chlenov, see *Novaia Rossiia*, No. 42-43, p. 24.
75   *The Great Purge Trial*, pp. 35, 699.
76   *Who Was Who*.
77   Gattiker, p. 221.
78   Olitskaia, Vol. 1, p. 268.
79   *Biulleten' Amerikanskoi Federatsii*, No. 2-3, p. 12.
80   *Lenin i VChK*, p. 649.
81   Olitskaia, Vol. 1, p. 268.
82   *Lenin i VChK*, p. 588.
83   Information received from his daughter, Mrs O. Iatsenko, during an interview on 6 May 1976 in New York. Mrs Iatsenko and her mother − Burevoi's widow − had emigrated from the Soviet Union to the USA shortly before this interview.
84   Interview with Mrs O. Iatsenko, 6 May 1976, New York.
85   Iziumov, *Dni*, 8 March 1928.
86   *RR*, No. 77-78, p. 31; *Lenin i VChK*, p. 635.
87   *RR*, No. 54, p. 36; *Dni*, 12 December 1926; *Katorga i ssylka*, No. 31, pp. 187-197; Idem, No. 34, pp. 185-188; *Bol'shaia Sovetskaia Entsiklopediia* (1-oe izd.).
88   See e.g. Sorokin, *A Long Journey*, pp. 61, 233; Solzhenitsyn, Vol. I-II, p. 62.
89   Verkhovskii, p. 430; *Who Was Who*.
90   Lazitch/Drachkovitch, p. 327.
91   Nekrich, pp. 125-134; see also: *Survey*, No. 100-101 (1976), pp. 313-320; letter by M. Svirskaia of 11 June 1978.
92   *Pamiat'*, No. 3, p. 523. For a letter written from Paris by his widow to Vandervelde, June 1937: Archives of the Emile Vandervelde Institute, Brussels, III/EV/F/34.
93   Vishniak, *Dan'*, p. 293.
94   *Bol'shaia Sovetskaia Entsiklopediia* (1-oe izd.).

Conclusion
pp. 186-195

1   Berman, p. 28.

2   Cf. Ziehr, pp. 50, 56.
3   Cf. Ulam, *Lenin*, p. 550.
4   *SV*, 1922, No. 4, p. 3; *Die Freiheit*, 23 April 1922.
5   In 1928 he took refuge abroad; in 1946 he was enticed back to Russia, arrested and executed: *Politicheskii dnevnik*, pp. 58-60. Cf. Schapiro, pp. 306, 327-328; Miasnikov, p. 3; *Pamiat'*, No. 3, pp. 281-282.
6   Stalin, Vol. 6, pp. 231-232.
7   *Pod znamenem marksizma*, 1924, No. 2, pp. 67-68.
8   See Medvedev, pp. 267-274, for a description of how Rubin was terrorized.
9   Svirskaia, *Vospominaniia*, pp. 33, 42-43, Archive of B. Sapir.
10   Letter by M. Svirskaia of 26 April 1978.
11   *The Great Purge Trial*, pp. IX-X. According to Tucker, the show trial is 'one of the special hallmarks of the Stalin era and of Stalinism', starting with the Shakhty trial in 1928. Kirchheimer also places, and on similar grounds, the 1922 trial in the older tradition of political trials (Kirchheimer, pp. 98-99). Sharlet takes the same position as Tucker and Kirchheimer (*Stalinism*, p. 166). Dewar also considers that there is a fundamental difference between the trial of the Socialist Revolutionaries and those of 1928 and after, the 'confession trials'; in his opinion, between 1922 and 1928 there was a 'process of change from the propaganda State Trial to the "confession" trial proper' (Dewar, p. 3). According to Reiman in 1928 a new element entered Soviet history: the political show trials. He thinks that the 1922 trial of the Socialist Revolutionaries 'belonged to another period in the history of the USSR' and calls the Shakhty trial 'the first of its kind' (Reiman, pp. 113, 116). Mandel considers that the political trials under Lenin and Trotskii 'were not show trials but cases of revolutionary justice'; he finds these trials 'a thousand miles removed from the caricatures of justice staged by Stalin' (*Die Sowjetunion*, p. 215; *New Left Review*, No. 86, p. 54). In an analogous manner, Rosmer stresses the difference between the 1922 trial and the later trials: the trial of the Socialist Revolutionaries, according to Rosmer, was one 'such as is customary in all revolutions', but 'not comparable at all' with the later trials in which Stalin made old revolutionaries confess to crimes that they had not committed (Rosmer, p. 307).
    With regard to the behaviour of the accused, these authors rightly draw attention to the difference between the 1922 trial (at least as concerns the 'first group') and those of 1928 and after. That difference had been discussed earlier by *Sovremennik*, pseudonym for a commentator for the Socialist Revolutionary-oriented emigré journal *Dni*, with regard to the 1931 trial of the 'Mensheviks' (*Dni*, 15 March 1931, pp. 14-16). Other authors also note the similarities between the 1922 trial and those that were held later.
    Kołakowski considers that 'show trials began at an early stage, for example, those of S.R.s and priests' (Kołakowski, Vol. 3, p. 55). Buber-Neumann calls the 1922 trial 'the first Soviet show trial' (Buber-Neumann, p. 57). According to Balabanova, the Stalinist pseudo-trials had 'their prototypes' in trials such as that of the Socialist Revolutionaries held under Lenin (Balabanoff, p. 138). Shteinberg points out that Krylenko organized the first show trials in the Soviet Union, including the trial of the Socialist Revolutionaries in 1922 (Steinberg, *The Fall of Krylenko*; idem, *The Fate of Krylenko*: Steinberg Papers, YIVO, New York). Shub calls the 1922 trial 'the first Moscow show trial' and considers that it 'prepared the ground' for the Stalinist trials (*Russkaia mysl'*, 2 October 1962). According to Baynac, the trial of the Socialist Revolutionaries was organized 'according to the recipe which, having been ameliorated, was to ensure the success of the future Moscow trials' (Baynac, *La terreur*, pp. 38-39). According to Ziehr, the trial of the Socialist Revolutionaries evinced the 'fundamental elements' of the show trial, such as that found its definitive form in the Shakhty trial in 1928; he also calls the 1922 trial a show trial, although with some reservations (Ziehr, pp. 69-70, 217). Ulam sees the trials of the 1930s as 'another stage in the development of a propaganda technique evolved as far back as 1922, at the trial of the Socialist Revolutionaries', and calls this trial 'perhaps the first of the Soviet "show" trials' (Ulam, *Stalin*, pp. 210, 411, 485). Elsewhere, Ulam discusses 'the great show trial of the Socialist Revolutionary leaders' (idem, *Expansion*, p. 163). Hingley considers that the 1922 trial was 'the first great Communist political show trial' in which certain characteristics of the Stalinist show trial arose 'in experimental and embryonic form' (Hingley, *The Russian Secret Police*, pp. 137-138; idem, *Joseph Stalin*, p. 188). Both Lapenna and Leggett call the 1922

trial 'the first of the show trials' (Lapenna, p. 256; Leggett, p. 318). Conquest also calls the trial of the Socialist Revolutionaries 'a show trial' (Conquest, *Lenin*, p. 107), as does Service (Service, pp. 160-161). According to Elleinstein, 'the mechanisms of this first Moscow trial [of 1922] in many respects announced those' of the Stalinist trials (Elleinstein, p. 71). 'And just as a foresighted painter proceeds from his first few brusquely drawn, angular strokes to create the whole desired portrait, so, for us, the entire panorama of 1937, 1945 and 1949 becomes ever clearer and more visible in the sketches of 1922', writes Solzhenitsyn when comparing the trial of the Socialist Revolutionaries with the later trials (Solzhenitsyn, Vol. I-II, p. 368).

Finally, according to Löwy, the trial of the Socialist Revolutionaries was 'the first great show trial in the Soviet Union'. Basing himself on Carr, however, he is of the opinion that, other than in similar trials in the 1930s, 'there seemed to be some basis for the charges'. If this latter opinion is disputable, Löwy is quite wrong in thinking that the 1922 trial seemed to give Bukharin 'a presentiment' of his own show trial that was to be held in 1938: Löwy erroneously sees Bukharin's performance in the 1922 trial as a defence of the Socialist Revolutionaries (Löwy, p. 186; also see Carr, *The Bolshevik Revolution*, Vol. 1, p. 190).

BIBLIOGRAPHY

ARCHIVES

(a) The International Institute of Social History, Amsterdam. Here were consulted: the PSR archives (including, under No. 212, a number of handwritten pieces reporting the trial); the LSI archives (including, under No. 96, the report made by Arthur Wauters of the first five days of the trial); the SAI archives; Chernov's archive; Rappoport's archive (including Ch. Rappoport, *Ma vie*, Paris 1926-1927); Kautsky's archive; die Kleine Korrespondenz.

(b) The Hoover Institution on War, Revolution, and Peace, Stanford, California. Here were consulted: the Nicolaevsky Collection (in particular, Nos. 7, 137, 218 and 232, and a number of uncatalogued illegal publications by the PSR); the Melgunov Collection; the Golder Collection.

(c) The Archive of Russian and Eastern European History and Culture, Columbia University, New York. Here were consulted: the papers of Vladimir Zenzinov; M. Fomichev, *Antonovshchina* (Box 7522).

(d) The YIVO Institute for Jewish Research, New York. Here I consulted the papers of Isaak Shteinberg.

(e) The Emile Vandervelde Institute, Brussels. For this, see Note 92 to Chapter 10.

Boris Sapir allowed me to see the memoirs of Mina Svirskaia. Mrs Oksana Iatsenko showed me some documents regarding Konstantin Burevoi.

I interviewed Boris Sapir on 3 September 1974 in Amsterdam; Mrs Olga Lang on 14 March and 2 May 1976 in New York; and Mrs Oksana Iatsenko on 6 May 1976 in New York.

I have received letters from Boris Souvarine, dated 22 December 1974, Paris; and from Mrs Mina Svirskaia, dated 26 April and 11 June 1978, Herzlia-Pituach, Israel.

PERIODICALS

Arkhiv russkoi revoliutsii; Bednota; Berliner Tageblatt; Biulleten' Amerikanskoi Federatsii P.S.R.; Biulleten' oppozitsii; Bulletin des Vereinigten Komitees zum Schutze der in Russland verhafteten Revolutionäre; Byloe; Canadian-American Slavic Studies; Clarté; De Communistische Gids; Delo naroda; Dni; Ezhenedel'-nik sovetskoi iustitsii; Die Freiheit; Golos Rossii; l'Humanité; Internationale Presse Korrespondenz (Inprekorr); Izvestiia Severo-Kavkazskogo nauchnogo tsentra vysshei shkoly, Obshchestvennye nauki; Izvestiia Ts.K.R.K.P.(b.); Izvestiia V.Ts.I.K.; Jahrbücher für Geschichte Osteuropas; Le Journal du Peuple; Katorga i ssylka; Kommunisticheskaia revoliutsiia; Krasnaia gazeta; Krasnaia nov'; Krasnyi arkhiv; Le Matin; Molodaia gvardiia; Nachrichten der Internationalen Arbeitsgemeinschaft Sozialistischer Parteien; Nakanune; Narodovlastie (Ekaterinodar); *Nasha zhizn'; The Nation; New Left Review; Novaia Rossiia; Novyi zhurnal; Ogonek; Le Peuple* (Bruxelles); *Pod znamenem marksizma; Pravda; Proletarskaia revoliutsiia; Prozhektor; Rabochaia Moskva; Revoliutsionnaia Rossiia; Rossiiskii demokrat; Die Rote Fahne; The Russian Review; Russkaia mysl'; The Slavonic and East European Review; Sotsialist-Revoliutsioner; Sotsialisticheskii vestnik; Sovremennye zapiski; Survey; De Tribune; Trud; Vestnik agitatsii i propagandy; Volia Rossii; Het Volk; Voprosy istorii; Voprosy istorii KPSS; Vorwärts; Vremia i my; Za narod; Za svobodu; Znamia.*

OTHER PUBLISHED SOURCES (INCLUDING MEMOIRS)

ABRAMOVITCH, R., *Les prisonniers politiques*, Bruxelles 1932.
ALEKSEEV (NEBUTEV), I., *Iz vospominanii levogo esera. (Podpol'naia rabota na Ukraine)*, Moskva 1922.
An den Pranger. (Zum Prozess gegen die Sozialrevolutionäre), Hamburg 1922.
ARGUNOV, A., *Mezhdu dvumia bol'shevizmami*, Paris 1919.
ARONSON, G., *Na zare krasnogo terrora*, Berlin 1929.

BALABANOFF, A., *Impressions of Lenin*, Ann Arbor 1965.
Belaia kniga po delu A. Siniavskogo i Iu. Danielia, Sostavitel' A. Ginzburg, Frankfurt a/M. 1967.
BELL, Th., *Pioneering days*, London 1941.
Bericht über die Tätigkeit des Präsidiums und der Exekutive der Kommunistischen Internationale für die Zeit vom 6.März bis 11.Juni 1922, Hamburg 1922.
BEZPALOV, N., *Ispoved' agenta G.P.U.*, Praga 1925.
BORISOV, P.A., *Chernym letom*, Moskva 1965.
BRUNOWSKI, W., *In Sowjetkerkern. Erlebnisse eines ehemaligen Sowjetfunktionärs*, Stuttgart usw., o.J.
BUBER-NEUMANN, M., *Kriegsschauplätze der Weltrevolution*, Stuttgart 1967.
BUREVOI, K., *Raspad 1918-1922*, Moskva 1923.
BYSTRANSKI, W., *Menschewiki und Sozial-Revolutionäre*, Hamburg 1922.

CHAIKIN, V., *K istorii Rossiiskoi revoliutsii. Vypusk I. Kazn' 26 bakinskikh komissarov*, Moskva 1922.
Cheka. Materialy po deiatel'nosti chrezvychainykh komissii, Berlin 1922.
CHERNOV, V.M., *Pered burei. Vospominaniia*, N'iu Iork 1953.
CHERNOV ANDREYEV, O., *Cold Spring in Russia*, Ann Arbor 1978.

Dekrety sovetskoi vlasti, Moskva 1957-
Delo Borisa Savinkova, Moskva 1924.
Dvenadtsatyi s"ezd RKP(b). Stenograficheskii otchet, Moskva 1968.
DVINOV, B., *Ot legal'nosti k podpol'iu (1921-1922)*, Stanford, Cal. 1968.

FOTIEVA, L.A., *Iz zhizni V.I. Lenina*, Moskva 1967.
FRIEDMAN, M., *The Pinkerton Labor Spy*, New York 1907.

Gosudarstvennyi perevorot admirala Kolchaka v Omske, 18 noiabria 1918 goda. Sbornik dokumentov, Sobral i izdal V. Zenzinov, Parizh 1919.

The Great Purge Trial, Ed. by R.C. Tucker and S.F. Cohen, New York 1965.

HERRIOT, E., *La Russie nouvelle*, Paris 1922.

IGNAT'EV, V.I., *Nekotorye fakty i itogi 4 let grazhdanskoi voiny (1917-1921 g.). Chast' 1. (Oktiabr' 1917 g.-Avgust 1919 g.). Petrograd, Vologda, Arkhangel'sk. (Lichnye vospominaniia)*, Moskva 1922.

Istoriia zakonodatel'stva SSSR i RSFSR po ugolovnomu protsessu i organizatsii suda i prokuratury. Sbornik dokumentov, Moskva 1955.

Iz istorii Vserossiiskoi Chrezvychainoi Komissii 1917-1921 gg. Sbornik dokumentov, Moskva 1958.

K prekrashcheniiu voiny vnutri demokratii. (Ufimskie peregovory i nasha pozitsiia), Moskva 1919.

KADT, J. DE, *Uit mijn communistentijd*, Amsterdam 1965.

Kak tambovskie krest'iane boriatsia za svobodu, B.m. 1921.

KERSTEN, K., *Der Moskauer Prozess gegen die Sozial-Revolutionäre, 1922. Revolution und Konterrevolution*, Berlin 1925.

M.L. Kogan-Bernshtein. Sbornik statei, Moskva 1919.

Kratkii otchet o rabotakh chetvertogo s"ezda Partii Sotsialistov-Revoliutsionerov (26 noiabria-5 dekabria 1917 goda), Petrograd 1918.

KRYLENKO, N.V., *Sudebnye rechi*, Moskva 1964.

—, *Za piat' let, 1918-1922 gg. Obvinitel'nye rechi*, Moskva-Petrograd 1923.

LATSIS, M., *Chrezvychainye komissii po bor'be s kontr-revoliutsiei*, Moskva 1921.

LEBEDEV, V.I., *Bor'ba russkoi demokratii protiv bol'shevikov. Zapiski ochevidtsa i uchastnika sverzheniia bol'shevistskoi vlasti na Volge i v Sibiri*, N'iu Iork 1919.

LENIN, V.I., *Polnoe sobranie sochinenii*, Izdanie piatoe, Moskva 1958-1970.

V.I. Lenin i VChK. Sbornik dokumentov (1917-1922 gg.), Moskva 1975.

Leninskii sbornik, Tom 37, Moskva 1970.

Letters from Russian Prisons, New York 1925.

LEVINÉ-MEYER, R., *Inside German Communism. Memoirs of Party Life in the Weimar Republic*, London 1977.

LOIKO, L., *Ot 'zemli i voli' k VKP(b). 1877-1928. Vospominaniia*, Moskva 1929.

LOSSKII, N.O., *Vospominaniia*, München 1968.

LUNACHARSKII, A., *Byvshie liudi. Ocherk istorii partii eserov*, Moskva 1922.

LUXEMBURG, R., *Die russische Revolution*, Berlin 1922.

MACKENZIE, F.A., *Russia Before Dawn*, London 1923.

MAISKII, I., *Demokraticheskaia kontr-revoliutsiia*, Moskva-Petrograd 1923.

MARX, M., *C'est la lutte finale!... (Six mois en Russie soviétique)*, Paris 1923.

MEL'GUNOV, S., ' "Sud istorii nad intelligentsiei" (k delu Takt. Tsentra)', *Rossiiskii demokrat*, 1954, No. 1 (sb. 25), pp. 36-63 (published before in *Na chuzhoi storone*, 1923, No. 3).

MEL'GUNOV, S.P., *Vospominaniia i dnevniki*, Parizh 1964.

MELGUNOW, S.P., *Der rote Terror in Russland, 1918-1923*, Berlin 1924.

MEYER-LEVINÉ, R., *Im inneren Kreis. Erinnerungen einer Kommunistin in Deutschland, 1920-1933*, Köln 1979.

Mezhdunarodnaia sotsialisticheskaia konferentsiia. (Ob''edinennoe zasedanie Is-polkomov trekh Internatsionalov). Stenograficheskii otchet, Moskva 1922.
MIASNIKOV, G.I., *Ocherednoi obman*, Parizh 1931.

NEKRICH, A., *Otreshis'.ot strakha*, London 1979.
NIESSEL, H.A., *Le triomphe des bolchéviks et la paix de Brest-Litovsk. Souve-nirs 1917-1918*, Paris 1940.
NOULENS, J., *Mon ambassade en Russie soviétique, 1917-1919*, Paris 1933.

Obvinitel'noe zakliuchenie po delu tsentral'nogo komiteta i otdel'nykh inykh organizatsii Partii Sotsialistov-Revoliutsionerov po obvineniiu ikh v vooru-zhennoi bor'be protiv Sovetskoi vlasti, organizatsii ubiistv, vooruzhennykh ograblenii i v izmennicheskikh snosheniiakh s inostrannymi gosudarstvami, Moskva 1922.
Odinnadtsatyi s''ezd RKP(b). Mart-aprel' 1922 goda. Stenograficheskii otchet, Moskva 1961.
OLITSKAIA, E., *Moi vospominaniia*, Frankfurt a/M. 1971.

Pamiat'. Istoricheskii sbornik, Vypusk pervyi (Moskva 1976), N'iu Iork 1978.
Pamiat'. Istoricheskii sbornik, Vypusk tretii (Moskva 1978), Parizh 1980.
PAUL-BONCOUR, J., *Entre deux guerres. Souvenirs sur la III-e République*, Paris 1945-1946.
PESHEKHONOV, A.V., *Pochemu ia ne emigriroval?*, Berlin 1923.
PLATONOV, A., *Stranichka iz istorii eserovskoi kontr-revoliutsii (Administrativ-nyi Tsentr). (Voennaia rabota eserov za granitsei v 1920-21 g.g.)*, Moskva 1923.
PLYUSHCH, L., *History's Carnival. A Dissident's Autobiography*, London 1979.
POKROVSKII, M., *Chto ustanovil protsess tak nazyvaemykh 'sotsialistov-revoliutsionerov'?*, Moskva 1922.
Politicheskii dnevnik (tom II) 1965-1970, Amsterdam 1975.
POPOFF, G., *Tscheka. Der Staat im Staate*, Frankfurt a/M. 1925.
——, *Unter dem Sowjetstern. Alltag, Kultur, Wirtschaft*, Frankfurt a/M. 1924.
POPOV, N.N., *Melkoburzhuaznye antisovetskie partii. (Shest' lektsii)*, Vtoroe is-pravlennoe izdanie, Moskva 1924.
Protokoll der internationalen Konferenz der drei internationalen Exekutivkomi-tees in Berlin vom 2. bis 5.April 1922, Wien 1922.
Protokoll des Vierten Kongresses der Kommunistischen Internationale. Petro-grad-Moskau vom 5.November bis 5.Dezember 1922, Hamburg 1923.
Protsess eserov. Vypusk vtoroi. Rechi zashchitnikov i obviniaemykh, Moskva 1922.
Protsess P.S.-R. Rechi gosudarstvennykh obvinitelei. Prilozhenie: 1) Prigovor Verkh. Rev. Tribunala, 2) Postanovlenie Prezidiuma VTsIK'a i 3) Vozzvanie Kominterna, Moskva 1922.
Puti revoliutsii. (Stat'i,. materialy, vospominaniia), Berlin 1923.

Rabota eserov zagranitsei. Po materialam Parizhskogo arkhiva eserov, Moskva 1922.
Rapport à l'Internationale Socialiste sur l'activité du parti en 1923-1925, Mar-seille 1925.
ROSMER, A., *Moscou sous Lénine. Les origines du communisme*, Paris 1953.
Russia. The Official Report of the British Trades Union Delegation to Russia and Caucasia, Nov. and Dec., 1924, London 1925.

SADOUL, J., *Les S.R. et Vandervelde*, Paris 1922.
SAVINKOV, B.V., *Bor'ba s bol'shevikami*, Varshava 1920.
Sbornik dokumentov po istorii ugolovnogo zakonodatel'stva SSSR i RSFSR 1917-1952, Pod red. prof. I.T. Goliakova, Moskva 1953.
Sbornik tsirkuliarov Plenuma Verkhovnogo Tribunala VTsIK za 1921 god, Moskva 1922.
SEMENOV (VASIL'EV), G., *Voennaia i boevaia rabota Partii Sotsialistov-Revoliutsionerov za 1917-18 gg.*, Berlin 1922.
SEMENOV, G., 'Vospominaniia byvshego esera', *Prozhektor*, 1923, Nos. 6-9.
SERGE, V., *Mémoires d'un révolutionnaire, 1901-1941*, Paris 1951 (Revised edition, Paris 1978).
SHKLOVSKII, V., *Sentimental'noe puteshestvie. Vospominaniia 1917-1922*, Moskva-Berlin 1923.
SHKLOVSKY, V., *A Sentimental Journey*, Ithaca-London 1970.
SHMERAL', B., *Chekho-slovaki i esery*, Moskva 1922.
SOKOLOV, B., 'Zashchita Vserossiiskogo Uchreditel'nogo Sobraniia', *Arkhiv russkoi revoliutsii*, Tom XIII (1924), pp. 5-70.
SOROKIN, P.A., *Leaves from a Russian Diary – and Thirty Years After*, Enlarged edition, Boston 1950.
—, *A Long Journey. The Autobiography of Pitirim A. Sorokin*, New Haven 1963.
Sovremennyi moment v otsenke Partii Sots.-Revoliutsionerov (fevral'-mart 1919 g.), N'iu Iork 1919.
SPIRIDOVITCH, A., *Histoire du terrorisme, 1886-1917*, Paris 1930.
STALIN, I.V., *Sochineniia*, Moskva 1946-1951.
STEINBERG, I.N., *In the Workshop of the Revolution*, London 1955.
STEKLOV, Iu., *Partiia sotsialistov-revoliutsionerov (pravykh eserov)*, Moskva 1922.
STEPUN, F., *Vergangenes und Unvergängliches. Aus meinem Leben*, München 1947-1950.
Sudebnye rechi sovetskikh obvinitelei, Moskva 1965.
SVERDLOV, Ia.M., *Izbrannye proizvedeniia*, Moskva 1957-1960.
SVIATITSKII, N., *K istorii Vserossiiskogo Uchreditel'nogo Sobraniia. Ocherk sobytii na vostoke Rossii v sentiabre-dekabre 1918 g.*, Moskva 1921.

TROTSKII, L., *Moia zhizn'. Opyt avtobiografii*, Berlin 1930.
The Trotsky Papers: 1917-1922, Edited and annotated by Jan M. Meijer, The Hague 1964, 1971.
Trotsky's Diary in Exile 1935, Cambridge, Mass. 1958.
TSCHERNOW, V., *Meine Schicksale in Sowjet-Russland*, Berlin 1921.

VANDERVELDE, E., *Avant le procès de Moscou. Notes au jour le jour*, Bruxelles 1922.
VANDERVELDE, E./A. WAUTERS, *Le procès des Socialistes Révolutionnaires à Moscou*, Bruxelles 1922.
VARDIN, I., *Eserovskie ubiitsy i sotsial-demokraticheskie advokaty. (Fakty i dokumenty)*, Moskva 1922.
VERKHOVSKII, A.I., *Na trudnom perevale*, Moskva 1959.
VISHNIAK, M., *Dan' proshlomu*, N'iu Iork 1954.
VOITINSKII, V., *Dvenadtsat' smertnikov. Sud nad sotsialistami-revoliutsionerami v Moskve*, Berlin 1922.
VORONOVICH, N., 'Mezh dvukh ognei. (Zapiski zelenogo)', *Arkhiv russkoi revoliutsii*, Tom VII (1922), pp. 58-183.

WINS, A., *Vermoorde onschuld.....?!!! Eenige staaltjes van 'revolutionaire' taktiek der Russische Sociaal-Revolutionairen. Feiten en bewijzen*, Amsterdam 1922.

Zakliuchenie sudebno-sledstvennoi komissii po delu Azefa, B.m. 1911.
ZAMIATIN, E., *Litsa*, N'iu Iork 1955.
Zelenaia kniga. Sbornik materialov i dokumentov. Istoriia krest'ianskogo dvizheniia v Chernomorskoi gubernii, Sobral N. Voronovich, Praga 1921.
ZENZINOV, V., *Iz zhizni revoliutsionera*, Parizh 1919.
ZETKIN, C., *Ausgewählte Reden und Schriften*, Berlin 1957, 1960.
—, *Wir klagen an! Ein Beitrag zum Prozess der Sozial-Revolutionäre*, Hamburg 1922.
ZINOV'EV, G., *Ob antisovetskikh partiiakh i techeniiakh. (Rech' na Vserossiiskoi Konferentsii R.K.P. s prilozheniem rezoliutsii)*, Moskva 1922.
ZORIN, S., *Potomki provokatora Azefa*, Peterburg [sic] 1921.

SCHOLARLY AND OTHER WORKS

AGURSKII, M., *Ideologiia natsional-bol'shevizma*, Paris 1980.
ASTRAKHAN, Kh.M., *Bol'sheviki i ikh politicheskie protivniki v 1917 godu*, Leningrad 1973.

Bankrotstvo melkoburzhuaznykh partii Rossii. 1917-1922 gg. Sbornik nauchnykh trudov, Chast' I-II, Moskva 1977.
BARIKHNOVSKII, G.F., *Ideino-politicheskii krakh beloemigratsii i razgrom vnutrennei kontrrevoliutsii (1921-1924 gg.)*, Leningrad 1978.
BAYNAC, J., *Les socialistes-révolutionnaires de mars 1881 à mars 1917*, Paris 1979.
—, *La terreur sous Lénine*, Paris 1975.
BERK, S.M., 'The Democratic Counterrevolution. Komuch and the Civil War on the Volga', *Canadian-American Slavic Studies*, 1973, No. 4, pp. 443-459.
BERMAN, H.J., *Justice in Russia*, Cambridge, Mass. 1950.
Bol'shaia Sovetskaia Entsiklopediia, 1-oe izdanie, Moskva 1926-1948.
Bol'shaia Sovetskaia Entsiklopediia, 3-e izdanie, Moskva 1970-1978.

CARR, E.H., *The Bolshevik Revolution 1917-1923*, Harmondsworth, Middlesex 1966.
—, *Socialism in One Country 1924-1926*, Harmondsworth, Middlesex 1970-1972.
CHEMERISSKII, I.A., 'Eserovskaia gruppa "Narod" i ee raspad (1919-1923 gg.)', *Bankrotstvo melkoburzhuaznykh partii Rossii. 1917-1922 gg. Sbornik nauchnykh trudov*, Chast' II, Moskva 1977, pp. 77-86.
COMPÈRE-MOREL, C.A., *Grand dictionnaire socialiste*, Paris 1924.
CONQUEST, R., *The Great Terror. Stalin's Purge of the Thirties*, Revised edition, Harmondsworth, Middlesex 1971.
—, *V.I. Lenin*, New York 1972.

DEUTSCHER, I., *The Prophet Unarmed. Trotsky: 1921-1929*, London 1959.
DEWAR, H., *The Modern Inquisition*, London 1953.
DONNEUR, A., *Histoire de l'Union des Partis Socialistes pour l'Action Internationale (1920-1923)*, Sudbury 1967.

F.E. Dzerzhinskii. Biografiia, Moskva 1977.

ELLEINSTEIN, J., *Staline-Trotsky. Le pouvoir et la révolution*, Paris 1979.
ETENKO, R.G., 'O roli melkoburzhuaznykh partii eserov i men'shevikov v aktivizatsii politicheskogo banditizma na Donu i Kubano-Chernomor'e v 1920-1922 godakh', *Izvestiia Severo-Kavkazskogo nauchnogo tsentra vysshei shkoly, Obshchestvennye nauki*, 1978, No. 2, pp. 74-79.

GATTIKER, A., *L'affaire Conradi*, Francfort a/M. 1975.
GOLINKOV, D.L., *Krakh vrazheskogo podpol'ia. (Iz istorii bor'by s kontrrevoliutsiei v Sovetskoi Rossii v 1917-1924 gg.)*, Moskva 1971.
—, *Krushenie antisovetskogo podpol'ia v SSSR (1917-1925 gg.)*, Moskva 1975.
—, 'Razgrom ochagov vnutrennei kontrrevoliutsii v sovetskoi Rossii', *Voprosy istorii*, 1968, No. 1, pp. 133-149.
GUSEV, K.V., *Partiia eserov: ot melkoburzhuaznogo revoliutsionarizma k kontrrevoliutsii. Istoricheskii ocherk*, Moskva 1975.
GUSEV, K.V./Kh.A. ERITSIAN, *Ot soglashatel'stva k kontrrevoliutsii. (Ocherki istorii politicheskogo bankrotstva i gibeli partii sotsialistov-revoliutsionerov)*, Moskva 1968.

HELLER, M., 'The First Warning', *Survey*, 1979, No. 3, pp. 159-189.
HILDERMEIER, M., *Die Sozialrevolutionäre Partei Russlands. Agrarsozialismus und Modernisierung im Zarenreich (1900-1914)*, Köln-Wien 1978.
HINGLEY, R., *Joseph Stalin. Man and Legend*, London 1974.
—, *The Russian Secret Police*, London etc. 1970.

Internationales Handwörterbuch des Gewerkschaftswesens, Berlin 1931-1932.
Istoriia sovetskogo kino, 1917-1967, Moskva 1969-1978.

KENEZ, P., *Civil War in South Russia, 1918. The First Year of the Volunteer Army*, Berkeley etc. 1971.
KIRCHHEIMER, O., *Political Justice. The Use of Legal Procedure for Political Ends*, Princeton, N.J. 1961.
KOŁAKOWSKI, L., *Main Currents of Marxism. Its Origins, Growth and Dissolution*, Oxford 1978.
KURITSYN, V.M., *Perekhod k NEPu i revoliutsionnaia zakonnost'*, Moskva 1972.
KUZNETSOV, I.V./E.M. FINGERIT, *Gazetnyi mir Sovetskogo Soiuza*, Moskva 1972, 1976.

LAPENNA, I., 'Lenin, Law and Legality', *Lenin. The Man, the Theorist, the Leader. A Reappraisal*, Ed. by L. Schapiro and P. Reddaway, New York etc. 1967, pp. 235-264.
LAZITCH, B./M.M. DRACHKOVITCH, *Biographical Dictionary of the Comintern*, Stanford, Cal. 1973.
LEGGETT, G., *The Cheka. Lenin's Political Police*, Oxford 1981.
LÖWY, A.G., *Die Weltgeschichte ist das Weltgericht. Bucharin: Vision des Kommunismus*, Wien usw. 1969.

MEDVEDEV, R.A., *K sudu istorii. Genezis i posledstviia stalinizma*, New York 1974.

The Mensheviks. From the Revolution of 1917 to the Second World War, Chicago etc. 1974.

MINTS, I., *Angliiskaia interventsiia i severnaia kontr-revoliutsiia*, Moskva-Leningrad 1931.

MORGAN, D.W., *The Socialist Left and the German Revolution. A History of the German Independent Social Democratic Party, 1917-1922*, Ithaca-London 1975.

Neotvratimoe vozmezdie, Moskva 1974.

NICOLAEVSKY, B.I., *Power and the Soviet Elite. 'The Letter of an Old Bolshevik' and Other Essays*, Ed. by J.D. Zagoria, New York 1965.

OBERLÄNDER, E., 'Nationalbolschewistische Tendenzen in der russischen Intelligenz. Die "Smena Vech"-Diskussion 1921-1922', *Jahrbücher für Geschichte Osteuropas*, 1968, No. 2, pp. 194-211.

ORLOV, B., 'Mif o Fanni Kaplan', *Vremia i my*, No. 2 (December 1975), pp. 153-163, and No. 3 (January 1976), pp. 126-159.

PERRIE, M., *The Agrarian Policy of the Russian Socialist-Revolutionary Party from its Origins through the Revolution of 1905-1907*, Cambridge etc. 1976.

PETROV, M.N., 'Vozniknovenie i raspad men'shinstva partii eserov', *Voprosy istorii*, 1979, No. 7, pp. 49-60.

PODBOLOTOV, P.A., *Krakh esero-men'shevistskoi kontrrevoliutsii*, Leningrad 1975.

POLONSKII, V., *Russkii revoliutsionnyi plakat*, Moskva 1925.

POPOV, F., *Chekho-slovatskii miatezh i samarskaia uchredilka*, Moskva-Samara 1933.

POPOV, F.G., *1918 god v Samarskoi gubernii. Khronika sobytii*, Kuibyshev 1972.

RADKEY, O.H., *The Agrarian Foes of Bolshevism. Promise and Default of the Russian Socialist Revolutionaries, February to October, 1917*, New York 1958.

—, *The Election to the Russian Constituent Assembly of 1917*, Cambridge, Mass. 1950.

—, *The Sickle under the Hammer. The Russian Socialist Revolutionaries in the Early Months of Soviet Rule*, New York-London 1963.

—, *The Unknown Civil War in Soviet Russia. A Study of the Green Movement in the Tambov Region 1920-1921*, Stanford, Cal. 1976.

RANDALL, F.B., *The Major Prophets of Russian Peasant Socialism; a Study in the Social Thought of N.K. Mikhailovskii and V.M. Chernov*, New York 1961 (Dissertation Columbia University).

REIMAN, M., *Die Geburt des Stalinismus. Die UdSSR am Vorabend der 'zweiten Revolution'*, Frankfurt a/M. 1979.

SCHAPIRO, L., *The Origin of the Communist Autocracy. Political Opposition in the Soviet State. First Phase, 1917-1922*, London 1955.

SERGE, V., *Destin d'une révolution. U.R.S.S. 1917-1936*, Paris 1937.

SERVICE, R., *The Bolshevik Party in Revolution. A Study in Organisational Change 1917-1923*, London etc. 1979.

SHESTAK, Iu.I., 'Bol'sheviki i eserovskaia gruppa "Narod". (O vzaimoot-nosheniiakh RKP(b) s men'shinstvom partii sotsialistov-revoliutsionerov)', *Voprosy istorii KPSS*, 1978, No. 8, pp. 95-105.

SHUB, D., 'Pervyi pokazatel'nyi politicheskii protsess v Moskve. K sorokoletiiu suda nad liderami partii sotsialistov-revoliutsionerov', *Russkaia mysl'*, 2 October 1962, pp. 2-3.

——, 'The Trial of the SRs', *The Russian Review*, 1964, No. 4, pp. 362-369.

SHVEKOV, G.V., *Pervyi sovetskii ugolovnyi kodeks*, Moskva 1970.

SIMONIAN, M., *Zhizn' dlia revoliutsii*, Moskva 1962.

SOBOLEVA, P.I., *Bor'ba bol'shevikov protiv men'shevikov i eserov za leninskuiu politiku mira (noiabr' 1917-1918 gg.)*, Moskva 1965.

——, *Oktiabr'skaia revoliutsiia i krakh sotsial-soglashatelei*, Moskva 1968.

SOLZHENITSYN, A., *Arkhipelag Gulag, 1918-1956. Opyt khudozhestvennogo issledovaniia*, Paris 1973-1975.

Sovetskaia istoricheskaia entsiklopediia, Moskva 1961-1976.

Die Sowjetunion, Solschenizyn und die westliche Linke, Reinbek 1975.

SPIRIN, L.M., *Klassy i partii v grazhdanskoi voine v Rossii*, Moskva 1968.

——, *Krushenie pomeshchich'ikh i burzhuaznykh partii v Rossii*, Moskva 1977.

Stalinism. Essays in Historical Interpretation, Ed. R.C. Tucker, New York 1977.

STEINBERG, I., *Spiridonova. Revolutionary Terrorist*, London 1935.

ULAM, A.B., *Expansion and Coexistence. The History of Soviet Foreign Policy 1917-67*, New York-Washington 1968.

——, *Lenin and the Bolsheviks. The Intellectual and Political History of the Triumph of Communism in Russia*, London 1966.

——, *Stalin. The Man and His Era*, New York 1973.

Velikaia Oktiabr'skaia Sotsialisticheskaia Revoliutsiia. Malen'kaia entsiklopediia, Moskva 1968.

VETOSHKIN, M.K., *Revoliutsiia i grazhdanskaia voina na Severe*, Vologda 1927.

VISHNIAK, M.V., *Vserossiiskoe uchreditel'noe sobranie*, Parizh 1932.

VLADIMIROVA, V., *God sluzhby 'sotsialistov' kapitalistam. Ocherki po istorii kontr-revoliutsii v 1918 godu*, Moskva-Leningrad 1927.

WHEELER, R.F., *USPD und Internationale. Sozialistischer Internationalismus in der Zeit der Revolution*, Frankfurt a/M. usw. 1975.

Who Was Who in the USSR, Metuchen, N.J. 1972.

WOLFE, B.D., *The Bridge and the Abyss. The Troubled Friendship of Maxim Gorky and V.I. Lenin*, New York 1967.

ZAND, H., *Z dziejów wojny domowej w Rosji*, Warszawa 1973.

ZIEHR, W., *Die Entwicklung des 'Schauprozesses' in der Sowjetunion. (Ein Beitrag zur sowjetischen Innenpolitik 1928-1938)*, Tübingen 1970 (Dissertation).

ZLOBINA, V.M., *Bor'ba partii bol'shevikov protiv melkoburzhuaznogo vliianiia na rabochii klass v pervye gody nepa (1921-1925 gg.)*, Moskva 1975.

INDEX